Dragon Slaying For Parents

TOM PRINZ

Dragon Slaying For Parents

T O M P R I N Z

P.O. Box 4123, Lancaster, Pennsylvania 17604

To schedule Author appearances write:
Author Appearances, Starburst Promotions, P. O. Box 4123,
Lancaster, PA 17604 or call (717)-293-0939.

Credits:
Cover art by Dave Ivey

We, The Publisher and Author, declare that to the best of our knowledge all material (quoted or not) contained herein is accurate; and we shall not be held liable for the same.

DRAGON SLAYING FOR PARENTS

First Printing, February 1992

ISBN: 0-914984-35-7
Library of Congress Catalog Number 91-75194

Printed in the United States of America

This book is dedicated to:

My loving and supportive wife,
Pam,
my partner in parenting and constant encourager.
We have worked together to implement the parenting strategies
and have helped each other to work toward
"slaying" our dragons;

to

Robyn, Matt and Chrissy,
our children,
who have been the recipients of our approach
to parenting, and who have given permission
for their personal anecdotes to be included in this book;

and to

Al and Esther,
my parents,
who provided me a solid foundation
from which to build my family.

Contents

Contents—cont'd.

Introduction

Why Another Book On Parenting?

Over the past 15 years as a graduate student, a school psychologist, a Marriage, Family & Child Counselor and the father of three children, I have read hundreds of books and articles on parenting. For much of this time I felt that the book store shelves were filled with almost any type book on parenting that one could possibly want. For over the past 10 years I have conducted successful lectures and seminars on parenting, utilizing many of these books. Parents who attended these seminars told me of the beneficial information they got from the seminars. However, the more I counseled with parents in individual and/or family counseling sessions, the more apparent that it became that something was missing from the books on parenting.

It is relatively easy to give parents the "How To's" of being a good parent. In fact, I once timed myself in a counseling session with the parents of a 5-year-old—it took less than one-half hour to highlight and explain the basic principles of being a good parent. Experiences with many frustrated parents who have struggled to apply what they have learned from "How To" books on parenting, and also from my seminars, has revealed to me that there are many hidden factors which can interfere with the application of simple and effective parenting strategies.

The main purpose of this book is to help the reader uncover and resolve the hidden issues that may be interfering with their successful application of parenting strategies. I have labeled these hidden factors, "Dragons." **Part I** of this book will cover the hidden factors, or "Dragons" that can interfere with the successful, effective and consistent application of the tools. Dragons also make it difficult, and sometimes impossible, for parents to remain calm as they deal with their youngsters. Each chapter on Dragons will illustrate how they will interfere with various parenting strategies. This book will also contain a brief review of proper parenting strategies and specific techniques that parents can utilize to improve parent-child and parent-teenager relationships.

Three Levels Of Counseling

In my counseling practice I describe counseling to my clients as consisting of three levels:

1.   SUPPORT
2.   EDUCATION
3.   DIGGING DEEPER

The first level of counseling is SUPPORT, where I will listen to and encourage parents. They need time to talk and to get out their feelings of frustration, anxiety, guilt and anger in their role as parents—they definitely need encouragement, because their feeling often is that they have tried everything and they don't know what else to try. I have to admit that when they've said "I've tried everything and nothing works," my initial reaction is panic. "Oh no! If they have tried everything what else could there be to try?"

My panic subsides in a few seconds however, as I've learned that the parents may need a review of proper parenting strategies (EDUCATION), and in all cases the exploration of DEEPER issues. It's definitely not time to give up and send their child to a grandparent or to a foster home. Encouragement is needed to motivate them to make another "run at it." People often say when they come for counseling, "I don't know why all of a sudden I'm not confident in my role as a parent," or "I don't know why the things I try aren't working." Rest assured, there is always a reason. Be patient, and you'll discover the reason(s).

The second level of counseling is EDUCATION. This applies to all types of counseling. Whether the goal is to improve parenting skills or to improve a marriage or whatever the goal, you will need to receive what I have called the "How To" information. In the case of parenting skills, this includes parenting strategies, or effective parenting tools. Many books have done this job adequately, however, I will briefly discuss the strategies I have seen applied successfully with many parents and then will refer the reader to other books that will provide additional information. Although there are many books on parenting *tools*, many parents do not know about the full range of parenting *skills*. Do not assume that you have all the tools, but be willing to add new tools to your tool kit as you read **Part II** of this book.

The third level of counseling is "Digging Deeper." A parent whom I recently counseled said, "I just wanted you to give me some simple charts to use to get my children to behave. I didn't think that I would need to talk about my *own* childhood." This is a common response on the part of many parents. However, one will not, and one can not, be successful as a parent, unless they look at their own childhood. The main purpose of this book is to help the reader to DIG DEEPER. To uncover and deal effectively with issues that may have interfered with applying the parenting strategies. In my counseling practice I used to stay at the EDUCATION level of counseling too long. Weeks, and sometimes months would go by, with little progress experienced by parents as they tried to apply parenting strategies. Today, I no longer wait weeks and months—but begin to DIG DEEPER during our very first sessions. I have come to the conclusion everyone needs to DIG DEEPER. An analogy is that of a ship heading across a harbor. The ship probably did not hit an iceberg and sink. Most people did not have one major childhood experience that may still be effecting them, but the ship picked up enough barnacles on the trip that it sunk. For most people, the digging deeper involves looking for and identifying the barnacles or subtle factors or issues that may have seemed to be insignificant.

Who Should Read This Book?

Then target population for this book is widespread. Obviously it is intended for all parents to assist them with the difficult task of raising responsible, confident children in the 1990's. Being a parent, child, or teenager in the 1990's is much more difficult than it was 20 or 30 years ago. It is very important for parents to realize this and understand that they face many issues that their own parents did not have to deal with. To name a few: television was not eating up more time in a child's life than school, the world was not seen as such a violent place as it is today with television broadcasting war live into your living room, drugs and alcohol were not as prevalent and available for our youth, the sexual revolution had not taken off, the Pill was not legalized, the divorce rate was lower, fewer mothers worked outside the home, and there was less pressure on youth to excel in school and sports, and less pressure was placed on them to grow up quickly. In short, the challenge for all parents is tremendous in the 1990's and they need to be well equipped to deal with the challenge.

This book has been written especially for parents who feel that they have "tried everything." It has been written to help them to identify, understand, and deal appropriately with hidden factors which may have been interfering with their ability to effectively and consistently apply the appropriate parenting tools.

The Small Society By Brickman

Reprinted with permission of King Features Syndicate, Inc.

"Today" is definitely different than 20 or 30 years ago. It's important to realize and accept this fact in order to understand the challenge we face as parents, and to help us to see that we may need to use different approaches with our children, than our parents may have used with us.

This book was also written for new parents who are eager to devote time and energy to being successful parents. In addition to learning and/or reviewing specific parenting strategies, you will begin to investigate issues early in your parenting career that may interfere with your application of the parenting techniques. This could save you months, even years, of grief and frustration and money needlessly spent on another "How To Parent" book. Another book or seminar is not the answer. The answer lies in looking at other issues that you have probably not yet considered.

A third, but equally important target population are the many counselors, therapists, educators, and pastors that attempt to counsel with parents to help them improve their parenting strategies. This book will help you to appreciate the complexity of your task, provide practical ideas for parents, and most importantly, help you to become aware of the "hidden" and "deeper" issues that must be addressed by all parents to some degree. You will be more efficient and successful in your efforts to help parents if you begin to incorporate this information in your counseling sessions at an early point.

What's The Most Important Thing To Consider—DRAGONS OR TOOLS?

Just as a carpenter or mechanic who has all the right tools is unable to utilize the tools if his arms are broken, so too is a parent unable to utilize proper parenting tools if their Dragons are in the way. This book will discuss all the proper parenting tools, but more importantly it will help parents to recognize their Dragons.

One of my favorite children's books is entitled, *There Is No Such Thing As a Dragon*, by Jack Kent. The book begins with a little boy, Billy, who notices a dragon on the end of his bed. He tells his mother about it, but she says "there is no such thing as a dragon." The dragon begins to grow and grow until it gets so large that it lifts up their house and runs away with it on its back. At this point, Billy's parents are finally forced to acknowledge that there really is a dragon in their house.

As they recognize and talk about the dragon, it gradually shrinks and becomes kitten size once again. The book concludes with the mother saying, "I don't mind dragons this size, why did it have to grow so big?" Billy replies, "I don't know mother, but I think it just wanted to be noticed." Recognizing and dealing effectively with your Dragons will help them to remain small so that they will not interfere with your application of the parenting tools.

This book is mainly about Dragons. We all bring Dragons into our adult life from our childhood that interfere with our relationships and our attempts at parenting our children in positive ways. The trouble with Dragons is that we frequently do not realize that we have brought them with us. If we do realize we have brought them with us, we frequently underestimate their effect on our lives. The Dragons may not interfere significantly in our lives for several years, sometimes not until our children are teenagers. At this point we often forget that we brought the Dragons with us, and they grow so big that they cause problems in our lives because, as in the story, "they begin to grow and run away with the house." Parents of teenagers frequently do not realize that the tools they used to parent young children are no longer effective with teenagers, and it is also at this stage that some Dragons really make themselves known. You could have all the right tools to deal effectively with parenting issues, but it's the Dragons that will inhibit your successful use of the tools. Some Dragons will cause you to overreact to your child and teenager, and cause you to be too angry, and therefore ineffective, in dealing with them. One of the biggest mistakes that parents make is the inappropriate use of anger in attempting to control children. All the "How To" books will mention this, but few give specific suggestions on how to stay calm. This book will give you specific answers on how to remain calm.

Part I of this book will help you to identify and deal effectively with the Dragons that you have brought into your role as a parent. The following Dragons will be discussed:

I encourage you to read all the chapters in order to identify all the issues you may need to deal with. The index of suspicion at the beginning of each chapter will help you to know more specifically which particular dragon is being dealt with in that chapter. Each Dragon chapter will conclude with a "Challenge to You!" You will become more aware of what impact that particular Dragon will have on your application of the parenting tools.

One of my favorite cartoons depicts one man saying to another, "I don't feel like mulling over mistakes today . . . Whaddya say we just dwell in the past?" Some adults make the mistake of never considering their past enough, while others dwell in the past too much. One needs to deal with their Dragons correctly so that they can move on and not be hampered by them in the future.

In **Part II**, I will review all the proper parenting tools that parents need to include in their tool kit. I will also refer the reader to the appropriate parenting "How To" books to help you refine your parenting tools. Do not assume that you have enough tools. When I discuss tools, I will also encourage you to investigate certain Dragons that may have been interfering with your use of that tool, or Dragons that could in the future interfere with the application of a particular tool.

Dragons And Tools! Both are important. Are you open and receptive to looking at your 'parenting' tool kit and adding additional tools as you learn of the full range of tools that are not only available, but necessary to be successful as a parent? Are you open and receptive to consider what Dragons you will need to deal with in order to become a more effective parent?

THE CHOICE IS YOURS TO MAKE!

Part I — Dragons

1

Codependency

Index Of Suspicion

- Have you experienced a great deal of difficulty with your youngsters as they have approached the teenage years?
- Are you often devastated when your child misbehaves?
- Do you have trouble letting go and allowing your youngsters to grow up?
- Do you try to control your youngsters so they will do the right thing and not make mistakes?
- Do you do things for your children that they can and should be doing for themselves?
- Do you tend to react to your youngster's misbehavior, rather than take action?
- Do you have trouble dealing with your youngsters when they express anger toward you?

If You Answered "Yes" To Some Of These Questions, One Of Your Dragons May Be Codependency.

All adults are codependents to some degree. The degree to which you are a codependent will obviously determine how detrimental this Dragon is in your effective and consistent parenting. Several "real life" examples may also help you to determine if this is one of your Dragons.

"One mother came into counseling along with her 14-year-old daughter. The mother was limping noticeably and she was very angry with her daughter. When I asked her why she was limping, she stated that she hurt her back doing her daughter's chores. She stated that since her daughter did not do her chores the mother *had* to do them, and in doing so hurt her back. Therefore, she was blaming her daughter for her back pains."

"When I explained to the mother of a five-year-old that young children will say things like, 'I hate you' when they are angry, and it is then necessary for her to remain calm and begin to teach the child how better to express his anger, she said she would be devastated if her 5-year-old said, 'I hate you.' "

"While counseling a couple, the mother stated that she was very frustrated and burnt out because she had put on 20 birthday parties. They have two children, ages 9 and 11, and she just couldn't bear the thought of putting on their nine-year-old's upcoming party. When I asked about having her husband put on the party, she couldn't fathom the idea. 'What if he doesn't do a good job? What if my son is unhappy with his party?'"

Another parent agreed to pick up her daughter at 1:00 AM at a party, even though the mother had been in bed all day with the flu. She was then angry at her daughter because she had to pick her up.

Well, have you identified with any of these situations? If not, you could skip this chapter, but I do not advise you to do that, for all of us are codependent to a certain degree.

These situations have several things in common. In all cases it appears that a child or teenager is doing something wrong and if he or she would change their behavior then the parent in each example would definitely become happier. In each case the "wrong" behavior is also pretty normal behavior for the age group. Also, the reaction of all the parents is very typical of codependents. They become very angry and/or stressed as a result of the behavior of their child and really want them to change their behavior. In fact, codependent parents frequently *demand* that their youngsters change their behavior.

Codependency has to do with our responses and reactions to people around us. It involves the effects people (alcoholics, gamblers, sex addicts, overeaters, etc.) have on us and how we try to affect them. Codependency affects ALL areas of a person's life, including their adult relationships and marriages, as well as the way they work and relate in the job market. One of the most popular books on codependency is *Codependent, No More*[1] by Melody Beattie. This chapter will focus only on how codependency effects parenting.

Codependent behaviors will make it very difficult for parents to apply many of the strategies discussed in **Part II** of this book. Additionally, parents will become very stressed, angry and will soon burn out unless they deal with the codependent traits that are interfering with their roles as parents. Codependency is definitely a dragon that parents bring into their adult lives from their childhood, and a dragon that interferes with the application of well-known parenting strategies that work.

Picture yourself as a young child getting ready to go out and play baseball for the first time. Your parents put you in a straight jacket and send you out the door. You don't know any better. You block the ball with your body, let it hit the ground and then kick it to first to get the runner out. You do this for many weeks and months and years and you get pretty adept at it. Being a codependent and trying to cope with life and parenting is a lot like trying to play baseball with a straightjacket. It is a lot harder than it needs to be.

Codependents left their childhoods in straightjackets, but with no idea that they were wearing them. Because they acquired it gradually over a period of time in their childhood, it felt normal. It was crazy, but it felt normal. The straightjacket is the irrational beliefs and other ideas that you picked up about life, other people and your responsibility toward others. The straightjacket is also the resentments that have built up in you because of the way you were treated as a child. The straightjacket is the "childish strategies" that you learned as a child to cope with your dysfunctional family situation. These "childish strategies" will definitely interfere with applying parenting principles effectively and consistently. The "childish strategies" are an assortment of maladaptive behaviors and beliefs, often labeled codependency.

The term codependency came about in 1979 to define "people whose lives had become unmanageable as a result of living in a committed relationship with an alcoholic." Growing up in a family with an alcoholic parent will cause one to develop destructive habits and/or irrational beliefs regarding relationships. Don't stop reading if your parents were not alcoholics, because characteristics can be developed from living in a family where you were neglected and/or rejected. You could have learned the traits or beliefs from a parent who is a codependent or from a parent with strict, unrealistic, religious beliefs. Some codependent behaviors could be learned as children, while others may pick up these traits later in life as adults.

Codependency is very difficult to define in one or two sentences. In her book, Beattie devotes one entire chapter to listing codependent characteristics. I will select certain traits that she has listed and discuss how those traits will cause you a great deal of frustration as a parent. You will be able to identify which traits are causing you difficulty and be on the way toward dealing more effectively with the trait, enabling you to become a more effective parent. Each codependent, like each person, is different. You will not necessarily identify yourself with all of the following behaviors. The important point is to identify the behaviors that you exhibit, recognize how they impact your role as a parent, trace the behavior or belief to its root (childhood experience), then work diligently to change that behavior.

Too Affected And Desire To Control

First, let's look at Beattie's one sentence definition of a codependent: "A codependent person is one who has let another person's behavior affect him or her and who is obsessed with controlling other people's behavior."[2] This sentence describes many of the reasons for the adverse reactions to the situations discussed at the beginning of this chapter. The parents were too affected by their child or teen's behavior and desired to control the child or teen's behavior in order that they, as parents, might feel happier and more successful. Frequently I hear parents of teenagers express a great deal of frustration and anger when their child has received a D or an F in a class at school. It is as though the parent has received a D or an F in parenting.

Remember, when parents become angry and/or frustrated then they are no longer effective in implementing a plan to help their teenager to become more successful in school. When parents try to force their teen to get better grades they will surely be unsuccessful. You may be able to "force" or "control" a 4 or 5-year-old and get them to do what you want, but you can not force a 14 or 15-year-old to do anything. Sometimes parents can even experience these same difficulties with a strong-willed younger child. So, often when parents experience difficulties with a child it is because they are trying to control them too much, and they feel that the entire problem lies with their youngster rather than their approach to parenting.

Ignore Behaviors And/Or Think Survival

Codependents may tend to ignore problems and pretend they aren't happening. They may pretend circumstances aren't as bad as they are and watch problems get worse.

In his book *Pain and Pretending*,[3] Rich Buhler states that when childhood victims have no one to talk to who can help them deal with the pain they are going through, they end up pretending when in pain. This same thing may happen when a parent is experiencing pain in relating to one of their children or when their children are misbehaving. The parent may pretend that it is not really that bad. Victims of childhood also frequently feel powerless as parents. As small children they were powerless to change anything in their lives, and very often bring these same feelings into their adult lives. They feel powerless to change anything, or to get their children to behave appropriately. They tend to let things happen rather than seek help in order to develop corrective strategies.

Tend To Ignore Their Personal Needs

Codependents tend to ignore their own needs and put the needs and wants of others before their own. The source of this trait is worth discussing, as it is very essential for parents to change this tendency. Often codependents grow up in families where their needs were not important or acknowledged. The needs of the alcoholic, drug abuser, or neglectful parent always took precedence, so the child becomes an adult who does not consider his or her needs as important. Sometimes codependents do not even know what they need. When their needs were ignored as children they soon learned to not even think about what they needed and therefore have difficulty figuring out what they need as adults.

Because codependents do not take care of themselves, they soon become fatigued and stressed out and thus are unable to parent effectively. Their life tends to be out of balance.

(See the chapter on "stress" in **Part II**). Not only do they become fatigued and stressed, but codependents often frequently blame their children and/or spouse for their stress and fatigue. This anger only adds to their difficulty in parenting effectively.

Codependents often give more than they receive. Since they anticipate and respond to the needs of others, they get angry that people don't take care of their needs. They rely on others to take care of their needs rather than looking after themselves and their own needs. They often feel that it is selfish to take care of yourself. However, if you do not take of yourself, then you will not be able to take care of your children and teenagers.

Codependents Are Caretakers Or Rescuers

Caretaking and rescuing mean the same thing. It means doing things for people or your children that they can and should be doing for themselves. I once heard a speaker say that if you do anything for your child that they can do for themselves then you are making them a marital cripple. One of the major things keeping children from growing up is their parents. Parents who give their children things that they don't need or do things for them that they can do for themselves keep them from growing up. Doing these things that they can be doing for themselves also erodes their self-esteem. According to Beattie,[4] the following acts constitute a rescuing or caretaking move:

- "Doing something for someone although that person is capable of and should be doing it for himself."
- "Meeting people's needs without being asked and before they have agreed we should do so."
- "Fixing people's feelings."
- "Doing people's thinking for them."

- "Suffering people's consequences for them."
- "Solving people's problems for them."

It is very obvious how these acts interfere with proper parenting strategies and will only cause continued frustrations on the part of the parent. Determine behaviors of which you may be guilty. Determine in what circumstances it affects your role as a parent, then actively work to develop healthier behaviors.

Refer to the section in **Part II** on self-esteem for additional information in this area.

SALLY FORTH by Greg Howard

Reprinted with permission of North American Syndicate, Inc.

Many parents try to control their children and teens far too much. Parents need to gradually let go of the controls as a child grows and see how they do with the added freedom. If the child or teen does not handle it well, then it may be necessary to take back some of the freedom. Parenting is like flying a kite. If you hold on too long the string will break, however, if you let go too fast the kite will fall, so parents need to realize that it is a trial and error process.

Codependents Are Controllers

Codependents tend to nag, lecture, scream, holler, cry, beg, bribe, coerce, hover-over, scold, remind, and hint. It is easy to see how these affect the parenting role. Instead of being able to give children choices, parents want to "force" them to make the "right" choices. As discussed in **Part II**, a key concept in parenting is to give children choices. Presenting them with both positive consequences and negative consequences for their behaviors allows them to exercise their choice.

Codependents have difficulty allowing children and teenagers to make choices. Sara Hines Martin in her book, *Healing For Adult Children of Alchoholics*,[5] gives a formula for effective parenting: "The parent teaches the child, allows the child to make choices, allows the child to reap the natural consequences of his actions (which would include making mistakes), then comes alongside to be a support system when the child makes mistakes and is in pain."

Parents often feel a great deal of guilt when they have to allow their child to suffer negative consequences for their behavior. When the child makes a "wrong" choice and suffers a negative consequence, the parents need to realize that he has made that choice. It's not **you** punishing the child, but the child choosing to misbehave.

A father, in counseling, shared that when he had to apply a negative consequence to his child's misbehavior, even though the technique was very appropriate, he felt tremendous pain for the child. Often he would back off on the consequence he had applied. When he punished his children he felt that they were experiencing the same pain that he felt from his very punitive father.

Codependents frequently try to force things to happen. They feel that they know best how things should turn out and how people should behave. They become afraid to let other people be who they are and allow events to happen naturally. Even an 8 ft. giant cannot get a 3-year-old to eat his/her dinner or go to the bathroom. To a 3-year-old a parent looks like an eight foot giant, but parents will be unsuccessful if they try to parent with force, even with young children.

Parents will often say they felt it was easier to parent when their children were younger. That's generally because they could somewhat control their child's behaviors. In my couseling practice I frequently see parents of teenagers experience a great deal of difficulty because they are trying to control their lives. They try to force them to act a certain way, to get good grades, and to make the right decisions. They often try to control their teen through guilt, coercion, threats, advice giving, manipulation, or domination.

Transactional Analysis[6] is a good model to help explain the controlling type of behavior. The diagram between a parent and their teen or child would be as follows:

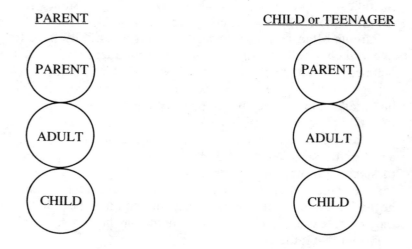

You will always be the parent of your child or teen. As a parent you will comfort him, praise him, give him advice, etc. However, with regards to rules and consequences, a change needs to take place as a youngster grows up. As a child gets older the parent needs to get out of the **parent mode** and into the **adult mode** as they relate to their child or teenager.

The more a parent stays in the **parent mode**, with regards to rules and consequences, they tend to nag, coerce, beg, yell, and scream at their child to behave. When they get into the **adult mode** they tend to set rules and consequences and calmly explain them to their youngster. When the youngster makes the wrong choice the parent calmly invokes the negative consequence. If the right choice is made, the youngster receives positive strokes. Another way of expressing this is that the parent is moving from a style of "high control" to a place of "low control."

Keep in mind the concept of "lag time." Just because you get in the **adult mode**, does not mean that your child will instantly get in the **adult mode** and become more responsible. In fact they may slip more in the **child mode** for a time to try and get you back into the **parent mode**. Don't get discouraged. Hang in there. You will also feel less stressed as you parent more from the **adult mode**, instead of trying to force things to go a certain way.

Codependents have difficulty in developing a de-parenting plan which is discussed in **Part II** and which is absolutely *essential* when dealing with teenagers. Remember the goal is not always to be in the **adult mode** with our youngsters. At times you will need to be a nurturing, supportive **parent**, while at other times you need to be in the **child mode** and play with your youngster.

Codependents Tend To React, Rather Than Take Action

Codependents tend to be reactionaries. Reacting to children causes parents to attempt to utilize anger and emotions, yelling and screaming, to change their behavior. Parents may tend to overreact (yell and scream) or underreact (keep quiet) when kids are misbehaving. "Acting," not "reacting," is needed in parenting. When we "act" we set rules and consequences and calmly follow through with positive and/or negative consequence.

A good example of how to "act" is presented in **Part II** under the discussion of chore charts and the school to home communication system. Codependents tend to rant and rave and react when chores are not done, rather than act or set up a chore chart and follow through consistently.

The following sections will discuss additional traits of codependency as discussed in Beattie's book, *Codependent, No More*. First, I'll list the trait, then state some of the behaviors that may go with that trait. Then I'll discuss how they effect parenting and some tips on changing the characteristic.

Obsessions

Codependents tend to:

- Feel terribly anxious about problems and people.
- Worry about the silliest things.
- Lose sleep over problems or other people's behavior.
- Feel unable to quit talking or worrying about other people or problems.
- Focus all their energy on other people and their problems.[7]

Codependents are often obsessed with the behavior of their children. They worry constantly about whether or not their children will be successful. They also spend much of their energy thinking about the problems and the behavior of their children.

As children, some codependents often felt very responsible for what was going on in their family. They often felt that what was happening was because of their actions rather than due to their parent's problems. Some tended to try and do all they could possibly do to somehow make the family and their parents all right.

Parents need to make sure that their lives are in balance and that they do not focus all their energy in one area of life, i.e. their children. The reader should be sure and read the section on "Is Your Life In Balance?" in Chapter 4. Parents must also realize that children need to learn to make choices and to become responsible for the choices that they make. In other words, do not become so focused on your son or daughter's behavior and ignore your own needs and the other six or seven areas of your life.

Dependency

Codependents tend to:

- Look for happiness outside themselves.
- Latch onto whoever or whatever they think can provide happiness.
- Desperately seek love and approval.
- Worry whether other people love or like them.
- Look to relationships to provide all their good feelings.[8]

This trait has been discussed somewhat in earlier examples and sections. Codependents may become terribly dependent on their children for their happiness. They may only feel successful as adults if their children are getting good grades, winning elections at school, getting invited to parties, hitting home runs in baseball, or scoring the goals in soccer. Parents often suffer more from a child's low grades than the youngster does. In fact, I believe that if parents demonstrate too much suffering about low grades it will have an adverse effect on their children.

Codependent parents may want to be friends with their children to such a degree that they forget to be parents. They may be hesitant to set limits and follow through with negative consequences for misbehavior because they are afraid their child will be mad at them. They may be reluctant to express their true emotions to their youngsters, expecially justified feelings of anger when the child has done something wrong to the parent, for fear that their child will not like them.

Codependent parents may be too wishy-washy in their parenting approaches and decisions because they are too concerned about what their friends may think of them and their children. They center their happiness around what others think of them, whether it be their children or other adults. They may try to "force" their children to wear the right clothes so they look right. They may give in to a child's demands when in public for fear others will look down on them if their child throws a temper tantrum.

Poor Communication

Codependent parents may:

- Blame, threaten, coerce, beg and bribe.
- Not say what they mean.
- Ask for what they want and need indirectly.
- Eliminate the word "No" from their vocabulary.
- Talk too much.
- Have a difficult time asserting their rights.
- Have a difficult time expressing their emotions honestly, openly and appropriately.
- Apologize for bothering people.[9]

This set of characteristics will affect codependent parents in many serious ways. It is very important for parents to clearly define rules in families. If rules are unclear then nobody knows what is expected of whom and/or when things will be completed. Clearly stated and understood rules are a prerequisite to any family discipline system.

Codependent parents may ask for what they want indirectly. One night I said to my daughter Robyn, "Do you think you'll have any time to iron some shirts for me?" If you had heard my tone of voice, which Robyn did, you would have known that I was being somewhat sarcastic. Robyn replied, "Dad, If you would like me to iron some shirts why don't you just ask me?" I was being too indirect.

Some codependent parents have difficulty saying "no" to their children. Remember, children and teens want and need clearly defined limits. They want you to be firm and be in charge. Although they may constantly test the limits and question your intelligence, deep down they do appreciate you, and need you to be firm. It lowers a youngster's self-esteem if they can manipulate their parent or appear to have power over their parents.

Some codependent parents have difficulty expressing their emotions honestly, openly, and appropriately. Remember that it is very important for parents to help their children learn to express their anger appropriately. Frequently codependent parents grew up in families where they could not express their emotions, especially anger. It is very important for parents to understand this in order to become more comfortable with their own emotions and thus become effective in teaching their youngsters to express their emotions. All emotions need to be expressed, not kept inside of you.

If you don't let them out then they will multiply and stomp around inside your body. After counseling a 6-year-old boy for several months after the death of his father, he came into my office and exclaimed that he had let some of the animals out that week; he had talked to his mom about his dad's death.

It may take quite a while for codependents to learn to identify their own feelings and develop the courage to express their feelings, before they will be able to help their youngsters to do the same.

Anger

Many codependents:

- Are afraid of their own anger.
- Think other people make them feel angry.
- Are afraid to make other people feel angry.
- Feel controlled by other people's anger.
- Repress their angry feelings.
- Punish other people for making the codependent angry.[10]

Although I discussed expressing feelings and emotions in the previous section, it is important to be aware of the traits you may exhibit in the area of dealing with anger. It is fairly obvious how some of the above traits will make it extremely difficult for you to stay calm while parenting. If you feel others make you feel angry, then you will feel very justified every time you get angry. You will not even take a look at youself and how you may be allowing others to cause you to become angry.

Codependent parents often respond inappropriately to their child's anger. Instead of remaining calm and discussing the situation with the youngster, the parent unloads their own barage of anger and emotion.

In the book *Codependent, No More*, Beattie lists several myths about anger that codependents and other people believe. These include:

1. It's not OK to feel angry.
2. Anger is a waste of time and energy.
3. Good, nice people don't feel angry.
4. We'll lose control and go crazy if we get angry.
5. People will go away if we get angry at them.
6. Other people should never feel anger toward us.

7. If other people are angry at us, we make them feel that way and we're responsible for fixing their feelings.

8. If we feel angry, someone else made us feel that way and that person is responsible for fixing our feelings.

9. If we feel angry at someone, that person has to change what he or she is doing so we don't feel angry any more.

10. If we feel angry, we have to shout and holler, or hit someone or break something.

11. If we feel angry at someone, it means we don't love that person any more.

12. If someone feels angry at us, it means that person doesn't love us any more.

13. It's OK to feel angry only when we can justify our feelings.[11]

Having rational beliefs about anger will not only help you to stay calm while parenting, but will also enable you to more effectively help your child to deal with their own anger appropriately.

Miscellaneous

Codependents tend to:

- Be extremely responsible or extremely irresponsible.
- Become martyrs, sacrificing their happiness and that of others for causes that don't require sacrifice.
- Have an overall passive response to codependency—crying, hurt, helplessness or
- Have an overall aggressive response to codependency—violence, anger, dominance.
- Find it difficult to have fun and be spontaneous.
- Vacillate in decisions and emotions.

- Be ashamed about family, personal, or relationship problems.
- Cover up, lie, protect the problem.
- Not seek help because they tell themselves the problem isn't bad enough, or they aren't important enough.
- Wonder why the problem doesn't go away.[12]

If you possess any of these characteristics, is it any wonder that effective parenting can really be a chore or totally impossible? I'll elaborate on a few of the traits.

When codependent parents are irresponsible they will tend to have a great deal of difficulty in following through with discipline strategies. They will not be consistent when following through and they will not present a very positive model to their youngsters of being responsible. When codependent parents are extremely responsible they may place unrealistic expectations on their youngsters and cause them much frustration. They may also be too rigid and expect young children to follow unrealistic schedules. They may expect young children to be extremely self-disciplined when in reality they are incapable of being so.

Another trait that greatly interferes with parenting is the tendency to avoid problems our youngsters are demonstrating, rather than develop an approach to deal with those problems. Nothing is more frustrating to a parent than to realize they are having a problem with their child but not know what to try in order to deal with the problem. If one is also reluctant to seek help, then the frustrations continue to mount. As stated earlier, many parents may "pretend" that things are not really as bad as they seem.

Detachment

A key concept for all codependents, which is also very true for codependent parents, is the need to detach from their children. In childhood, codependents were nearly always affected by the behavior of their parents. In other words, they were very attached to their parents' moods and behaviors. When codependents grow up they may become too attached to someone else. In other words, they continue to be too affected by another's behavior and/or moods. The following quote by an Al-Anon member begins the chapter on Detachment in Beattie's book. "It (detachment) is not detaching from the person whom we care about, but from the agony of involvement."[13]

Often when I counsel with parents about parenting concerns, I assure them that we can develop the necessary strategies which will work to change their child's inappropriate behavior. We can develop strategies that work to help youngsters improve their grades in school. However, I remind them that in this process their child will be making his/her own choices. I tell parents that part of my goal is to make sure they don't go crazy while their child or teen is deciding whether or not to get his/her life on a better course.

As Beattie states, "Sometimes detachment even motivates and frees people around us to begin to solve their problems. We stop worrying about them, and they pick up the slack and finally start worrying about themselves. What a grand plan! We each mind our own business."[14] Detaching is very scary for parents to do, since in their minds they are giving up control, and they are sure things will get worse. (And they might, for a time). One recent counseling situation illustrates this point. I was counseling a codependent mother and codependent stepfather, trying to get them to "back off" of their 16-year-old daughter and "detach." The daughter's grade point average when she came to counseling was about 1.86 (An A average is 4.0). After three months of counseling with the parents and seeing the daughter occasionally, her grade point average dropped to 1.50. The mother was about to demand a refund! Three months later, the daughter received an award because her grade point average jumped a whole number to 2.80. This is an example of the "lag time" that I discussed earlier.

Teenagers and younger children will not automatically become responsible immediately after parents begin to detach and act ADULT-like. Detaching does make a difference, both to the child who must become more responsible for the decisions they make, and to the parent, who is no longer dependent on their child or teenager for their own personal happiness.

Another way of explaining detachment is through Transactional Analysis. The parent moves out of the **parent mode** and begins to deal with the youngster from the **adult mode**. Nagging and reminding is replaced with setting rules and consequences. Remember, consequences need to be both positive (rewards for grades, etc.) and negative (restrictions for low performance in school for example).

Parents frequently ask, "But how do I detach?" These points may help you with this process. (1) Recognize when doing your family of origin work how affected you were or how attached you were to what was happening in your childhood family. You may still be continuing this tendency, as it is still the **child** in you that becomes too affected by those around you. (2) Recognize and accept that detaching is hard work. Picture yourself in a large swimming pool, ten times the size of a regular one. This one also has ten different drains.

You are swimming along peacefully, when suddenly someone opens a drain (a child gets an F in a class), and it forces you to swim harder to keep from getting affected by the drain, then someone opens another drain (your teenager doesn't want you to take them to the basketball game and sit with them), and you have to swim even harder to avoid being affected by this second drain. I am sure you get the point. Detaching takes work and effort.

All adults are codependent to some degree. The degree to which you are codependent determines how this trait affects your parenting. I am sure that you have identified traits and beliefs in this chapter that affect your role as a parent. It's hard work to change, but necessary and well worth it, for the happiness and welfare of you and your children.

Conclusion: The Road To Successful Parenting Involves Three Things:

1. *Change Your Behavior*

All parents need to learn about and develop proper parenting strategies. All parents lack a sufficient number of tools to "go the distance" with their children. This book is mainly about the Dragons that will interfere with applying the parenting tools, but **Part II** of this book reviews all the proper parenting strategies. Do not skip the section on tools, be open to adding some new ones to your parenting tool kit. Dragons will keep you from being able to apply the tools effectively and consistently. Dragons will cause you to overreact and resort to anger and emotion to change behaviors.

In general, Dragons can be labeled **Irrational Beliefs And Unresolved Resentment**.

In addition to utilizing proper parenting strategies you will need to:

2. *Change Your Beliefs (Expectations, Tapes, Beliefs About Yourself, Or Self-Esteem)*

The chapter on Codependency has helped to point out many beliefs that need to be changed in order to be effective as a parent. Beliefs are also discussed in the following chapters on Dragons. I encourage you to read all the chapters in order to best identify your irrational beliefs and learn the strategies to change your beliefs. You may identify your dragons in more than one chapter.

3. *Heal The Hurts Of The Past*

All parents have been hurt at some point in their lives. Possibly the hurt was from our own parents, or possibly it was from a sibling or another adult whom we lived with as a child. It could even have been from an ex-spouse who divorced us or died unexpectedly. Many parents have been hurt by the actions or failures of their children to perform up to their expectations and/or society's expectations.

Sidney Simon describes cycle breaking as change. "Change is cycle breaking. When we keep on doing what was done to us, we keep the cycle alive. When we change what we do that is different from how we were raised, we break the cycle." Simon further states, "Cycle breakers have dealt with those hurts and have been on a healing journey that involves a ruthless examination of what and who has hurt them, and they have moved into it and then out the other side. Some of it is forgiveness work."[15] We deal effectively with this Dragon when we label the hurts of the past and work through them to the other side. In other words, we resolve our resentment toward one who has hurt us.

To effectively deal with the Dragon of codependency, one needs to change his/her belief system and heal the hurts of the past. Chapters 2 through 8 deal with other Dragons and will help the reader to identify their Dragons. A key ingredient in dealing with each Dragon is to identify the beliefs that need changing and the pain that needs to be resolved.

A Challenge To You,
And A Time To Reflect:

1. Reread this chapter and mark the codependent traits that apply to you.

2. Recognize the ways in which the codependent traits have impacted on your role as a parent.

3. What are you doing for your children that they could be doing for themselves?

4. What decisions are you currently making for your children that they could and should be making for themselves?

5. Do you worry excessively about a child or teenager?

6. Who do you need to detach from?

7. What do you feel might happen if you detach?

8. What do you need to do (specifically) in order to detach?

9. Read the following chapters on Dragons and identify Dragons that you may need to deal with.

ENDNOTES

1. Beattie, Melody, *Codependent, No More*, Hazelden Foundation, 1987.
2. Ibid., p.31.
3. Buhler, Rich, *Pain and Pretending*, Nashville: Thomas Nelson Publishers, 1988.
4. Beattie, pp. 78-79.
5. Martin, Sara Hines, *Healing For Adult Children of Alcoholics*, New York: Bantam Books, 1988.
6. Harris, Thomas A., *I'm OK, You're OK, A Practical Guide to Transactional Analysis*, Harper & Row, Publishers, 1967; **and** Harris, Amy Bjork, and Thomas A. Harris, *Staying OK*, Harper & Row, Publishers, 1985.
7. Beattie, adapted from p. 39.
8. Ibid., p. 41.
9. Ibid., pp. 41-42.
10. Ibid., p. 43.
11. Ibid., pp. 141-142.
12. Ibid., pp. 44-45.
13. Ibid., p. 51.
14. Ibid., p. 57.
15. Simon, Sidney, *Cycle Breaking*, ASCA Counselor Newsletter, Delores Ehrlich, ed., October 1989. Published by American School Counselor Association (a Division of the American Association of Counseling & Development) Alexandria, Virginia, pp. 18-19.

2

Recreating Your "At Home" Feeling

Index Of Suspicion

- Do you find yourself yelling and nagging at your children just as your mother or father yelled at you?

- Do you find yourself taking sole responsibility for parenting and excluding your partner, because one of your own parents was the main parent?

- Dads, do you find yourself working long hours and being away from home a lot just as your own father was?

- Have you identified one child in your family as the problem child, just as your parents singled out one of your siblings as the major cause of problems in your own home?

- Do you demand perfection from your children, just as your parent/s did of you?

If You Answered "Yes" To Some Of These Questions, One Of Your Dragons May Be Recreating Your "At Home" Feeling.

One of the most helpful books that I have found in working with adults is one by W. Hugh Missildine, entitled *Your Inner Child of the Past*.[1] Missildine describes various parental attitudes, which, when they are used to an extreme degree, will cause maladjustments in children which then can be carried into adulthood. One of the author's common themes throughout the book is that adults, both consciously and subconsciously, attempt to recreate their "at home" feeling in their adult relationships. This "at home" feeling is not necessarily a healthy atmosphere, but it's the only one the person feels comfortable with. It's scary to think about how you might be trying to recreate your childhood feelings in your adult relationships, but I see it happening over and over again in all the adults I counsel.

This can happen in minor ways such as serving dinner in bowls, which may have been the custom in your house, rather than putting the food on plates and then bringing the plates to the table, not allowing a child to play in the house or living room, not allowing a child to sleep in your bedroom, even when they are afraid, etc. It can also happen in major ways, such as always arguing with your spouse over something, because there was always arguing and fighting in your home while you were growing up. If your parents did not work together on parenting issues, then you may tend to try and parent alone, without working together with your spouse.

It is very important for parents to look back at their childhood experiences in order to make sure that they are not simply repeating a pattern that they observed growing up and accepted as healthy and normal. Recreating your "at home" feeling is definitely a Dragon that will interfere with applying effective parenting strategies consistently. Missildine describes various pathogenic parenting styles. You may be consciously or subconsciously recreating these styles in your current role as a parent.

A common thread of all of the following pathogenic parental attitudes is that they erode the self-esteem of the child. Another common thread through most of the pathogenic parenting styles is that parents are doing what they do because they love their child. As you consider which of the following pathogenic parental attitudes you may fall into, it is also important to consider what style your parents exhibited. In this way, you will begin to understand more about your current parenting style and this in itself may help lead you to healthy changes.

I will discuss the following pathogenic parental attitudes that are covered in much more detail in Missildine's book *Your Inner Child of the Past.*

- Perfectionism
- Overcoercion
- Oversubmission
- Overindulgence
- Punitiveness
- Neglect
- Rejection.

It is important to realize that you were undoubtedly raised in more than one of these styles and these parental attitudes may be occurring in your own home at this time. One parent may exhibit one style while the other may demonstrate another, or a combination of others. Determine which of the following "at home" feelings you may be recreating in your current family.

PERFECTIONISM:
Children need to receive approval and praise from their parents. Perfectionist parents often withhold praise until a child or teen has completely mastered a task. Frequently they may praise a child, but always add "next time you should do this and it will be even better." During my training to become a School Psychologist I observed, through a one way mirror, a father playing blocks with his 5-year-old son. I will never forget the experience. Each time the son stacked one block

on top of the other, the father would readjust it so it fit "perfectly." This parental attitude obviously will destroy a child's self-esteem and the child will constantly strive to make things perfect, and end up belittling himself when they aren't. Trying to be perfect will cause the youngster much stress, and lowered self-esteem. Perfectionist parents may also use overcoercion and punitiveness in an effort to get the child to do better.

The origins of perfectionism can be several. One excellent book is by Dr. David Stoop, entitled *Living With a Perfectionist*.[2] According to Stoop, one source is summarized by the following sentences, "Sometimes a parent will be so aloof from the parenting role that a child experiences a cold, unpredictable, and even dangerous environment. When a child has these types of early experiences, the conditions of perfectionism are already set in motion." Obviously, growing up with perfectionist parents will cause you to be a perfectionist. As Stoop also points out, you may not necessarily be a perfectionist in the areas that your parents were, but may instead gravitate toward different areas. Rich Buhler, in *Pain and Pretending*,[3] also discusses how the origin of perfectionism can come from being victimized in some way as a child. The child may consciously or subconsciously make a vow that "When I am old, I will do everything perfect, then nothing bad will happen to me."

If you suspect you are a perfectionist, you need to Face it, Trace it (understand where it comes from), then work hard to Erase it. Chapter 6 on Irrational Beliefs will also give you some additional ideas for dealing with perfectionism as it discusses how one can identify irrational beliefs and work toward changing them. Chapter 1 on Codependency may also help you, as codependents frequently feel that things should always go a certain way and they tend to want control over the situations and people. The books previously mentioned by Stoop and Buhler will also be helpful, in addition to Missildine's book.

OVERCOERCION:

According to Missildine,[4] the most common pathogenic parental attitude in America is Overcoercion. The overcoercive parent constantly supervises, directs, reminds, and nags the child with an endless stream of commands. This leaves the child with little opportunity to initiate and pursue his own interests and activities. Overcoercive parents often had overcoercive parents.

The Overcoercive parent may also feel very anxious about their capabilities as a parent, and try to force their child to "turn out right." The overcoercive parent tries to maintain high control on a youngster when it is no longer needed and constantly reminds youngsters of chores and other responsibilities, instead of allowing youngsters to make choices and experience the consequences of those choices. The overcoercive parent would have difficulty utilizing chore charts and would also have difficulty using the technique of logical consequences.

Children raised in an overcoercive environment often resort to dawdling, procrastinating, daydreaming and "forgetting" in order to deal with the constant parental demands. They tend to wait for the teachers to nag and remind them, and may also resist the teachers in the same way they resist their parents.

Parents may tend to be overcoercive if that is what they experienced as children. Recognizing this connection may help one toward changing, provided he/she also adopts appropriate parenting tools, such as chore charts and logical consequences. Codependents also tend to be very controlling and frequently overcoercive, so you should read Chapter 1 on Codependency, if you have not done so already. The chapters on Low Self-Esteem, Irrational Beliefs, and Unresolved Resentments will also help you recognize possible sources of this type of parental attitude.

OVERSUBMISSION:

According to Missildine, "Almost as common as the overcoercive parent, the oversubmissive type capitulates to the child's immature whims and demands, ignoring and sacrificing his/her own needs and rights. Such a parent attitude makes the child the 'boss,' the parent the slave. The child responds to this parental attitude by demanding more, becoming impulsive, and flying into temper outbursts if his demands are not met. He has difficulty in considering the rights of others." Parents often have difficulty saying "no" and are overly concerned that their child will love them. They do not realize that the child needs limits and needs parents to enforce those limits.[5]

Several other chapters will help the reader to overcome this parental attitude. Chapter 1 on Codependency will help since codependents often have difficulty setting limits and saying no to their children. Chapter 8 on Dealing with a Loss (and the guilt feeling associated with it), may also be helpful to some, because if one is working through the grief cycle and feels guilty, he/she may give in too much to the children.

Many parents want to make up to their children what they themselves did not get as children, and therefore give in too often to their demands, which is discussed in Chapter 5 on Frozen Needs. Other parents made vows as children that when they become parents they would give their children things that they never had, thus some parents may relate to Chapter 3 on Vows. Chapter 4 on Low Self-Esteem will also be helpful to some, as low self-esteem parents are often unsure of setting limits and being firm with their children.

OVERINDULGENCE:

A paragraph from Missildine's book summarizes this behavior; "A parent with this attitude constantly showers the child with presents, clothes, 'treats,' and services—often without the child's desiring them and with out any consideration of the child's needs to develop his own ways of affecting his environment. While the overly submissive parent waits for the child's demand—and obeys it—the overly indulgent parent showers gifts and presents without the child's asking. The child eventually responds to this inexhaustible cornucopia with bored, blase behavior. Both as a child and later as an adult, he has difficulty in initiating any effort and has little persistence."[6] Does this describe you as an adult? Does it describe your child or teenager now? If so, then this may definitely be one of the pathogenic parental attitudes that you will need to change. Oversubmissive parents create a child who is active and demanding, while overindulgent parents create a child who is bored, passive, and often discontent.

Overindulgent parents would probably not require a child to work toward goals, and would probably not utilize chore charts or an allowance system.

Several other chapters will help you deal with this parental attitude as well. Chapter 5 on Frozen Needs discusses how parents try to make up to their children what they did not get as children. If they were deprived as children then they may try to give their child everything that they did not have. They may not require the youngster to work toward any long term goals. Vows and Frozen Needs may overlap in some areas. Some parents, as children, may have made a vow such as, "When I am old my children will have this or that."

Therefore, Chapter 3 on Vows may be helpful to some parents. Some parents may overindulge their children out of guilt. Therefore, Chapter 8 on Dealing with A Loss may help some parents. If a parent has gone through a divorce or is going through a divorce, they may try to make it up to their child and overindulge them. Codependents (Chapter 1) and parents with low self-esteem (Chapter 4) may strive too hard to be a friend to their child and may overindulge their child "out of love."

PUNITIVENESS:

According to Missildine, "Punitiveness is an excessively strict, stern and harshly punishing viewpoint toward a child on whom a parent consistently vents his own recurring personal hostility and aggressive feelings."[7] Punitiveness does not refer to only excessive physical punishment, but also to endless, strict moralizing and the creation of guilt and feelings of utter worthlessness in a child because of his behavior. Harsh scoldings, angry beatings, and punishments for behaviors that are normal for the child's age are part of a punitive parent's approach.

The effect of all punitiveness is to create in the child an excessive guilt and feelings of being no good, worthless, contemptible, and not worth loving, according to Missildine. Punitiveness is not effective for several other reasons. The child begins to rely on an outside force to guide his/her behavior and does not develop an internal guiding system. Children also tend to avoid parents who are very punitive and thus will not want to go to them when they have a problem, for fear of punishment. When punishment is severe, children and teens may lie to their parents to attempt to escape severe punishment. Punitiveness gives a child a very poor role model for dealing with things that one does not like. It says that it's OK to use physical force to get someone to change his/her behavior.

Often a parent who has been severly punished as a child, although he swears not to do the same to his children, frequently ends up doing so. This parent may honestly feel that it is necessary and proper to be punitive in order to raise a healthy and obedient child. Therefore, a major souce of this parental attitude is one's own childhood experiences. Parents may also be punitive as a reaction to the stress in their own lives; thus Chapter 11 on Self-Esteem And Stress may be important for some parents to read.

Another major source of this parental approach is due to unresolved resentment toward someone in the past. Parents frequently reassign anger that they have toward a sibling to one of their own children. Chapter 7 on Unresolved Resentment deals with this situation. Parents frequently react angrily to their child because of irrational beliefs, unrealistic expectations, and negative interpretations of their behavior. For these parents, Chapter 6 on Irrational Beliefs will be very helpful.

NEGLECT:

According to Missildine, "Neglect is usually a parental attitude—often expressed as a preoccupation with work or 'duties'—which results in the parent having little time for, interest in, or awareness of the child's need for a continuing attachment with an adult to whom he can turn for help in satisfying his needs."[8] Children can experience neglect for a variety of reasons. When one parent dies, a child will experience neglect due to the absence of that parent. Children can also experience neglect due to a parent's job, social activities, alcoholism, sickness, etc. Children and teens experience some neglect in cases of divorce and living with a single parent. When neglected, a child often feels that there is no one there for him. They may keep feelings inside having no one available to share them with.

As stated above, some forms of parental neglect are unavoidable. Others are not. If you were neglected as a child, then you may not fully appreciate the importance of being involved with your children. Identifying the degree of neglect you may have experienced will help you to avoid this with your children. Neglect is the absence of something as a child, therefore it can be difficult for adults to identify that they were neglected. Few adults that I counsel readily accept, at least initially, that they were neglected as a child.

As parents move through the grief cycle due to divorce or death of a spouse, they may tend to neglect their child. This is understandable. However, it points out the importance of parents accepting their need to work through the grief cycle, in order to be better equipped to be there for their children.

Thus, Chapter 8 on Dealing With A Loss would be good to read for those who are going through a divorce or dealing

with the death of a spouse. Some parents try to make up
to their children what they did not get when they were children.
This may require them to spend many hours at work to make
money to provide the material things that they never got.
Chapter 5 on Frozen Needs will be helpful to you if you
spend a great deal of time away from your children trying
to give them what you never had.

REJECTION:

"Rejection is a parental attitude that denies the child any
niche of acceptance; he is considered and treated as an unac-
ceptable individual and an unwanted burden, a nuisance and
a source of trouble," according to Missildine.[9] True rejection
seldom occurs, however there are certain situations where it
may occur. A rejected child will definitely experience low
self-esteem.

A parent may reject and act negatively toward a child if
they are reassigning anger that they had toward a sibling to
one of their own children. This happens, and it is discussed
in Chapter 7 on Unresolved Resentments. When parents are
going through a divorce, they may temporarily reject a child
that may remind them of their ex-spouse. For those of you
in this situation, Chapter 8 on Dealing With A Loss will be
very important for you to read. Irrational beliefs and faulty
expectations may also cause a parent to reject a child. Chapter
6 on Irrational Beliefs discusses how this happens and suggests
steps toward acting with less anger toward a child.

As stated earlier, some parents may identify one child in
their family who is labeled as "the problem" because this
was done in their family of origin. If this happens, the child
may definitely feel rejected.

A Challenge To You, And A Time To Reflect:

1. In what way(s) have you been recreating your "at home" feeling?

2. How has your spouse been attempting to recreate his/her "at home" feeling?

3. Which of the seven pathogenic parenting styles might you be recreating?

4. Which of the seven pathogenic parenting styles might your spouse be recreating?

5. Discuss the above questions with your spouse and compare answers.

6. Read the other chapters that were suggested under each discussion of a pathogenic parenting style.

ENDNOTES

1. Missildine, W. Hugh, *Your Inner Child of the Past*, New York: Pocket Books, 1963.

2. Stoop, Dr. David, *Living With a Perfectionist*, Nashville: Thomas Nelson Publishers, 1987, p. 63.

3. Buhler, Rich, *Pain and Pretending*, Nashville: Thomas Nelson Publishers, 1988.

4. Missildine, p. 101.

5. Ibid., adapted from pp. 125-144.

6. Ibid., p. 156.

7. Ibid., p. 204.

8. Ibid., p. 232.

9. Ibid., p. 266.

3

Vows and Parenting

Index Of Suspicion

- Do you remember ever deciding as a child that when you had children you would not do certain things to them that were done to you?

- Do you find yourself trying to explain everything to your children?

- Are you determined to never use physical punishment on your children?

- Do you stay up to all hours in the night cooking or cleaning house or helping your youngsters with school projects?

- Do you feel tremendous guilt if you happen to miss one of your youngster's school functions or sporting events?

If You Answered "Yes" To Some Of The Above Questions, One Of Your Dragons May Be Vows.

As a child you undoubtedly made many observations while traveling the course from childhood to adulthood. You observed how your parents interacted with each other and you especially observed how your parents treated you and your siblings. During your trip through childhood you consciously and subconsciously made certain vows as to what you would do in your adult life, your marriage, and with your children. Some of you could rattle off the list of vows fairly rapidly. Others may require some counseling sessions and/or somewhat deeper introspection to identify the vows.

Everyone makes vows at some point, either conscious, or within their subconscious. Some of the vows you made are very healthy vows. These vows make your life a lot easier as an adult. However there are many vows that will get in the way of becoming an effective parent. These are the vows that you need to uncover, analyze, recognize that they are unhealthy, and work hard to discard. Vows will definitely get in the way of effectively applying the tools in your "parenting tool kit."

Another way to look at vows, how they may get you in trouble, and why they might not work for you now, is through looking at the Transactional Analysis model again:

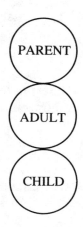

As previously stated, the child in you made the vows. As you experienced things as a child you made the vows: When I am older I will always . . . , or I will never . . . . What I am asking you to do at this point is to get into the Adult and look at these vows objectively, evaluate them, and discard the unhealthy ones. It's not as easy as you think. You have lived with the vows for so long that you may honestly feel that you didn't make any vows as a child, or that whatever vows you made are OK. Remember too, that in most cases someone did not force or encourage you to make the vow, but you made it within your own mind as a strategy to help you to cope with the pain.

In his book *Pain and Pretending*, Rich Buhler describes how victims of childhood abuse make vows and he lists four categories of vows. The four are:

Vows of Silence:

"That (the abusive situation) did not happen, and I will never say that it did." This is the reason that counseling is required to help adults uncover the "secrets of the past." The child made a vow when experiencing pain, that he/she would never speak of it again and blocked it from his/her conscious memory. Frequently, adult victims may not even remember the painful experience until adulthood, when they may observe a show on TV that may remind them of it, or their own child may experience a similar trauma at the hands of a neighbor, grandfather, etc. Even though the adult victims may have pushed the painful event to their subconscious, that does not mean they are not affected everyday by that event.

Vows of Revenge:

Victims often make a vow of revenge. "When I am older I will get that person." The only problem is, that person is often not around, so adults frequently take out their anger on someone in the present. One mother who was verbally and physically abused by her brothers found herself always siding with her daughter when her son and daughter got into an argument. She was taking out her revenge on her son. This type of behavior is also discussed in the chapter on Unresolved Resentments and Parenting.

Vows of Perfection:

Childhood victims often strive for perfection so that they will not be hurt again. Trying to be "perfect" as a parent is very stressful and produces much anger as the parent becomes frustrated and his/her self-esteem sinks lower and lower. Expecting children to be perfect is often a result of this vow, which causes parents and children much anguish.

Vows of Safety and the Need to Control:

This vow has a tremendous impact on parenting. According to Buhler, "One of the most powerful vows of the abandonment stage is, 'I am not going to hurt like this ever again.' And from that point on, the victim directs every ounce of energy, skill, and intelligence to remain safe. This, in turn, produces a need for the victim to be in control of the people and circumstances in his life, because if they are potentially out of control, he or she feels the threat of more pain."[1] The need and/or desire to control is definitely a Dragon that gets in the way of effective parenting, especially when their youngster hits the teenage years. I do a great deal of counseling with parents of teenagers and a typical response from parents at this stage is: "I was doing a great job as a parent when they were young. In fact, friends would say our children were better behaved than most kids."

When children are younger, parents can "control" them a lot more than when they become teenagers. In some cases a strong willed 7 or 8-year-old will give the parent as much trouble as a teenager would if the parent tries to "control" the child's behavior.

The desire and need to control is also discussed in the chapter on Codependency, since codependents are by definition, "too affected by someone's behavior, and want to control that person's behavior." Another way of describing the control issue utilizes the Transactional Analysis Model of Parent, Adult, and Child. This was also described in Chapter 1 on Codependency, but is such a common problem that it is worth repeating. The tendency to want to control our children can be due to several different Dragons.

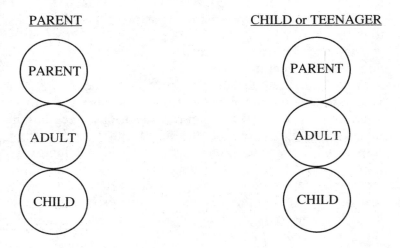

You will always be the parent to your son or daughter, make no mistake about that. However if you try to control them, then you parent them out of the **parent** part of your personality. Your approach might be, "Do it now," "Do it because I said so," "Why do I always have to remind you to do your chores?" "Don't forget to do your chores today, OK . . . OK, did you hear me, I don't want to have to remind you again." Do any of these statements sound familiar?

Parents can begin to deal with their children out of their own **adult** when children are young. For example, "When you finish your meal, then you can have dessert" allows the child to then decide what they will do. "When you clean up your room, then you can go out and play" allows the child to make a choice.

As mentioned in **Part II** on parenting Tools, it is important to develop a parenting strategy that allows and encourages children to make choices. If parents have not experienced any difficulties when trying to control youngsters, they will undoubtedly experience it in the teenage years. Trying to control or force a teenager to do something, is like trying to push a wet piece of spaghetti up a slight incline. Young children are more like a hard piece of spaghetti; it's easy to push a hard piece of spaghetti up an incline, but whenever you try and push a wet piece, it never seems to go in the direction you want it to.

When you parent teenagers, you definitely need to get into your **adult** mode and hope that they will also get into the **adult** and learn to make appropriate decisions. Keep in mind that as you get more into the **adult** and turn over more responsibilities to them, they generally will not jump right into the **adult** and begin to make healthy decisions. There may be some lag time. It may take them a while to realize that they are responsible for the decisions they make in their lives. Many teenagers do not want to accept responsibility for their decisions.

I once counseled a very frustrated mother who said that parenting her daughter was like trying to pull a stubborn mule. Since the daughter was in the room with us, I felt that the word picture of a mule was not too complimentary, and I asked the daughter what kind of an animal she liked. She described a big, fluffy dog which we decided to use in place of the mule. It would be one thing if, after the mother stopped pulling the dog, it just sat there and did not move. Most parents wouldn't worry too much about that situation.

However, most parents picture the dog on the edge of a cliff, and believe their failure to pull their youngster will result in them going over the cliff. It's scary when we think that our teenagers may fall off the cliff. The thing that parents do have some control over is how far the youngster will fall. In other words, don't put your head in the sand and wait three months to see what choices your teenager made regarding their grades, but utilize the school-to-home communication system that is described in **Part II**. Weekend privileges and rewards will depend on what happened in school that week. In this way inactivity results in a shorter fall off the cliff, and it will not be as devastating.

Before getting to parenting vows that may be less obvious, I would like to point out a vow that I have observed many times in counseling. Many adults have been raised in an overly coercive environment, where their parents always stayed in the PARENT mode and constantly told them what to do. W. Hugh Missildine describes this type of environment and the vow in his book *Your Inner Child of the Past*.[2] Oftentimes when parents were overly coercive, the child makes a vow such as "When I get old, no one will tell me what to do."

This vow can get in the way of counseling as well, because even though one may go to counseling, they may still look at the counselor as an overly coercive parent who is trying to tell them what to do; their vow kicks in and they do not do anything the counselor has encouraged them to do. Frequently, I recommend to people that they ought to read some books on a particular subject. I get all kinds of excuses, "I don't like to read," "I don't have time to read." However, the most frustrating for me is, "Sure, I'll read that," followed by three of four weeks of excuses as to why they didn't get around to reading. They are using the same strategy with me that they used with their own parents. I used to be really naive to this game, but now I am able to recognize it fairly soon and frequently point it out to the client.

Often at the end of a session I will kiddingly say to a client, "This is a good book, you can read it if you want. I really don't care." Since I have removed the command (You should), it helps to take away their resistance (I will say I will do it, but I won't do it). If your spouse made this vow as a child, you will probably have a very difficult time trying to suggest to him/her that they do something different. The best approach might be to say, "I have tried to do the following with our son and it seems to be working. You may want to try it." Or, "I've read this book on parenting and it seems to make sense to me. If you would like to read it and discuss it, let me know." With this approach you are trying to avoid "commanding" your spouse to do something. The more you make commands the more they will resist.

It is impossible in any book to list all the vows that children could have made while growing up. I will attempt to list many that I have heard in counseling or that were shared with me following a parenting seminar. The following vows will relate only to parenting issues and I will discuss each of them briefly. The key to dealing with vows is to first recognize them, realize where they came from, and then evaluate them as to their relevance now and continually attack and eliminate the useless ones so they do not interfere with effective parenting.

1. *I will never spank my children.*

   If you were frequently spanked as a child, this is a pretty obvious vow that you might have made. Spanking is definitely an appropriate tool for parents to use, when used at the right time, the right age, and in the right manner, as is discussed in **Part II**. This vow would get in the way of spanking your children, even when the situation called for it. Never spanking a child is just as wrong as always spanking a child. There are situations when spanking is the only and most appropriate technique to use.

2. *I will always explain everything to my children.*

   It is very important to explain our rules and beliefs to our children, although some parents go overboard in this area. One day in my office, a woman spent five minutes explaining to her 2½-year-old son why he should not play in the trash can. She should have given him a firm "No," and moved him to another part of the room. When asked about this, she said that her parents never explained anything to her, so she was going to explain everything to her kids. This could cause a parent to get into too much explaining and even arguing, which is ineffective. Explaining reasons for your rules to kids is OK, but trying to convince them that your rule is necessary and fair is impossible. It promotes something that you do not want—constant arguing and debating within the house.

3. *I will not pressure my kids about their grades.*

If you received a lot of pressure from your parents to get good grades then maybe you have gone overboard to not pressure your kids. One mother said her parents made her feel that if she didn't do well in second grade she would never go to college. This mother hasn't wanted the same thing to happen to her own kids so she has probably erred by not encouraging them enough in school. She let her children decide for themselves what they wanted to do in school at an age when they were too young to make wise decisions.

4. *I won't have my children do chores.*

One mother said that as a child she had to do everything around the house, so she vowed that when she had kids they would not have to do much work around the house. She ended up with three teenagers that were not responsible for any jobs at home, which carried over into school where they were not responsible in getting their work done there. Having children do chores around the house is not set up simply to get some cheap labor. It is designed to help children become responsible and accountable for their actions. Accountability and responsibility are requirements for children to become successful in school and later life.

5. *I will be involved in all my children's activities.*

The attempt to try to make up to your kids what you did not get will not work. It is OK to try to be involved in your children's activities, but if you happen to miss one or two, don't put yourself down or go on a guilt trip. It's impossible to be involved in all their activities. Another trap here is that you may expect your child to praise you constantly for your attendance at school activities. Generally, children will not do this, which may cause the anger to swell in you. This vow is similar to Frozen Needs which are discussed in Chapter 5.

6. *I will let my kids do what they want.*

Obviously, this will result in chaos and unruly, obnoxious, children. It is easy to see how one could make this vow if their parents were very dictatorial and called all the shots for their child. Parenting is like flying a kite. It can be disasterous if you let out too much line too fast as the kite will fall. Kids will fall if they are put in situations to make decisions that they are incapable of making at that point in their life. In other words, giving youngsters too much freedom too quickly can be very harmful.

7. *I will give my children everything I didn't have.*

This is another vow that can be related to Frozen Needs which are discussed in Chapter 5. This vow often results in having a child who not only has everything, but has had to put forth very little effort to get it. Frequently, they wait around as a teenager or adult for someone to take care of them. If this is one of your vows, then it may be difficult for you to set up a chore chart and let your child or teen work for the things that they want. It will help them to learn to make choices and experience the consequences for those choices. If they have to choose between two toys, and the one they choose breaks right away, they will learn to make better choices. If you run out and buy them a toy right after one breaks then they will not learn that valuable lesson.

8. *I will make sure that my kids love me.*

If you felt a great deal of anger toward a parent and "hated" them, you may have made a vow that your kids would always love you. This can result in your not setting limits and not following through with appropriate consequences. Someone shared with me that on one Bill Cosby show, the father said, "If my kids always love me when they are children, then they will probably hate me when they are adults." There is a lot of truth to that quote. Your role as a parent is not to be loved by your children, but to help them develop into healthy responsible adults. You may not get praised for your role as a parent until your children have children of their own. That's a long time to wait, isn't it?

A Challenge To You,
And A Time To Reflect:

1. What vows did you make as a child?
   List the vows and continue to give it some thought so you
   can add vows as you think of them.

2. To help you think of the vows you might try to complete
   the following sentences:
   When I was a child I decided that I would always . . .
   When I was a child I decided that I would never . . .

3. Once you've identified the vows, try to identify where they
   came from. This identification will help you to realize that
   you can eliminate them. I read once in a book that to deal
   with something you need to: Face It, Trace It, and Erase
   It. That's exactly what we need to do in order to eliminate
   the unhealthy vows. Keep in mind that childhood vows die
   a slow death. You will need to continuously recognize vows
   and attack them to apply the parenting strategies effectively.

4. Discuss with your spouse what vows he/she may have made
   as a child. This may help you identify the root of some
   of your conflicts in parenting.

ENDNOTES

1. Buhler, Rich, *Pain and Pretending*, Nashville: Thomas Nelson
   Publishers, 1988.
2. Missildine, W. Hugh, *Your Inner Child of the Past*, New York:
   Simon and Schuster, 1963.

4

Low Self-Esteem

Index Of Suspicion

- Do you frequently feel unsure of what to do as a parent?
- Are you constantly second guessing yourself after setting a punishment for one of your youngster's misbehaviors?
- Are you often reluctant to attempt a new idea when dealing with your children?
- Do you feel devastated when one of your youngsters is mad at you and refuses to speak to you?
- Are you unable to ask your spouse for help in dealing with the children?
- Do you ignore your own personal needs, leaving yourself frequently tired and stressed out?

If You Answered "Yes" To Some Of These Questions, One Of Your Dragons May Be Low Self-Esteem.

Low self-esteem is a Dragon that many individuals bring into their adult lives. Low self-esteem can have an important impact on one's ability to apply the parenting tools.

In addition to the areas listed above in the Index of Suspicion, those with low self-esteem may:

a. Have difficulty setting limits on their children and following through with the consequences to misbehavior because they want to be liked by their children.

b. Have difficulty expressing their ideas and concerns to their spouse in order to resolve conflicts with regard to parenting strategies.

c. Take things that their children and spouses say personally, resulting in anger and/or guilt feelings, and therefore be unable to resolve differences with their spouse.

d. May tend to get artificial feelings of self-worth from helping others, which may cause them to feel unworthy when someone does not request or need help.

e. May tend to take responsibility for others' failures and/or disappointments and feel guilty and inadequate because of someone else's behavior.

As you can see, the effects of low self-esteem on parenting can be very significant.

Low self-esteem is a Dragon that most parents have to deal with to some degree. I will make an effort to summarize significant points regarding low self-esteem and some tips for you to build your self-esteem and that of your child, but strongly encourage that you do more reading in this area, as good self-esteem is a major key to all areas of your life.

What Is Self-Esteem?

Self-esteem is the beliefs that an individual holds true about himself. How do you feel about yourself? Do you feel you can solve problems? Do you feel that your opinions and ideas are important and are you willing to share them with others? Self-esteem is the confidence of knowing your worth as a human being, coupled with a healthy concern to maintain that posture. Self-esteem is a key to our marriages, our jobs, how we deal with stress and changes, how we deal with losses such as divorce, and how we deal with mid-life transition. It is definitely a key to successful parenting and to building positive self-esteem in your children. One cannot develop youngsters with high self-esteem unless one's own self-esteem is healthy.

Where Does Our Self-Esteem Come From?

In order to change and evaluate our self-esteem we need to do some family of origin work and determine how our self-esteem was formed. Self-esteem is like a package that you put together about how you feel about yourself. Looking back at your childhood is like opening up the package and seeing all the parts, and how they were put together into the package. We then have more power over the process of taking out things we don't like, rearranging the package, and adding more positive things to the package.

Our self-esteem has come from our parents, friends, teachers, television, and society. We sometimes perpetuate a low self-esteem by the way we continue to treat ourselves. Your self-esteem may be low if your parents:

- compared you to a more successful brother or sister,
- criticized you more than praised you,
- gave you conditional love, rather than unconditional love,
- did not accept your feelings or allow you to express them,
- did not allow you to do things that you were capable of doing for yourself,
- seemed to emphasize skills or traits that were not your strengths (For example, you might have been a great

musician, but your parents valued sports, so you may have felt inferior.),

- had expectations for you that were unrealistic and unattainable (Youngsters do not—cannot question their parents' expectations. They simply feel inferior if they do not live up to those expectations.),
- were too busy with their lives to respond to your needs and feelings,
- were physically or emotionally abusive to you.

A daily devotional from the book *Days of Healing, Days of Joy*[1] by Earnie Larsen and Carol Larsen Hegarty summarizes some of these points:

"When they didn't love me, I thought there was something wrong with me. Donna B."

When we felt unloved, we didn't have the sophistication to wonder whether our parents loved themselves. We didn't have any way of knowing that loving has much more to do with the capacity of the giver than it does with the deservedness of the receiver. Children don't reason that way. "If you don't hold me," we assumed, "it must be that I am not holdable. Other kids are loved. The fault must be with me."

One of the greatest challenges for a counselor is to help adults to realize that there was nothing wrong with them as children and there is nothing wrong with them now. As I helped her overcome her low self-esteem, one woman said to me, "How do I know that what you are telling me about myself is the truth? How do I know that I am a worthwhile person like you say?" I was stumped at first for an answer.

Then I stated that just because she first picked up some negative views about herself in life as a child, that did not mean they were accurate. It just means that she picked them up first. She could develop a different view of herself and not simply perpetuate the first view she picked up from her parents.

Another writing which describes some of the sources of our low self-esteem comes from the book, *A Life Worth Waiting For!* by Dwight Lee Wolter. In the book, Wolter describes how growing up in an alcoholic family has affected him in various areas in his life. One of his entries, Keep 'em Guessing, gives an illustration:

> My mother made two fists behind her back, then brought them around to the front and said, "Guess which hand my love for you is in?" After playing this game several times and never guessing the correct hand I said "Hey! Wait a minute! Open both hands at the same time." She did, and I bet you aren't surprised, but I sure (was surprised) to discover that both of her hands were empty. Just because someone is withholding something from you doesn't mean they have it to offer.[2]

Children do not realize that parents may not have "love" in either hand. We take it all on ourselves and assume there is something wrong with us. We feel low self-worth and then perpetuate these feelings by the way we treat ourselves.

How Do You Improve Your Self-Esteem?

To improve your self-esteem, awareness, courage, and decision need to be coupled with action. You need to dig deeper and determine specific reasons as to why you developed a negative view of yourself. This step and steps of change definitely will require courage, because it will be a painful process, and trying to treat yourself differently will be very difficult. You need to decide to do something about your low self-esteem. Family of origin work or digging deeper is not done to find someone to blame. When a person gets stuck in the blame game, then they will do very little to develop a more positive self-image. They continue to blame someone else for their problems. They do not accept responsibility for themselves. "Family of Origin" work involves looking back at your childhood in order to understand how your self-esteem was affected as a child. In doing so, you will be more able to change this image of yourself.

One of the clearest ways to explain how an adult will enhance their self-esteem is through the use of the model of *Transactional Analysis.* As you remember from previous chapters, a person can be divided into three parts:

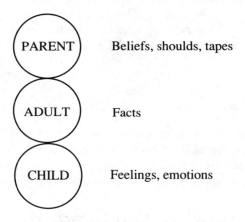

PARENT — Beliefs, shoulds, tapes

ADULT — Facts

CHILD — Feelings, emotions

Remember, it is important to have all three parts. The Adult in you does some family of origin work and identifies how your self-esteem was formed. It finds out some additional information about your parents in order to more fully understand why they acted the way they did. Possibly it investigates to find a little more information about your grandparents and how they treated your parents.

Then you need to recognize how you are currently parenting yourself. What kind of a parent are you to the child in you? Are you a nurturing parent or a critical parent? Grown-ups with a low self-esteem are typically very critical parents to *themselves.* Helping someone to become a better parent to *himself* is a very difficult and often long process. But if you do not become a positive, nurturing parent to *yourself* then you will not be able to be a positive, nurturing, parent to your children.

A woman was referred to me by my friend, who also was a counselor. She stated that the counselor was helping her to know herself better and enhance her own self-esteem. Since he did not feel as comfortable dealing with parenting issues, she wanted to see me for help with parenting her children. I took the challenge, but refuse to do this anymore because it's impossible to help someone parent her children more effectively without investigating both her own self-esteem and how she is parenting herself.

What does it mean to be a positive, nurturing parent to yourself? It means:

- praising yourself when you do something well, and/or try something new;

- excusing yourself if you make a mistake, not kicking yourself around the block for two weeks;

- setting goals for yourself that are reasonable and measurable, and rewarding yourself for their attainment;

- seeking new opportunities for responsibility and success (encouraging the child to try something new);

- allowing the child in you to avoid negative influences (If some of your friends or parents are very critical of you, avoid them. Stay away from them. It may not be necessary forever, but only until you are able to develop the confidence and assertiveness skills to not allow other adults to put you down.);

- accepting your feelings (A woman recently told me that she had been very depressed over the weekend and couldn't figure out why. She tried to do things that had worked before to help with her depression—such as listening to music, taking a walk, etc. Nothing seemed to work. She was not accepting her feelings.

She felt that she shouldn't be depressed. When she simply said to herself, "I'm depressed and I know it will pass," her depression lifted. Granted, dealing with depression is not always this easy, but as nurturing parents to ourselves we need to accept our feelings. That not only may allow the feelings to pass more quickly, but we are also having a positive impact on our self-esteem.);

- looking after the needs of the child in you. Allowing that child to eat the right kinds of food, allowing it proper time to sleep and relax, and even occasionally buying it a gift or two;

- giving yourself private support talk (One of the best books on self talk is by David Stoop, entitled, *Self Talk*.).[3]

We may talk out loud at the rate of 200 to 300 words per minute, but our self-talk, that internal dialogue, is going on at the rate of 1200 to 1300 words per minute. Usually the majority of those words are negative. "You dummy, why did you do that," "You don't deserve to relax," "You won't be able to write a book." That last sentence is some negative self-talk that I have had to deal with in writing this book. When you recognize that the child in you is talking in this negative way, the positive parent needs to kick in and say, "That's not true, you can do it!" You not only need to become aware of what you are saying to yourself, but consciously give yourself better self talk. I strongly encourage you to investigate this area further.

A cartoon I once saw depicted a boxer saying to his trainer *before* the fight, "This is going to be the shortest title bout in the history of boxing . . . I feel faint already." This fighter has very negative self talk and I'm sure that he must have lost the fight.

Investigating the "shoulds" that may be controlling your life is another way to enhance your self-esteem. Many adults, especially perfectionists, have long lists of "shoulds": "I should fix this, I should make three well-balanced meals a day, I should sew all the kids clothes, etc." Lists of "shoulds" become little clubs that adults beat themselves over the head with. Instead of praising yourself for accomplishing something, the critical parent will say, "Why haven't you finished your list of 'shoulds?' " Investigate your "shoulds," write them down, decide where they came from, (i.e. parents, friends, society) then decide which ones you really want or need to keep. Get rid of the rest and realize they will die a slow death. You may feel guilty at first as you eliminate them, but if you continue to not beat yourself over the head with them they will disappear.

Is Your Life In Balance?

Having a "life in balance" is also essential to developing and maintaining positive self-esteem. Evaluate the following areas of your life:

- Spiritual
- Physical
- Professional
- Marital
- Social
- Personal
- Financial
- Your Relationship With Your Kids

How do you feel about each area. Are you:

- In the pits?
- Average?
- Soaring?

Parents often try to get all of their self-esteem from their children and then feel devastated if their child is not doing well. It is important to have a "life in balance" so that your esteem comes from a variety of places. This is also discussed in **Part II** when I discuss building self-esteem in your children.

It is hard for an adult to change his self-esteem for many reasons. If someone praises you, and your self-esteem is low, you will negate that praise. You won't accept it because it doesn't jive with your internal feelings. That's why changing your self-esteem has to begin with learning to parent yourself in a more positive and healthy way. You must have the courage to begin to treat yourself in a better way and take specific steps to make the changes happen.

The power of decision to stay the same or change is up to you. Do you accept the challenge?

I hope that you will. It will be a key to your success as a parent, as well as all other areas of your life.

A Challenge To You, And A Time To Reflect:

1. Rate your self-esteem on a scale of 1 to 10, 10 being high.

2. List several ways that your parents affected your self-esteem in a positive way, and several ways that they affected your esteem in a negative way.

3. State specifically how you will become a better parent to yourself.

4. Is your life in balance?
   Set goals for yourself in areas where you scored yourself "in the pits."

5. Read the chapter in **Part II** on building self-esteem in you and your child.

ENDNOTES

1. Larson, Earnie, and Carol Larson Hegarty, *Days of Healing, Days of Joy*, Hazelden Foundation, 1987, March 30th devotional.

2. Wolter, Dwight Lee, *A Life Worth Waiting For!*, Minneapolis: CompCare Publishers, 1989, p. 5.

3. Stoop, Dr. David, *Self Talk*, Old Tappan, New Jersey: Fleming H. Revell Co., 1982.

5

Frozen Needs
and
Their Impact on Parenting

Index Of Suspicion

■ Do you find yourself trying to make up to your children things that you did not have as a child?

■ Do you find yourself getting resentful when your youngsters do not show appreciation for all the things that you do for them?

■ Do you always put the needs of your youngsters ahead of your own needs?

■ Did you miss out in childhood on things such as attention, praise, love, and/or material things, such as toys and nice clothes?

If You Answered "Yes" To Some Of These Questions, One Of Your Dragons May Be Frozen Needs.

According to W. Hugh Missildine, in *Your Inner Child of the Past*[1] and also discussed by H. Norman Wright in *Marital Counseling*:[2] "Sometimes people enter adulthood with needs that were not adequately met in childhood. Such needs might include love, security, belonging, or acceptance. Frequently such unmet needs develop into rigid behavior patterns. These patterns are called frozen needs, and they are like recordings that play over and over. Frozen needs cannot be met in the present."

Do "Frozen Needs" affect parenting? Definitely! The impact can be as damaging to children as it can be to the parents.

What needs did you have as a child that were not met?

- Did you need attention and not get it?
- Did you need praise and not get it?
- Did you need affection and not get it?
- Did you need more clothes and not get them?
- Did you need someone to explain things to you and not get it?
- Did you need to live in a clean house and not get it?
- Did you need your parents to attend your athletic events, cub scout meetings, brownie groups and not get it?
- Did you need your parents to become more involved in your school work and not get it?
- Did you need your parents to help you to have more friends when you were young and not get it?

Have I left something out? What did you need that you felt you did not get from your parents?

Write it down: _____

_____

_____ .

Don't skip over this and try to go on without looking at Frozen Needs. You won't be able to effectively apply the parenting tools, unless you identify and control this Dragon. Most adults will have to spend some time on this. If possible, get some pictures of yourself and other family members when you were young, get some place by yourself, and really spend some time thinking about yourself as a 4-year-old, a 7-year-old, a 15-year-old, etc. Sometimes when our needs weren't met as children we started to not even think about what we might need. To continue thinking about what we needed, while never getting it, would be more painful than if we were to just "numb out" and not think about what we needed at all. You may gain a great deal of input on what your Frozen Needs are by observing your own children and what your priorities are for them.

Obviously, all of the above are needed by a child to some degree. Your perception of what you did not receive is what you have to deal with. The question is, "Did you feel that you did not receive _____ ." Don't feel that you have to prove it or have your parents and/or siblings agree that you did not receive it.

Before describing how to effectively deal with Frozen Needs, let's look at how they get in the way of using the parenting tools.

Going back to the 2½-year-old toddler I spoke about in Chapter 3 (under #2—*I will always explain everything to my children*). We had been talking about the boy's tendency to bang his head on the floor when he didn't get what he wanted. In fact, he had developed a pretty large knot on his forehead. However, I was planning to just see the mother and give her some strategies. I hadn't planned on a 2½-year-old running around my office while I talked to his mother. Remember! Frozen Needs can not be met in the present. It's OK to explain things to your children, but there is a time to just take action. (It was not necessary to go to great length lecturing him on the hazards of garbage.) Trying to take care of a Frozen Need in the present was diverting this mother from the action she needed to take with her toddler.

I remember counseling a mother who appeared to be spending too much time with her daughter. Her daughter was feeling smothered and did very few things on her own. Additionally, the mother was not taking care of her own personal needs, so she was always tired and stressed out herself. In digging deeper, she realized that since her mother did not spend time with her, she was going to make it up to her daughter by spending all her time with her daughter. Again, this was harmful to both daughter and herself.

Many children may have longed for their parents to attend their sporting events, dance recital, school play, etc. They later try to make it up to their children and heal their own hurt by attending all of their children's activities. It's definitely OK in my book to be supportive of your children and be involved in their activities. In fact, it's extremely important.

As stated in Gary Smalley's book *The Blessing*: "a parent can tell a child that school or sports are important, but unless they (the parent) show an active commitment by spending time at these places, their words will not have much impact."[3]

The problem that parents often get into by trying to meet this Frozen Need in the present is two-fold. One, you may feel intense guilt if you happen to miss one of these activities, and two, you may feel that they are not appreciative enough because they don't run and jump in your arms and thank you. Remember, they don't know that you did not have this experience as a child. They don't know that your parents didn't come to your activities and/or understand the depth of your feelings about this.

Another common Frozen Need is not getting enough clothes, toys, or presents as a child. Here again the effects of trying to make up for this in the present is harmful to both children and parents. Parents may overextend their budgets by trying to get too much for their children, and children may become very spoiled and lazy if given everything they want. Parents may not require children to do chores and earn money to save for long term goals or toys.

You might try to make up to your child the piano lessons that you never had. That might work out if your child has interest and ability in that area, but it could turn into a disaster if he/she has interests in other areas. If you didn't get piano lessons as a child and wanted them, then remember this saying which is posted in my office, "It's never too late to have a happy childhood." Take piano lessons yourself.

Another example of the impact of trying to make up to our kids what we didn't get is illustrated by the following letter that was written to Abigail Van Buren:[4]

"Every Day is A Father's Day Now"

Dear Abby:

This is to tell you about a letter you never received. Some time ago I received a call from my son's third grade teacher asking me to stop in at school to discuss a letter my son had written in letter-writing class and was addressed to *you*. It reads:

"Dear Abby,
My dad works all the time. He is never home. He gives me money and lots of toys, but I hardly ever see him. I love him and wish he would not work all the time so I could see him more."
signed Jeff

That was the entire letter Abby. I was very poor when I was a boy. I always wanted my children to have it better than I did, so in addition to my regular job, I worked two part-time jobs—almost doubling my income. I managed to provide my wife and two sons with many luxuries, but I realized after reading Jeff's letter that I was depriving them of something far more important—myself. And my time. For instance, I had never attended a report card conference, nor visited school. I took no part in scouting, although both sons were Cub Scouts.

I have never reprimanded my sons. This responsibility was entirely their mother's. Sometimes days would pass without my seeing the boys awake.

Because of the standard I had set for my family, I felt I couldn't lower those standards without first discussing it with them, so we held a family meeting. The result, I quit both part-time jobs and we adjusted our standard of living accordingly.

That was nearly two years ago, and now I realize what a wonderful family I have. I have earned the respect of my sons. But more important, I have learned that the greatest gift a man can give his children is himself and his time.

Today I am a happier man, and I want to thank you, Abby, because if it were not for the letter my son wrote to you, I might never have known what I was missing.

Signed,
Dad.

In trying to give his children and wife what he did not get as a child, he was depriving them of something more important than material things: himself. All his efforts would not serve to alleviate the pain he experienced as a child.

Parents who were not encouraged to do well in school, and/or did not do well in school become obsessed with their children being successful in school. They may pressure their children to succeed in school, become easily frustrated, and attempt to use anger to get their children to do better. Remember, anger and emotion are ineffective when trying to change a child's behavior. Dealing with school problems requires indentifying the problem and setting up positive and negative consequences based on the choices your child makes. This works far better than nagging, threatening, or trying to coerce them into getting better grades.

Another mother I counseled tended to stay up till wee hours of the morning cleaning house, making breads, and cooking for her two teenagers. Her mother was never there for her, and they had very little food in the house, so she was going to make it up to her kids. The only thing she did was stress herself out and become frustrated when her teenagers did not show her the type and amount of appreciation that she expected for all her sacrifices.

One of the greatest deterrents, or obstacles, keeping teenagers from growing up is their parents. Parents often inhibit their teenagers' growth by giving them something they don't need. Of course they may want something, a car, a big allowance, etc. and the parents may give these things to their teenager because they (the parents) didn't get such things as a child. When this frequently happens, the teenager has not been given initiative or motivation to work for things, or the ability to delay gratification and work for a goal.

One problem with Frozen Needs is that it's like putting a bandage over a deep cut that actually requires 20 or so stitches. The bandage doesn't stop the flow of blood and isn't the right approach to healing the wound. The wound never heals and you go through lots of bandages needlessly. A stitchery hanging in my office which my mother made for me states, "You can't heal a wound by saying it's not there." That's what parents often try to do. In the process, they may cripple their child, and become so guilt-ridden and stressed out that they aren't effective.

Unmet childhood needs cannot be met in the present. No matter what you do in the present with your own children, it will not erase the pain of your unmet childhood needs. The only way to deal with the Frozen Needs is to grieve their loss. Grieving losses is also discussed in Chapters 7 and 8, but let's look at aspects relative to dealing with the Frozen Needs. Here are the stages of grief and a few comments:

DENIAL:
Denial can mean several things with regards to Frozen Needs. A person may have (a) completely forgotten or blocked out childhood memories, (b) remembered that certain needs

weren't met but have ignored or forgotten how they felt about it, or (c) remembered that certain needs were not met, how they felt about it and thought they dealt with the issues (reached forgiveness) when they had not.

ANGER:

To move through the grief cycle one needs to identify specific Frozen Needs and feelings about those losses. Sometimes it is necessary to talk with a counselor to get help in discovering Frozen Needs. Since each of us had only one childhood we can tend to take our childhood experiences as "normal," and therefore not feel that we missed anything. Many books on resolving anger suggest writing a letter to your parents regarding your resentments. It's a good way to help identify the feelings, direct them at the the person/s they need to be directed at, and help the feelings flow out of your body through the pen and onto paper. Most of us should not send the letter to our parents. Read the letter to a friend, a counselor, or read it to any empty chair pretending your parents are sitting in the chair, listening and accepting your feelings. Remember, to deal with Frozen Needs we must identify them, and our feelings about them. We must get the feelings out into the open, and not try to cover them up with present-day actions. Harold Bloomfield's book *Making Peace with Your Parents*[5] is an excellent book that goes into more detail on the letter writing aspect of dealing with resentments. Another way of dealing with our anger is to become more assertive (in the present) with our parents regarding Frozen Needs.

One client of mine rarely got presents or special attention on her birthdays. That was one of her Frozen Needs and she went overboard on her own children's birthdays. She worked hard to resolve her resentment toward her mother that she felt as a child. Then, one birthday she failed to receive a birthday card from her mother. Her mother said she was sorry that the card would be late. It never came. I encouraged the woman to confront her mother and say, "It really hurt my feelings that you did not send the card you said you did for my birthday."

This is an example of becoming more assertive (in the present) towards our parents for this type of behavior. Being assertive means you respond out of love. Love for yourself, so you will speak up for yourself. Love for your parent in that you will not call them a name or put them down when telling them your feelings. You need to be assertive, not aggressive and attacking. You also should not be passive and remain silent. That's what you did as a child, and if you keep acting like you did as a child, it will be very difficult to ever forgive your parents. Be patient. It takes time to build up the courage and resolve to begin to be assertive. Your parents may always sing the same song that they did during your youth, but you do not have to dance the same way you did as a child.

DEPRESSION:

Nobody likes to deal with the anger or resentments they have toward their parents. It is depressing to confront the old wounds that we tried to ignore. Being depressed as you work through this, although it hurts, is normal. Decide that you want to move on. Make a decision to do what you need to do to forgive your parents.

UNDERSTANDING:

As you move through the grief cycle, it may help to find out more about your parents. Ask them or other relatives questions about what their childhood was like. You may find out that although you felt that you did not get some things, your parents were able to give you things that they never got from their parents. Adults often feel their parents deliberately did this, or forgot that, when in reality they may never have had the idea given to them as to what to give to their children. I remember the story of a man going to a friend's house and asking for a seven course meal. The man opened the cupboard and nothing was in it. Although he wanted to serve his friend a seven course meal, he didn't have it in the cupboard. Your parents could not give you something that they did not have.

ACCEPTANCE:

The final stage of the grief cycle is acceptance or forgiveness. "I forgive my parents for not getting me _____ , and I accept that I did not get _____ ." Claudia Black, in her book, *It's Never Too Late To Have A Happy Childhood* says "Forgiveness is not forgetting, it's remembering and letting go."[6] We also accept that we cannot make up to our children what we did not get, and we look objectively at what they really need to help them mature into healthy adults.

Resolving the resentments toward our parents is necessary in order to deal appropriately with Frozen Needs. Dealing with Frozen Needs affects our effectiveness as a parent. Adults rarely feel like forgiving someone, so don't wait until you feel like forgiving them, because you will probably never feel like it. Forgiveness begins with a decision to let go of anger and resentment.

Although you need to forgive, you'll also need to realize and accept that you can't make up to your kids what you didn't get.

A Challenge To You, And A Time To Reflect:

1. Do you identify Frozen Needs as one of your Dragons?

2. List the Frozen Needs:

3. How have you tried to make these things up to your own child or teen?

4. Have you made the decision to forgive someone in your past who hurt you?

5. Frozen Needs and Childhood Vows are similar in some respects, so be sure to have read Chapter 3 on Vows. Some readers may relate to one concept better than the other.

ENDNOTES

1. Missildine, W. Hugh, *Your Inner Child of the Past*, New York: Simon and Schuster, 1963.

2. Wright, Norm, *Marital Counseling*, Denver: Christian Marriage Enrichment,, 1981, p. 153.

3. Smalley, Gary, and John Trent, *The Blessing*, Nashville: Thomas Nelson Publishers, 1986.

4. Letter to Abigail Van Buren.

5. Bloomfield, Harold, *Making Peace With Your Parents*, New York: Ballantine Books, 1983.

6. Black, Claudia, *Its Never Too Late To Have a Happy Childhood*, New York: Ballantine Books, 1989.

6

Irrational Beliefs

Index Of Suspicion

- Do you frequently react with anger and/or feel tremendous guilt when your son or daughter misbehaves?
- Do you sometimes feel that you overreact to their misbehavior?
- Do you find yourself blaming your son or daughter for your anger and frustrations?
- Do you have difficulty consistently using parenting techniques such as praise, logical consequences, and chore charts?
- Do you feel that your youngsters should do what they are told, when they are told to do it?
- Do you resent it when your youngsters test the limits?

If You Answered "Yes" To Some Of These Questions, One Of Your Dragons May Be Irrational Beliefs And Unrealistic Expectations

Most parenting books emphasize the importance of remaining calm when applying parenting strategies. Yet few books instruct parents on how to remain calm. Some psychologists feel that the biggest mistake that parents make is trying to use anger and emotion to change a youngster's behavior. Applying the principles discussed in this chapter will help you to remain calmer while parenting and therefore allow you to be much more effective as a parent.

Dealing with the Dragon of *Irrational Beliefs* is very difficult, but if you are able to consistently apply the principles discussed in this chapter you will definitely see progress in your ability to parent more effectively. You will remain much calmer and become less irate at your youngster's behavior. Additionally, you will feel less stressed and anxious as a parent.

Before you begin this chapter on Irrational Beliefs, let me warn you what will be required for you to successfully consider and then apply the concept.

You'll need to:

1. Accept that you'll be effective as a parent only if you can remain calm when you deal with your child's behavior.

2. Accept that it's your irrational beliefs, myths about parenting, expectations, self-talk, and/or possibly your interpretation of your youngster's behavior that causes you to react angrily to the behaviors, not the behavior itself.

3. Be willing to work hard at identifying the irrational beliefs, parenting myths, and self-talk that cause you to react angrily.

4. Replace those statements with more rational or positive self-talk.

It is difficult to objectively identify irrational beliefs because you have lived with them so long that you do not believe that any of them are irrational. Often parents need help identifying their irrational beliefs and a willingness to try to develop more rational beliefs.

Interpreting your child's behavior rationally is a major key toward remaining calm—regardless of the behavior. It's not that I want you to remain calm and learn to accept everything your child does, and not get angry about it. (That's often a misconception parents have.) I want you to remain calmer and become less hostile so that you will be able to effectively apply the parenting tools discussed in **Part II**.

The theory of counseling that deals with irrational beliefs is called *Rational Emotive Therapy*. According to the theory, it is not the event (A) in our life which causes our feelings (C). In other words:

A (The Event) $\longrightarrow$ Does not Cause $\longrightarrow$ C (Our Feelings)

This obviously applies to emotional pain and not physical pain. For if you hit your finger with a hammer, the event would definitely cause the pain or (C) your feelings. With regards to emotional pain, our perception—*belief* (B) of the event, is what causes our feelings. Diagrammed as before, it would look like this:

A (The Event) $\longrightarrow$ B (Beliefs) $\longrightarrow$ C (Our Feelings)

We process the event through our belief system or perceptions which will then cause our feelings. Therefore, if you tend to overreact to your children or get angry too easily because of their behavior, then looking at and changing your beliefs (B) will help you remain calmer.

Albert Ellis developed a system to attack irrational beliefs and thoughts, and called it Rational Emotive Therapy. It was first introduced in *A Guide To Rational Living* with co-author Robert A. Harper in 1961.[1] Ellis' basic thesis is that emotions have nothing to do with actual events. In other words, it's our beliefs/thoughts/self-talk that we "feed" the event through which causes our emotions. Our own thoughts create anxiety, anger, and depression. Ellis and Harper have updated their original work in *A New Guide to Rational Living*, published in 1975.[2]

But how does all this apply to parenting? Remember, a key to parenting is to remain calm and unstressed. It is only when we calmly deal with our children's behaviors that we will be effective. Before giving you specific examples which will make this clearer and more applicable for you, I'd like to define "B" or Beliefs, with several other words and give examples after each one. In this chapter, I will look at four different aspects of how beliefs effect your feelings. The five areas are:

- Expectations
- Irrational Beliefs
- Myths About Parenting
- Your Interpretation of your child's behavior
- "Shoulds"

EXPECTATIONS

Another word for Beliefs could be the word "expectations." Are your expectations of your child realistic or unrealistic? Rational or Irrational? Realistic or rational expectations will generally leave you feeling much less angry and frustrated than will unrealistic or irrational expectations. In order to have realistic expectations of children it is important to be aware of the various stages of child development. It is important to know at what age children will walk, talk, be able to tie their own shoes, dress themselves, etc. One good resource in this area is a book by Ilg and Ames, *Child Behavior, Specific Advice on Problems of Child Behavior.*[3] It discusses what is normal behavior in a variety of areas for different age levels.

If you expect a two-year-old to tie his shoes, or sit quietly in a restaurant for one hour, then you will become very angry when these things do not happen. The child's behavior does not cause your feelings, rather it's your expectations of that child.

Your pediatrician or a child counselor will be able to assist you in this area by telling you what's normal and what's abnormal development. When your expectations are realistic you will react much more calmly to your child and then be more effective with parenting strategies. Children rarely question your expectations. If they are falling short of your expectations, they will automatically assume that something is wrong with them, not you. A personal example should adequately illustrate this point. When my son, Matt, was about 10 or 11-years-old I was helping him work on some merit badges for scouts.

The only problem was, we were working on 5 merit badges at one time. He was getting really frustrated and so was I. Matt wasn't able to realize and tell me that I was unrealistic, but I was. I finally said to him, (in my infinite wisdom) that I was wrong, and that it was my fault for having unrealistic expectations of a 10-year-old. It is therefore up to parents to determine and realize that their expectations may be unrealistic. The child should not be expected to be able to verbalize this.

The Born Loser

Reprinted with permission of NEA, Inc.

Unrealistic expectations on the part of parents will cause parents to become very angry, over emotional and ineffective as a parent.

IRRATIONAL BELIEFS

Albert Ellis has suggested 10 basic irrational beliefs which are thoroughly discussed in *A New Guide To Rational Living*.[4] Another excellent resource is the *Relaxation and Stress Reduction Workbook*.[5] The authors, Martha Davis, Elizabeth Eshelman, and Matthew McKay, also provide a "beliefs inventory" to help the reader identify which of the 10 basic irrational beliefs they may be living with. Additionally, they list other irrational ideas that they have identified. It can be extremely difficult for adults to accept that they have irrational beliefs. We live with our beliefs for so long that they become part of us. We think that everybody has the same beliefs and that there cannot possibly be any other way to look at life. You must be determined to continue reading to identify thoughts or beliefs that can help you to not only deal with life more effectively, but also help you to be a more effective parent.

I will list the 10 basic irrational beliefs that can affect adults and children that are discussed by the above authors. Each of these irrational beliefs will have an impact on all areas of your life, however I will make a comment or two only about how these irrational beliefs can adversely affect your role as a parent. I will also include a comment or two on what a more rational belief might be for you to develop. An excellent resource for this is a book by Jill Anderson, entitled *Thinking, Changing and Rearranging*.[6] Her book discusses irrational beliefs in a language that children can understand. Ms. Anderson describes irrational beliefs as *Junk Thought*. I think that is a very good way to look at it. We all know what Junk Food is. Junk Thought is probably just as bad for you as Junk Food.

I will discuss the 10 Irrational Beliefs, and then look at some additional beliefs that the authors have identified that impact our role as parents.

1. *It is an absolute necessity for an adult to have love
   and approval from peers, family and friends.*

   This belief can cause you lots of grief as a parent.
   You undoubtedly will need to and want to do some things
   different from peers, family, and friends when parenting.
   If you need their approval, you will become very frustrated
   and suffer low self-esteem if others do not approve of
   the choices you are trying to make. If you have to have
   love all the time from your children you definitely will
   not be effective as a parent. You may have a tendency
   to give in to their every wish, do their chores for them,
   not set rules and limits, etc. etc., because you want them
   to love you.

   A more rational belief would be, "Not everyone will
   always like me or like what I do. I am still a worthwhile
   person, even if adults or children disapprove of what
   I am doing." Also, remember that your goal as a parent
   is to raise healthy, responsible children, not have children
   that love everything you do. Children do not always love
   parents who hold them accountable for specific chores,
   but it's extremely important for parents to do so.

2. *You must be unfailingly competent and almost perfect
   in all you undertake.*

   The results of believing you must behave perfectly as
   a parent will paralyze you from trying new things and
   cause you much guilt and lowered self-esteem when you
   "blow it" as a parent—which we all do. You may tend
   to also expect perfection from your children. The tendency
   toward perfectionism is very common for many adults
   who came from a dysfunctional family and/or who were
   abused in some way as a child.

   A more rational belief would be, "It's OK to make
   mistakes, everybody make mistakes. I am worthwhile,
   even if I do make mistakes. I can learn from my mistakes
   and keep trying new things."

3. *Certain people are evil, wicked, and villainous,
    and should be punished.*

The effect this belief has on parenting is significant, and so important that it will be discussed later in this chapter when I discuss how "shoulds" cause much anger and frustration.

A more rational belief would be, "Just because people do things differently from me does not mean they are bad and should be punished. People will do things that they are not supposed to do and will need to experience the consequences for their behavior. Again, be sure to read the upcoming section on "shoulds" for a more indepth look at this belief.

4. *It is horrible when people and things are not the way
    you would like them to be.*

This has been described as the *spoiled child syndrome.* Any inconvience, and there are many with children, is likely to be met with such negative statements. The result is intense irritation and stress. When things don't work out the way you had planned you may become extremely irritated and resentful toward your children.

A more rational belief would be, "Things will not always turn out the way I want them to. I can handle it when things don't turn out the way I think they should."

5. *External events cause most human misery—people simply
    react as events trigger their emotions.*

Ascribing unhappiness to the actions of your children relieves you of any responsibility for your emotions and causes you to focus entirely on a change in their behavior to make you feel better. If this is one of your beliefs you will have difficulty accepting that you can change your beliefs in order to help you respond more calmly when your children misbehave.

A more rational belief would be, "I am responsible for my day. I can choose how I will let the behavior of others affect me."

6. *You should have fear or anxiety about anything that is unknown, uncertain or potentially dangerous.*

All parents worry and fear for the safety of their children. A certain amount of fear and worry is normal and healthy, as it will cause you to be careful as a parent. However, when the fear grows too large, it may cause you to hold on too tight and try to control your children, which could cause them anxiety and lower their self-esteem. You may become afraid to let them ride their bike to school, spend the night with a friend, go swimming in the ocean, etc.

A more rational belief would be, "I don't need to worry about what may go wrong, things usually go well, and I can handle it if something were to go wrong."

7. *It is easier to avoid than to face life's difficulties and responsibilities.*

Ascribing to this belief may cause parents to not take action when they notice that their child or teenager is having a problem. Hoping that it will go away, or that they will outgrow it, is not facing the problem. Many parents tend to ignore problems or wait too long to begin to address them. Many times I find myself trying to "save someone from drowning." They have waited so long to address a problem, it's like they are going down for the third time and only beginning to look for help. It's easier to teach people how to swim than to save them from drowning. I encourage parents to seek help and/or consult parenting books at the first sign of any difficulties, as well as encourage them to learn about parenting strategies or tools and Dragons before the problems begin.

A more rational belief would be, "All children and parents will have problems. I will identify the problems and develop a strategy to deal effectively with that problem."

8. *You need someone stronger or greater than yourself to rely on.*

This belief may cause parents to avoid relying on themselves and their own knowledge of their children when deciding what action to take with certain problems. Its OK to seek help from others, but do not constantly second guess yourself and question every move you make.

A more rational belief would be, "I am capable of dealing responsibly with a problem. I do not need to constantly second-guess myself and always rely on others."

9. *The past has a lot to do with determining the present.*

The best explanation of this is to quote from the book by Davis, Eshleman, and McKay: "Just because you were once strongly affected by something, that does not mean that you must continue the habits you formed to cope with the original situation. Those old patterns and ways of responding are just decisions made so many times they have become nearly automatic. You can identify those old decisions and start changing them right now. You can learn from past experience, but you don't have to be overly attached to it."

This has direct bearing on your role as a parent, because to improve as a parent you must strive to break some old patterns of doing things and responding to situations.

A more rational belief would be, "I can change. Just because I did something a certain way in the past, does not mean I need to continue the pattern." Also remember, "It's never too late to do what's right."

10. *Happiness can be achieved by inaction,
    passivity and endless leisure.*

    Sometimes parents try to ignore their child's misbe-
    havior instead of doing something about it. Many adults
    felt powerless as a child, and they bring that same feeling
    into their role as a parent, remaining inactive or passive
    in the face of problems, rather than taking action.

    A more rational belief would be, "Problems will not
    go away by ignoring them. I can take action to solve
    any problem that comes up, provided that I seek
    appropriate help and stick to it until the problem is
    resolved and not give up."

Other irrational beliefs discussed in *The Relaxation and Stress
Reduction Workbook* that relate to parenting include:

11. *You are helpless and have no control over
    what you experience or feel.*

    Ascribing to this belief will cause you to feel that you
    can not do anything to change your child's behavior and
    have little choice as to how their behavior will effect
    you.

    A more rational belief would be, "I do have some
    control over interpersonal relations and I can choose how
    I will respond to someone's actions."

12. *When people disapprove of you, it invariably
    means you are wrong or bad.*

    This can affect parenting in several ways. Husbands
    and wives will have different ideas about how to parent.
    When a spouse disagrees with you, it does not mean
    you are bad or wrong, it just means you have a different
    idea and the two of you must work toward resolving
    your differences. When your child disapproves of you
    it does not mean you are wrong or bad. You may be
    doing exactly what you need to do as a parent, but it

may be going against something your children want, or think they want.

A more rational belief would be, "Others may not always agree with what I say or do. That does not mean I am wrong, nor does it mean I am a bad person. It does not mean that I need to change anything that I have done."

13. *You shouldn't have to feel pain, you are entitled to a good life.*

This statement from the *Stress Reduction Workbook* best describes the problems with this belief; "The realistic position is that pain is an inevitable part of human life. It frequently accompanies tough, healthy decisions and the process of growth. Life is not fair, and sometimes you will suffer no matter what you do."[7] Therefore, ascribing to this belief would cause one to become terribly upset when dealing with pain in a parent/child relationship, and therefore not be effective in dealing with the situation.

A more rational belief would be, "Life is not always fair and I may suffer in spite of what I try to do to avoid it. I can deal with pain, work through it, and learn from the experience."

14. *Your worth as a person depends on how much you achieve and produce.*

One reason why this belief gets parents in trouble is that they may feel they are worthless when their children or teenagers have problems. This will often cause them to become very angry and thus ineffective in parenting. When a parent derives much of their own self-worth from their children then they may tend to try and force them to always do the "right" thing.

A more rational belief would be, "I am worthwhile no matter what. My worth does not depend on what I accomplish or what my children accomplish."

15. *Anger is automatically bad and destructive.*

If parents truly believe that anger is bad, then they will not take on the enormous responsibility of teaching their children how to best deal with anger. Many adults grew up in families where they could not express anger and thus do not realize the importance of dealing with anger in appropriate ways. It is crucial for parents to teach their children to express anger appropriately and this is discussed in Chapter 10.

A more rational belief would be, "Anger is an honest emotion. It is not wrong to be angry, but we need to deal with our anger in appropriate ways."

16. *It is bad or wrong to be selfish.*

No one knows your needs better than you do. Selfish has become a bad word, but parents need to take care of themselves if they are to be effective with their children. In order to take care of yourself you will probably appear selfish at times. When you go jogging, to a gym, or on a shopping trip, people may think you are selfish, but you need to take care of yourself.

A more rational belief would be, "My needs are important. I need to take care of myself so that I will be more relaxed and healthy which will enable me to be more effective with my family members."

These 16 Irrational Beliefs have been identified by counselors over the years and many adults have been helped through identifying their beliefs and changing them to more rational ideas. I have described how these 16 beliefs can effect your role as a parent. Sometimes it is important to identify where the beliefs have come from. Many of the beliefs were picked up in your childhood through observing your parents and how they parented you. When parents are able to determine where the beliefs have come from, they will often realize that they have more ability to change their belief system.

Recognizing and identifying the irrational beliefs that you have is only the first step. It takes work to change a belief. The belief is like a tape that plays over and over in your head. To change it you need to erase that old tape and replace it with a new one. Some people have found it helpful to write down the more irrational beliefs to help them get rational ones into their belief system. Others have recorded the more rational beliefs on a personal tape recorder and played the tape while they were getting ready for work or while driving to work. Replacing irrational beliefs with more rational beliefs will definitely improve your effectiveness as a parent, but remember, old beliefs die slowly and only through hard work on your part.

MYTHS ABOUT PARENTING

Through my counseling over the past years I have become aware of other irrational ideas that parents have which cause them many problems. To help differentiate them from the first 16 irrational ideas I have previously discussed, I'll call them myths. Identify the myths that you may believe in, recognize them as myths or irrational beliefs, and work hard to eliminate the myth and replace it with a more realistic idea.

Myth #1:

Children will see what needs to be done around the house and do it willingly.

It would be nice if this happened, but it doesn't. Children need to have chore charts to follow and parents need to have both positive and negative consequences which are dependent on the child's behavior. Hopefully, our youngsters will see what needs to be done and do it when they have their own house, but it's irrational to expect young children to do this now.

Myth #2:

If I state the rules then there shouldn't be any problems.

Rules don't change people, it's the resulting positive or negative consequences that bring changes. It's amazing how many parents feel that the rules will change behavior and do not follow through consistently with consequences. Many parents have said to me that they told their children the rules or outlined their chores, but nothing changed. They neglected to set up and follow through consistently with positive and negative consequences.

Myth #3:

If I do a lot for my children, they'll realize that it's better to give than to receive and will in turn be nice to me.

Wrong. It seems like mothers buy into this belief more than fathers. If your child has been disrespectful to you and treated you like "dirt," then upon their next request simply state, "No, I will not do that for you and I'll tell you why." One night I was on my way to a meeting so I asked my oldest daughter, Robyn, if she would do the dishes for me. She said she didn't have time.

The very next night when she asked me to drive her to a friend's house to get some clothes she'd left there, I said I wouldn't but I'd tell her why. I said, I wasn't going to do something for her, if she was going to respond to me like she did the night before. I told her I didn't like playing the game this way, and that I'd rather we willingly did things for each other.

As I write this it seems unloving, heartless, but it teaches a valuable lesson. Two weeks later when Robyn asked me to cover a book for her she said, "Dad, here's a piece of gum if you'll cover this book for me." The point is not that you always need to get something from your kids for what you do, but to realize that children do not learn the correct message if you always do things for them and allow them to be disrespectful to you. Additionally, your anger and resentment will grow and grow, and probably come out at an inappropriate time if you do not express it calmly and rationally.

Myth #4:

Children will change quickly.

The rule of thumb to remember about changing a child's behavior is that "for each year a child is old, it will take at least one month to change the behavior." For example; it will take at least four months to change a particular behavior in a four-year-old. This is on the outside, but most parents tend to error on the inside and think behavior will change in a few days. Then they become angry when the behavior doesn't change and they switch too quickly to another technique.

Myth #5:

If I'm a good parent and do everything right my child won't experience any problems or have any difficulties.

Its easy to see how this belief or myth will cause anger the first time your child experiences a problem. It's impossible to keep kids from having problems. Our role as parents is to determine what problems our children have, then develop a strategy to deal with that problem, not become unglued or angry at them. Additionally, there is no guarantee that good parenting will "produce" good children. Sometimes in spite of all the proper techniques, children may experience many difficulties. I often encourage parents to evaluate themselves based on what parenting strategies they are using and what they are trying to do with their children. Do not evaluate yourself on what your child is doing.

Myth #6:

If I do a good job as a parent, my teenager won't have mood swings, question and reject my values, or swing back and forth from being dependent on me to wanting to be independent.

Good or bad parenting has nothing to do with the aforementioned behaviors. It's normal for teenagers to experience all of these things. Getting angry will only serve to increase your stress, and will surely not help your relationship with your teenager.

Myth #7:

If I've taught my teenagers right from wrong, and the harmful effects of drugs, smoking, and alcohol, then they won't try those things. Surely they won't ever steal anything, either.

What's wrong with this? Well, it's simply not true. Part of the process of growing up is to experiment. I'm not condoning experimentation or suggesting you should encourage your teenagers to experiment, just don't come unglued and overreact when they do. Overreactions and anger won't be effective tools to help steer your teenager on a correct course. Parents often overreact to them for fear their teenagers may turn out like a relative who went to jail or became a drug addict or an alcoholic.

When you assume the same will happen to your teenager, you'll try too hard to control him or her. You can't control them. You can only guide them. In fact, trying to control them will generally result in more rebellion than outlining the consequences of their choices to them and allowing them to decide. Parents should not just look at the above problems and deal with them alone. Parents need to look at the areas of self-esteem, dealing with stress, and helping your child deal more effectively with their anger. These are the underlying factors that may be causing teenagers to abuse alcohol or drugs.

Myth #8:

My children will appreciate the things I do for them and show me their appreciation.

Often we do things for our children because our parents didn't do these things for us. We may go out of our way to attend their sporting or musical events. We may overextend ourselves to buy them a special present or to keep them in the best clothes, or pay for expensive trips or lessons—the list goes on and on. Don't become unglued because they don't show you appreciation the way you might expect. It is OK to expect a thank you; in fact, you should require it. But remember, they won't feel the same about the items described above as you might have if you'd have received it as a child. Some reasons for this have also been discussed in Chapter 5, Frozen Needs.

I remember a story in a book by Charlie Shedd. A father and son had spent the whole day together, walking, talking, fishing, and having lunch. At the end of the day, the father wrote in his diary that not much had happened. The son wrote in his diary that it was the best day of his life. Children will generally not show appreciation for things we do in the ways we might expect.

Myth #9:

My children won't test the limit.

Wrong. All children will test the limits. You can count on it. It's ironic and sometimes confusing that children want and need limits, but they will still test them. Don't panic, just follow through with a short-term consequence. For example, if your son or daughter comes home 20 minutes late, then have him/her go to bed 20 minutes early that night. Don't rant and rave for hours. If your son or daughter "forgets" to do his or her chores, follow through with docking their allowance or apply a heavier fine, then start again the next day as discussed in the section on chore charts.

Myth #10:

My words should speak louder than my actions.

At first I felt it was unnecessary to discuss this one, until one day a mother said she was angry that her son wouldn't put on his seat belt in the car. I asked her a dumb question: "Do you wear your seat belt?" She said, "No, but my son (14-years-old) should know that it's best to wear your seat belt."

I never cease to be amazed at how many parents expect me to change a behavior their child displays that they are unwilling to change in themselves.

Myth #11:

A parent can use the same parenting approach with all their children.

Parents really need to study their children and understand them. One cannot and should not use the same parenting approach with all children. Each child has a unique temperament which needs to be considered when applying parenting strategies. One child may need a stiff penalty for a rule infraction while another may require only a stern look of disapproval to cause the child to change their behavior. The saying, "Don't take an elephant gun to kill a fly" definitely applies. Consider your child's temperament when considering both positive consequences as well as negative consequences for misbehavior.

Myth #12:

I am totally responsible for the happiness of my children.

Many parents feel that when their child says he/she is bored that as parents they need to do something about it. This is not only unnecessary but unhealthy. Youngsters need to accept some responsibility for their own happiness. Children must be allowed to make decisions about themselves and live with the consequences of those decisions. Parents need to require youngsters to make decisions in areas where they are capable and where a wrong choice would not be psychologically or physically damaging.

What myths or irrational beliefs do you have? Remember irrational beliefs, myths, or unrealistic expectations will cause you to be angry and/or stressed as a result of your child's behavior, and then cause you be be ineffective in dealing with them.

INTERPRETATION OF YOUR YOUNGSTER'S BEHAVIOR

Another term that can be used in place of beliefs is interpretation. How do you interpret your son/daughter's behavior? A few examples will best illustrate how our interpretation can lead to a calm feeling or a more hostile angry feeling.

A (The Event) ⟶ B (Interpretation) ⟶ C (Feelings)

The event is: your son/daughter forgets to do their chores. If your belief or interpretation is "he or she did it deliberately to make me mad," then you definitely will be mad. If your interpretation is that children will be irresponsible and test the limit, you'll be somewhat frustrated, but not so angry that you'll be ineffective in changing the behavior.

A mother and stepfather of a teenage boy complained that their son did not call home when he was going to be late. The mother stated he was possibly having too much fun and/or maybe there wasn't a phone available. She was frustrated. The stepfather was livid, because he felt that the boy purposely did not call home to make him angry.

A mother of a hyperactive five-year-old boy called me frantically one day, because she felt like beating her son. I asked what he did and she said he forgot to bring some papers home from school. I asked her to put into words what his behavior was saying to her. She replied very quickly with the response, "He's trying to make a fool out of me." How incorrect she was. The boy was being irresponsible and acting like any five-year-old hyperactive boy would.

When my son Matt threw a ball and broke a window in our den when he was five, my belief was that children are uncoordinated and irresponsible at his age so I was frustrated, but not full of anger or rage. If I'd have felt he did it on purpose to upset me, I would have been livid, and therefore ineffective, when dealing with his behavior.

One father's interpretation of his son's poor school grades was that his son was "lazy." He stated that he was angry at his son. When I encouraged him to find another interpretation that would make him less angry, he missed the point. Remember, to be effective in helping our children change (i.e. to do better in school) we need to approach our children calmly, not with anger. Changing his interpretation would definitely help this father to be able to approach and deal with his son more effectively. When the father asked me to see his son in order to determine if he was lazy, I told him I would see his son, but that he still needed to change his interpretation if he wanted to be effective as a parent. Even if the boy was lazy, the father's belief that he should not be lazy was causing the trouble. This leads to the last category:

SHOULDS

A fifth concept which is so predominate and powerful and thus deserves special attention comes out of the third Irrational Belief listed previously. If parents could eliminate some words from their thoughts and discussion their lives would be much less stressful. They are the words **should** and **should not**. Anytime you get angry you could probably trace your reaction to the use of the word should. For example;

"My teenager should take a shower."

"My children should appreciate all the things I do for them."

"My children should do their chores without a reminder."

When parents of a teenager said to me, "Our son should take a shower." I replied, "Why? Where is it written down that teenagers should take a shower?" I'm sure they thought I was crazy, but their use of the word "should," and their belief that he should take a shower was causing them so much anger when he didn't take a shower, that they were ineffective in dealing with his behavior. Change the word should to "it would be nice," or "one would expect," and you'll see a big difference in your emotional reaction to your child's behavior. This change in your emotions will result in a more effective reaction on your part. The difficult part in understanding and applying this concept is that usually we are right, a teenager should take a shower, and children should appreciate what we do for them. However, being right doesn't mean they will do those things.

In the book, *A New Guide to Rational Living*, Ellis and Harper state this regarding "Shoulds," "Even if you rightly see Joe's acts as wrong or immoral, your belief that he shouldn't act wrongly and your subsequent anger will hardly serve to stop him from acting badly again (in fact, it may give him an incentive to continue acting wrongly just because you hate him and he hates you back.) It will almost always stir up your guts, lead to possible ulcers or high blood pressure, and deflect you from the real problem: how can you determinedly and effectively induce Joe not to act badly again?"[8]

Remember, the purpose in eliminating your "shoulds" is to help you remain calmer and therefore help you to be more effective in getting your child to stop an inappropriate behavior.

Many parents have trouble accepting this concept right away because, as stated above, they are usually right with regards to what a child will do. Being right, however, does not mean that the child will do what is right or what you expect of him. Using the word "Should" is commanding a change, which will cause immediate anger in you when the change does not occur. When you are angry you will not be effective in changing the behavior. Thus the first step is to help you to remain calm, in spite of your child's behavior. Once calm, you will be able to effectively use the tools discussed in **Part II**.

The purpose of this discussion on Irrational Beliefs has been to give you an approach to look at your own behavior and emotions, as a result of something your child has done. A key to successful parenting is to remain calm as you deal with your children. When your self-talk and beliefs are rational you remain calmer and thus can be more effective as a parent.

We have already discussed various types of irrational beliefs. The steps necessary to overcome these beliefs include:

1. Realization and acceptance that in order to be an effective parent you need to remain calm and less stressed.

2. Acceptance that your own thought patterns are contributing greatly to your emotions and therefore to your difficulty in effectively applying the parenting principles.

3. The ability to identify the irrational beliefs, myths, unrealistic expectations, negative interpretations, and "shoulds."

4. A determined effort to consistently attack and refute the above and replace them with rational beliefs, realistic expectations, correct, rational interpretations, and eliminate the "shoulds."

The above four steps are definitely not "mastered" in one week or one month. Parents will need to constantly and consistently work at improving their self-talk and changing their irrational beliefs to rational ones. Beliefs take time and effort to change. But remember, your behavior toward your child will definitely not change unless your beliefs change first. Remember too, that your behavior toward your youngsters may remain the same for a certain time period, during which you are consciously trying to develop a more rational belief system.

A Challenge To You, And A Time To Reflect:

1. State one or two Irrational Beliefs from the list of 16 that you need to work on.

2. State one or two myths that you need to change in order to become a more effective parent.

3. State a behavior that your child is demonstrating, and a healthier, positive way to view that behavior.

4. State a "should" that you need to eliminate, and revise your thought to say, "It would be nice if my son did . . . ," or "One would expect teens to do . . . ."

ENDNOTES

1. Ellis, Albert, and Robert A. Harper, *A Guide to Rational Living*, Englewood Cliffs, New Jersey: Prentice Hall, Inc., 1961.

2. Ellis, Albert, and Robert A. Harper, *A New Guide to Rational Living*, No. Hollywood: Wilshire Book Company, 1975.

3. Ilg, Francis, and Louise Bates Adams, *Child Behavior, Specific Advice on Problems of Child Behavior*, New York: Harper & Row Publishers, 1981.

4. Ellis and Harper, 1975.

5. Davis, Martha, and Elizabeth Robbins Eshelman, and Matt McKay, *The Relaxation & Stress Reduction Workbook*, Oakland: New Harbinger Publications, 1982.

6. Anderson, Jill, *Thinking, Changing, Rearranging, Improving Self-Esteem In Young People*, Eugene, Oregon: Timberline Press, 1981.

7. Davis, Eshelman and McKay, p. 108.

8. Ellis and Harper, p.11.

7

Unresolved Resentment

Index Of Suspicion

- Do you tend to overreact with anger when one of your youngsters misbehaves?
- Are you still angry at your brother or sister because of some of the things that he or she did while you were a child?
- Are you resentful that your mother or father did some things that you did not like as a child?
- Are you resentful toward your ex-spouse?

If You Answered "Yes" To Some Of These Questions, One Of Your Dragons May Be Unresolved Resentment.

All of us have been hurt at some time in our lives. Many adults have had hurtful experiences at the hands of our parents and/or our siblings. Sometimes the only way we were allowed to deal with pain as children was to keep the feelings inside of us or become involved in fantasy play or some compulsive behavior. One man that I counseled resorted to playing baseball for hours at a time to deal with his pain. In order to deal effectively with this Dragon, you may have to give yourself some time and permission to think about your relationship with your siblings or your parents or other adults that may have hurt you. You may need to make a conscious effort to remember events of your childhood that you may have repressed or discounted as meaningless.

A woman that I was counseling explained that she was very angry at her brother for things that he had done to her when she was a child. She said that someday she would need to do something about it. Few parents see the connection between those painful childhood memories and their effectiveness as a parent. I told her that "someday" needed to be now. If she really wanted to become a more effective parent, she had to deal with the painful memories, understand how they have affected her current approach to parenting, work through the grief cycle, and forgive her brother.

I am almost afraid to bring up the word "forgiveness" with clients who have resentment toward people in their past because their initial response (whether it is verbalized or not) is usually, "you've got to be kidding me, why should I forgive them for what they did to me?" I remind them that forgiveness is not the first thing to do, but it is definitely necessary in order to utilize parenting tools effectively and consistently. A parent may be able to apply the tools effectively and consistently for a week, or even a month, but not for much longer unless the resentment is identified and resolved. Sometimes the effect of unresolved resentment does not show up for five or even fifteen years, so one can never be sure that resentment is not interfering with parenting effectiveness. Giving parenting tools to a parent who is resentful to someone in their past is a lot like giving a saw or hammer to a carpenter and then noticing his arms are broken. The broken arms need to be healed before the carpenter can use the tools, much like past resentment needs to be healed before one can successfully apply the parenting tools discussed in **Part II** of this book. Forgiving someone who has hurt you is necessary for the benefit of you and your family. It is not done in order to benefit the person or persons who have hurt you.

Most adults bring fear, guilt, and anger that they picked up along the way in their relationships with the significant other people in their lives into their roles as parents.

Several examples will serve to illustrate how resentment affects parenting. The examples will illustrate how fear, guilt, and anger brought into our parenting role will not only make it difficult, but impossible to apply the parenting strategies calmly, effectively, and consistently. I will also discuss how to deal with the resentment, in order to keep this Dragon small and manageable.

I counseled one woman for nearly four months about what parenting strategies might be the most effective to use for her teenage son. I also spent some time counseling the teenager. I met with the woman and her husband and helped outline very specific strategies that they could use together to deal with their son. As a reminder that things are never really simple, this woman had never "talked" to her father when she was a child. Her father was either at work or doing his own things. She had very little experience in communicating with a man, especially in a family situation. Additionally, her mother handled all the issues regarding her and her siblings when she was a child. She never saw her mother and father discuss the children, and certainly never saw her father get involved with the children.

Consequently, she felt that she needed to be the parent, and did not need her husband's involvement. She was recreating her "at home" feeling by deciding she should be the parent in the family. That strategy worked fairly well when the children were younger, but now it was becoming more difficult. Now she was blaming her teenage son for these difficulties. She did not realize that she did not have enough tools to deal with a teenager, and that she had brought some Dragons into the marriage from her childhood. The clincher to her difficulties happened one day in counseling when she blurted out, "I say every hateful thing to my son that I would like to say to my brother. He was the main problem in our family. He was always in trouble and he caused our family to be in turmoil a lot." This woman not only had trouble working together with her husband to develop appropriate parenting strategies, but felt she should be the primary parent in the family. She also overreacted to her son's behavior because she would look at her son and "see" her brother. It was appropriate for her to be upset by her son's behavior, but to go (in my words) "bonkers" was an overreaction. Obviously, going "bonkers" means that you have not remained calm and unemotional, and therefore will not be effective in whatever action you take. Unresolved resentment to someone means that you are still handcuffed to that person. Picture that! How can you be effective as a parent if you are still handcuffed to someone from your past? It was impossible for this mother to have a positive relationship with her son, because her own brother kept getting in the way.

A second example illustrates the impact on parenting when unresolved guilt is brought into the parenting role. One woman I counseled was having a great deal of difficulty with her teenage stepdaughter. The teenager definitely did not "make things happen" in school. She was very passive with her school work and had little motivation or self-discipline to complete her work. Having counseled the daughter as well, I discovered with the daughter that one of her beliefs was that "if you don't do something, it will either go away, or someone will do it for you."

We determined, along with the stepmother's help, that the girl learned this as a 5 to 7-year-old. When someone would ask her to complete her chores, she would procrastinate and dawdle, and then someone would either do them for her or not bug her anymore. The stepmother realized in counseling that she was very angry and resentful toward her own mother who had died of alcoholism. Her mother had simply let things happen and did not do anything to help herself. Eventually, her inability to take action and do something for herself resulted in her death. The stepmother was bound and determined that this would not happen again in her life. But it was happening to her stepdaughter. The teenager was getting lousy grades and did not seem to care at all about herself or her future.

Consequently, the stepmother would go "bonkers" over the teenager's behavior and was ineffective in her approach to parenting. Incidentally, she also lacked a few important tools to use with teenagers, but that really didn't matter, as the resentment she carried toward her mother would have gotten in the way of applying any tools successfully. This stepmother also realized that she was overreacting to her stepson's behaviors because of unresolved anger that she still carried toward her own brother. Her stepson, although being a very typical teenager, possessed several characteristics that her brother also exhibited. It is obvious that the stepmother had brought anger into her current situation as well as the guilt regarding her own mother. She felt much guilt that she could not get her stepdaughter to "snap out" of her passive approach to life, and became over-emotional when dealing with her stepdaughter's behavior. She felt much anger toward her stepson because he reminded her of her own brother who had been very mean and cruel to her while growing up.

In another situation, the mother would get very angry at the oldest daughter, whenever the younger daughter would complain of being harassed by the older sister. Whenever there was a fight, the mother would immediately get angry at the older daughter, and had difficulty seeing that sometimes the younger daughter would provoke the situation. Why was this happening? Now, it seems pretty obvious and it will to you as I explain it, but these types of things are going on in all families and all parents need to realize it and deal with their resentment appropriately.

The mother had an older sister (in fact the age difference between the two daughters and the mother and her sister was very similar) toward whom she still harbored some resentment. She felt that her own older sister did not show her much attention as a child, had excluded her from her activities, and had been mean to her at times.

Consequently, when her own younger daughter would complain, the mother would immediately feel the way that she had felt as a child, and respond to the older daughter with the additional anger that she had carried into her adult life. The more that this mother talked about the resentment she had toward her older sister and how she felt about the things her sister had done, the more effective she became as a parent to her own daughters. When fights occurred between the two daughters she no longer jumped to the defense of the youngest child, but looked at the situation more rationally and unemotionally. Therefore, she became more effective in applying some of the parenting tools that are discussed in **Part II** of this book. The mother became much calmer and less stressed as a parent and was much fairer to both of her daughters.

We all carry resentment into our adult lives that will influence our effectiveness as parents. However, the effect of this resentment might not, and generally does not, show up right away. It may take several years or certain specific situations may need to arise before the resentment has an impact. This can make it difficult for parents to understand that they are really dealing with a Dragon that has been with them all the time, and as taken some time to grow to the size of impacting their roles as parents. It is easy to focus entirely on the present and feel that your emotions (going bonkers, or intense guilt or fear) are not only appropriate but also that they are solely due to what is happening in the present.

Another example will illustrate how fear that is brought into our roles as parents will adversely affect our responses to our children.

One mother that I counseled became very upset and would overreact when her teenage son would simply sit on the couch and stare into space. He'd simply be daydreaming. Additionally, because of a learning disability that had gone undetected for some time, he struggled in school and was therefore not very motivated to achieve well academically. His mother worried a great deal about whether or not he would be a success in school, and about his future. All parents worry about their youngsters, however her worry was way beyond what was helpful to either of them. Why did this mother respond so negatively?

The answer became clear as we talked about her own family of origin. She had a brother who, at the age of 17 (her son's age), had been diagnosed as schizophrenic. She was extremely fearful that her son would turn out like her brother. When she saw her son take on some behaviors her brother had exhibited, she would panic and try to force him to snap out of it and do better in school. Her efforts, due to panic, were ineffective and only caused her son, a strong-willed teenager, to dig his heels in even more.

Most family situations have additional factors that are involved and this situation was no different. Some additional factors may include the following:

1. When I gave the teenager a battery of psychoeducational tests I discovered that he had difficulties in the fine motor areas. He had trouble writing quickly, which affected his note-taking in class, and would become tired quickly when he had to write a report long hand. I believe that his low fine motor skills have caused him to become discouraged about school and have caused him to develop

low self-esteem. I have encouraged him to use the family computer, which he has been doing recently. This is an example of helping a youngster learn to compensate (use the computer) for a weakness (handwriting skills). Additionally, his parents and teachers have interpreted his lack of school work production to laziness instead of realizing that the main reason was that his slow fine motor skills made writing hard and frustrating for him, so he would give up easily.

2. It does not appear that his parents have discussed goal-setting very much with their son. Parents need to be good models to their children, and one area where this is important is in goal-setting. Share with your children what goals you have and your progress toward those goals. Additionally, help them to set goals for themselves. Setting realistic goals and reaching them is a great boost to their self-esteem. This teenager felt that if he set a goal and didn't reach it he was a failure, so we discussed this and the fact that he needed to look at it differently and not see it as a failure so frequently.

Many people bring fear into their role as parents. Some fear that their child will turn out like one of their own siblings who got into trouble, or that they will turn out like a niece or nephew. This fear will usually cause a parent to overreact to their youngster's misbehavior. Overreacting then diverts you from effectively helping your child or teenager with their situation.

What do all these situations have in common? Yes, each parent is looking at their son or daughter, but is really seeing someone from their past. One of the best ways to summarize the chapter is to quote from Rich Buhler's book, *Pain and Pretending*. In all situations parents are "reassigning the fear, guilt and anger to someone in the present." Buhler's book describes what is happening in these situations perfectly. "Even though a person can forget or ignore memories of abuse, the painful effects of that season of destruction do not go away. Fear, guilt, and anger persist. As a result, the pretending victim (who is now an adult, and a parent) is faced with a dilemma. In front of his own children, he acts as though nothing painful happened. He wants to live in a new world where the reality of what happened and what he fears it means about him will not have to be acknowledged.

Yet even if the memory is left in the old world, the fear, guilt, and anger are stowaways that come along to the new world. What can the victim (you may have trouble thinking of yourself as a victim, but read on) do with them? He can't admit what they mean. That would be too painful and would violate his commitment to pretend the past did not happen. So what now? He reassigns them. He attaches the fear, anger and guilt to things that are in his new world and acts as though the new things are the cause. That is, he practices a new form of pretending."[1]

In all of the cases discussed previously, parents have reassigned either fear, guilt, or anger to someone or some situation in the present. In doing so, their effectiveness as parents has been diminished. They respond to frustrating situations with too much anger, or try to force someone to change quickly out of fear, or carry tremendous amounts of guilt because they cannot change the situation immediately.

When a child goes through pain, there is frequently no one available to help them to deal with the pain. Consequently, many adults turned to pretending during childhood in order to cope with the painful situations that they experienced. Thus pretending is not a conscious act, but rather a strategy learned as a child to cope with a difficult situation. This strategy then gets carried over into adulthood, where it is no longer needed and certainly no longer effective. The "pretending" is carried into parenthood, by thinking and believing that all your anger, fear, and guilt are due solely to your child.

Even if a parent was using the correct parenting tools, using them with anger, guilt, and fear will render him or her ineffective. Adults can also reassign guilt, fear, and anger to their spouses, then obviously the parents will not be very effective in working together to help their son or daughter.

Another factor which makes it difficult for some people to parent effectively is an overwelming feeling of being powerless. As a child, victims felt powerless to do anything about their situation. Victims frequently carry that same feeling into parenthood. They feel powerless to do anything about specific situations. Helping parents to realize that they are no longer powerless is often a first step toward their road to better, more effective parenting.

What Does A Parent Do With The Feelings Of Fear, Guilt, And Anger That They May Be Reassigning To Their Child Or Teen?

If you have read this far then you have undoubtedly begun to recognize that you may be reassigning feelings of anger, guilt or fear to your own children. That is the first step. Next it is important to take the time to write down specific events that you remember happening to you as a child. Don't worry at this point about how you might have felt as a child, because you may have started pretending a long time ago, and might feel, at first that certain events did not really bother you. Don't try to evaluate them as to whether or not those events bothered you, just write the ones down that come to mind. Take several days or even weeks to do this.

You don't have to get it all done at one sitting. If you were unable to express feelings as a child, it may take you several weeks or months of giving yourself permission to write down events, before you will actually be able to sit down and write anything. One exercise that might be helpful is to write down a description of your mom and/or dad and write down a description of the ideal mom and/or dad. Compare the two lists. How do they compare? Or write down the ideal brother or sister and compare that list to how your own brother or sister was toward you.

Three books that are very helpful in resolving resentment toward people in your past are Rich Buhler's book, *Pain and Pretending*, Harold Bloomfield's book *Making Peace with Your Parents*[2] and Norm Wright's book, *Making Peace With Your Past*.[3] In effect, what you will need to do is work through the grief cycle, which will also be discussed in Chapter 8. In this case the stages may be described as follows:

CONFUSION:

You may feel confused about what is happening with your approach to parenting and your effectiveness as a parent.

DENIAL:

Many adults are at the stage of denial. One can be at denial in several ways. You may have repressed all memories of your childhood because they were too painful, or you may deny that your childhood has anything to do with your role as a parent. Many parents, especially men, are in this category. They may remember what happened to them as a child, they may even remember how they felt about it, but they deny that those experiences may be affecting them now. Another form of denial is when a person remembers his or her childhood, and remembers the pain and resentments, but thinks that they have dealt with the pain when they really haven't. Which category do you fit into? All are forms of denial.

ANGER/GUILT:

This is the stage that you must go through in order to release the effects of your childhood. Many adults try to go around this stage. Writing down some of the events of your childhood that may have been painful is a first step toward dealing with the anger and resentment. Bloomfield also suggests writing a letter to the person or persons you resent as an additional step toward recovery. In the letter, you are directing your feelings toward the person/s you need to direct them toward so you don't reassign them to your own son or daughter or spouse. You do not need to send the letter to the person to resolve the anger and resentment. In fact, one should probably not send the letter. Share the letter with a friend, a counselor, or your spouse. Talk about your resentment. It is another way to get those feelings out of you.

Again, if you were unable to express any anger as a child, then you may need to give yourself permission and possibly receive permission from a counselor in order to be able to sit down and write the letters. You may also have an opportunity to share your feelings with your own brother, sister, mother, or father, but it should only be done after you have worked through some of the anger and have gained some insights into why your brother, sister, mother, or father acted the way they did.

When you approach them it is more effective for all parties if you are assertive. That means that you approach them out of love for them and love for yourself. You do not accuse them or dump anger on them, but attempt to discuss the childhood situations openly, honestly, and objectively.

DEPRESSION:

Naturally, doing all of the above and grieving your loss (Comparing the ideal parent to your parent, or realizing your brother or sister weren't what you would have liked) saps energy from you and will leave you in a state of depression. This time gives your body time to rest and regain energy.

UNDERSTANDING:

Resolving anger and resentment from the past will require you to find out more about your parents and siblings. Realizing that your parents had parents will help you to realize that they too came into parenthood without all the necessary tools, and undoubtedly with some Dragons of their own. Many adults today do not realize that they lack the tools to be effective as a parent, so we need to realize that many of our parents also did not know they lacked the necessary tools for parenting and that they too brought Dragons into their adult life.

Counseling and parenting classes were generally unheard of for many of our parents.

Are you ready to forgive your parents or do you want to stay angry longer? What about your siblings? It is important for you to think about what your brothers and sisters were experiencing in your family of origin. In all dysfunctional families, each child tends to take on a different role; scapegoat, hero, clown, etc. Most books for adult children of alcoholics discuss these roles. Remember, children assume roles subconsciously, not deliberately, and children develop coping strategies to deal with parents in whatever way they can. Hopefully, this understanding will enable you to decide to forgive a sibling that has hurt you. As Buhler says, forgiveness is not something you do for your parents or siblings, it is something you do for yourself. Unless you make a decision to forgive your parents or siblings, you will not reach the next and final step. Forgiveness begins with a decision to forgive.

ACCEPTANCE OR FORGIVENESS:

Forgiveness does not mean forgetting, it means remembering and letting go. Forgiveness begins with making a decision to forgive people who have hurt you in the past. If you are angry toward anyone in your past, then you are connected to that person with a 60 foot piece of rope or as previously stated, you are handcuffed to that person. It's pretty hard to move forward if you still are connected to someone in your past. Have you made the decision to cut that rope? To unlock the handcuffs? It's your decision, but to be effective as a parent, it is required. It is not an option, or something to put off until you feel like it.

A Challenge To You,
And A Time To Reflect:

Dealing with painful childhood experiences can be extremely difficult. It is an area that many people choose to avoid looking at, but healing the hurts of the past is definitely a necessary stop on the roal to successful parenting. A quote hanging in my office reads, "You can't heal a wound by saying it's not there." Remember, healing the hurts of the past is done for your sake and for the sake of your children. Don't take out your own childhood resentments on your children. They don't deserve it and you don't need to continue to carry the resentments around. It's your choice. Continue to be angry and resentful or work hard to forgive people who have hurt you.

1. List five qualities of the ideal mother.
2. How did your own mother compare to those qualities?
3. List five qualities of the ideal father.
4. How did your own father compare to those qualities?
5. Do you have any resentments towards any sibling?
6. If "yes," to whom?
   For what?
7. Read the following chapter, as it too deals with resolving feelings due to experiencing losses.

ENDNOTES

1. Buhler, Rich, *Pain and Pretending*, Nashville: Thomas Nelson Publishers, 1988.
2. Bloomfield, Harold, *Making Peace With Your Parents*, New York: Ballantine Books, 1983.
3. Wright, Norm, *Making Peace With Your Past*, New Jersey: Fleming H. Revell Co., 1985.

8

Dealing With A Loss
And
Its Effect On Parenting

Index Of Suspicion

- Has your child been recently diagnosed as having a mental or physical handicap?
- Have you recently been divorced, or are you currently going through a divorce?
- Has your spouse just died?
- Are your children performing in school or sports below your expectations?
- Have you been placed in a situation in life that you did not expect?

If You Answered "Yes" To Some Of These Questions, One Of Your Dragons May Be Unresolved Grief.

When a person experiences a loss in their life, he or she will need to grieve that loss. The stages of grief in resolving a loss, are to some degree, very predictable and similar for each person.

In order to be effective as a parent, one needs to move through the grief cycle. Your effectiveness as a parent will be somewhat dependent on the stage of grief you are in. Parents need to first understand the grief cycle, accept their need to work through it, and obtain whatever help or information they need in order to move through the stages of grief.

Elisabeth Kubler-Ross, in her book, *On Death and Dying*, was one of the first to analyze and describe the stages of grief. Her work came as a result of interviewing terminally ill patients, doctors, and relatives of the terminally ill. She listed the stages as follows:

First Stage: Denial and Isolation: Our first reaction to catastrophic news is, "No, it's not true, it cannot involve me."

Second Stage: Anger—When the first stage of denial cannot be maintained any longer, it is replaced with feelings of anger, rage, envy, and resentment. A patient will ask the question, "Why me?" and dis- place anger in all directions, including toward God.

Third Stage: Bargaining—This is an attempt to postpone the situation. The plea might be, "If you get me through this I promise to stop smoking," or, "I will attend church every week," etc.

Fourth Stage: Depression—Numbness or stoicism (denial), anger, and rage will soon be replaced with a sense of a great loss or a sense of hopelessness.

Fifth Stage: Acceptance—If a patient has had
enough time (i.e. not a sudden, unex-
pected death), and has been given some
help in working through the previously
described stages, he will reach a stage
during which he is neither depressed
nor angry about his fate."[1]

Many parents that I have counseled have been dealing with a loss in their lives. Their effectiveness as parents is always reduced to some degree as they deal with their loss. It is impossible to go through the stages of grief and still be calm, rational, and fair in parenting issues. As previously stated, in order to deal effectively with a loss, parents need to:

1. Recognize that they have experienced a loss in their life.

2. Understand the stages of grief that they will need to work through (this will help them to be more effective with their child while they are working through the stages).

3. Understand how the different stages will affect their role as a parent.

4. Accept the fact that (regardless of how they currently feel) they will need to work through the various stages of grief.

The need to work through the grief cycle applies in a variety of situations, such as:

A. A child is thought to be mentally or physically handicapped.

B. Parents going through a divorce, or have been divorced.

C. A spouse has died.

D. A child does not achieve or behave at a level you had expected.

E. Special circumstances put you in a place you hadn't expected.

The stages of grief are essentially the same for all of the above, although each situation possesses its own unique components. I will review each example listed above, describe the stages, and discuss things to look out for as you work through the stages.

A Child Is Thought To Have A Mental Or Physical Handicap

Mary Leydorf, M.D.,[2] has described the following stages, with a brief description about each stage, that occurs when parents are told that their child has a mental or physical handicap. The amount of time spent at each stage varies widely from a few seconds to many years. This fact is further complicated in two-parent families, when each parent may be at a different stage and may be unaware of the stages and their need to work through them.

Stage	Description
1. Confusion	A reality before a diagnosis is made. Often professionals are unsure, and require a planned time interval for study of the child. Parents are uncertain and bewildered.
2. Denial	When presented with the diagnosis, the parents do not accept it and may comment, "He'll outgrow it." "How could the doctor know, he only spent five minutes with the child." "Great-uncle Herman's third child had the same thing, and he's OK." Attention is often focused on one small item and the total picture is ignored: i.e., "He can spell 'CAT,' therefore he is not retarded," etc.

3. Anger-Guilt

An aggressive, out-going parent will turn his dismay outward, often against the doctor who made the first diagnosis of abnormality. Also common is to turn against the spouse, possibly blaming him or her for the problem. Occasionally, the obstetrician is accused. The passive parent will turn his disappointment inward: "What did I do wrong?" "Did I really want this child?" "Maybe I should have . . . "

4. Hope

There may be excessive hope for a miracle. Frantic searching for a "cure," "shopping" from doctor to doctor, or medical center to medical center, without allowing consistent treatment is characteristic of this stage.

5. Depression

In this stage there is a resigned attitude, but an unhealthy one. May range from "blue," or "listless" to real withdrawal and attempt to hide the child. This indicates that the diagnosis of the child's abnormality is accepted.

6. Acceptance

This stage suggests the beginning of a good parent-child relationship. On this firm basis, help may be given to the child. The parent accepts the child "for what he is." The parent realizes both the normal areas and abnormal areas. "He is a child first and handicapped second." A relaxed attitude predominates.

7. Understanding   The parent not only understands his own child, but is enriched by having to strengthen his own ability to cope with life. A parent is now able to help his child. This is the final stage. Fulfillment is reached, and there is a new dimension now added to this parent's personality.

As stated above, the beginning of a good parent-child relationship can only begin at Stage 6, "Acceptance." If you are at "Denial" (denying there is a problem), then you may have unrealistic expectations of your child and interpret his behavior inappropriately, which could lead to anger on your part. Unrealistic expectations and anger get in the way of effective parenting strategies. When a parent is at Stage 3, "Anger," they may direct some of the anger toward the child, while guilt could cause the parent to be too lenient toward the child's misbehavior.

Obviously, depression leaves a parent incapable of responding positively to any situation. As stated previously, an added complication to dealing with one's grief in a two-parent family is that each parent will probably go through the stages at a different rate. They may have trouble understanding that each person expresses his or her emotions in a different manner and one may take longer than the other to reach acceptance or understanding. I am not referring to "rights and wrongs" but rather to the fact that each person is different, and thus may grieve in a different manner and speed.

It definitely takes time to work through the grief cycle, however, time alone is not enough. Grieving is an active process. One needs to cry and get angry and express those feelings, not keep them bottled up. It can be very helpful for parents to join a support group of other parents that have gone through and are going through a similar situation. It is also important to realize that once you reach Understanding, you will still go back to some of these emotions, depending on your child's handicap and how it affects him as he progresses through various development stages.

Accepting this fact as normal should be of some comfort to you. Remember, to be effective as a parent you'll need to reach Understanding and Acceptance. In other words, reaching Understanding and Acceptance is not an option if you want to be an effective parent. You will need to do whatever it takes, and get whatever help is necessary to reach Understanding and Acceptance.

This description applies to a child that is born with a birth defect and has a mental or physical disability. It can also apply to conditions diagnosed well after birth, such as a heart problem, a learning disability, Attention Deficit Disorder with or without Hyperactivity, Diabetes, etc.

Remember, it is crucial to your effectiveness as a parent to work through the grief cycle. It is not an option if you desire to be effective as a parent. Dealing with the pain is hard work, but definitely worth the effort.

Parents Who Continue To Fight Because Of A Divorce

This is one of the most common situations that can contribute to a parent's ineffective parenting. The reasons for this are several. The first has to do with working through the loss of the marriage, and for the child, the loss of daily contact with one of the parents. The second has to do with the different parenting styles of the mother and father. The combination of the different parenting styles, and the unresolved anger, and the guilt will definitely interfere with effective parenting. I'll first discuss the different parenting styles, then the grief cycle and dealing with the loss of the marriage.

Husbands and wives usually divorce one another because they were unable to resolve their differences. They were unable to reach compromises on issues that they differed on. One of the major areas where differences can occur is in the area of parenting. The reader may also refer to the section in **Part II** where I discuss the issue of partners reaching agreements on parenting. If you asked all parents what they wanted their children to be able to do when they are 18, you would probably get pretty similar answers.

However, if each parent is trying different approaches to parenting, the likelihood of reaching those goals is reduced. When a divorced father in counseling said to me, "I'll raise the kids the way I want to, and she can raise the kids the way she wants to when they are with her," he obviously was not thinking of what is best for the kids. When couples with children divorce, they often fail to realize that they still need to work at resolving conflicts that involve the children, and the lives of their children will be filled with continuous stress and disharmony.

The more divorced couples can agree on common rules and consequences, the easier the task of each parent will be, and the children will definitely be much better adjusted as a result. Divorced parents could list different areas of parenting or concerns and attempt to negotiate compromises. Obviously, if they were unable to resolve conflicts in their marriage, they may need the help of a counselor and one or both of them may need to acquire better tools for resolving conflicts. If one spouse can develop effective tools for resolving conflicts, he or she can often be successful in approaching the other spouse in a more constructive and effective manner. Remember, few parents realize that they do not have enough tools in their tool kit to deal with life. Most people when they run into difficulties with a spouse or child will blame it on someone besides themselves. They seldom realize that they themselves could develop a few more effective tools. The difficulty in agreeing on a parenting approach is further compounded in situations of divorce by the need for all parties, including the children, to work through the grief cycle.

I will describe the stages of grief in the case of divorce as follows:

CONFUSION:

Usually at least one spouse, sometimes both, are very confused when divorce is suggested or initiated. One may have been caught off guard by the other's action.

DENIAL:

Denial follows closely to confusion. "No, it really isn't happening. My spouse is just joking." A word about the children is important here. When parents tell their children that they are going to get a divorce, the children are definitely in Confusion and Denial. Many parents will think that the kids are handling it just fine when in reality they are in shock or Confusion and Denial. One couple said that they told the kids the night before seeing me that they were getting a divorce and "the kids took it very well."

You may ask why they were calling me after telling the kids about the divorce. The wanted to make it easy on the kids, so they sought counseling. It is possible to make divorce *easier* for children. In my opinion, it is impossible to make it *easy*. Regardless of their ages, divorce is traumatic on children, and will have an impact on the rest of their lives. I believe that many couples would spend more time trying to make their marriage work if they truly understood the impact that divorce can have on the lives of children for the rest of their lives. Some adults still carry scars from their parents' divorce that occured when they were children.

ANGER AND GUILT:

When parents are at this stage of grief, it is nearly impossible to be effective. When parents are in Anger, they will often be unfair toward their children as they may reassign the anger they have towards their spouse to their children. Being angry at the situation their lives are in may cause them to immediately respond with anger when their child misbehaves. One will not be an effective parent if he is utilizing anger and emotion to try and change the child's behavior. A parent may also use the child to get back at the other parent.

You may try to keep your child from seeing your spouse because you know your spouse will be mad. The only problem is, you end up hurting your child with this action. Anger may cause you to say very negative things about your spouse. This also can be devastating to your child. Each child is made up of each parent. When you criticize your spouse you are inevitably criticizing a portion of your children, which may damage their self-esteem.

An excellent book that can help you deal with anger at this stage and the loss of a loved one is *Making Peace With Yourself*, by Harold H. Bloomfield. One comment he makes about this anger is, "To heal from the loss of a love, anger must be accepted and ventilated so that the pain of the hurt can be fully let go. When the anger is denied, the price is incomplete healing and chronic depression."[3]

A client of mine recently followed one of Bloomfield's suggestions, one that is in many books about grieving a loss. She wrote an angry letter to her ex-husband, went to the spot where they were married, and read it to him. No, he wasn't there, but she visualized him being there, and accepting her anger. She felt a great deal of relief after doing that. She may need to do this periodically as she feels the anger coming back.

The best way to deal with this anger would be to read the letter to your ex-spouse, but only if he or she would **accept** your anger, and not counter attack immediately with their own excuses or reasons for their behavior. When an ex-spouse will not or cannot do this, the next best thing is to write the letter and read it to a counselor, a friend or anyone who will simply accept your feelings.

Simply writing the letter helps people to get the feelings out of their body, onto a piece of paper, and away from themselves. It helps to get rid of the anger. Bloomfield states,

"The psychological importance of working through painful resentments cannot be underestimated. Not to release suppressed feelings of hurt and anger is to remain imprisoned by them."[4]

Feelings of guilt also cause parents to be ineffective. When you feel guilty, you might go overboard to "make it up" to your children. You may give in to their every demand and have trouble setting limits on their behavior. You may have trouble following through with a punishment when they misbehave. Guilt may cause you to want to make up for the parent that is no longer in the home. Trying to be "super-mom" or "super-dad" to your children will cause you additional stress, which will also make it difficult to be effective as a parent.

DEPRESSION:

Depression usually causes one to be listless, tired, unmotivated, and unresponsive. An "I don't care" attitude may develop. Little energy is left to deal with parenting issues. Remember too, that one does not work through the stages in a 1, 2, 3, etc. sequence as listed here. You may work through to Understanding, then slip back to Anger, when your child has a birthday party and your ex-spouse does not show up or forgets to send a present. Then you have to work through the stages again.

Usually it becomes easier to work through the stages, if you have the right tools and realize the need to work through the stages. By right tools, at this point, I refer to the ability to write a letter to your ex-spouse stating that you felt a lot of disappointment that he or she did not remember the child's birthday. In this way, you have expressed your anger in an assertive way, and you haven't let it remain bottled up inside you. Even if your spouse won't read anything from you, or you feel he or she will just laugh, send the letter. The main reason for writing the letter or telling your spouse your feelings about the party is to help you get the feelings out. A second major goal is that you would be modeling the effective way to deal with anger for your youngsters to see. This will help them to learn to deal with their anger more effectively. It is not productive to continually bring up the past with an ex-spouse, but it is important to be assertive regarding behaviors they exhibit in the present.

If you can be assertive, not aggressive or passive, then there will be less tendency that your own resentments will continue to grow. Being assertive, not aggressive or passive, is a skill many people lack. You may require some counseling or classes to master this technique.

UNDERSTANDING:

Understanding means you have taken the time to figure out what really went wrong in your marriage. You know what you did wrong, you know what your mate did wrong. You have come to accept that it takes two to make a marriage and two to break it up. If you continue to blame your ex-spouse for all the problems in the marriage, then it will be almost impossible for you to work through the grief cycle. Additionally, if you blame your ex-spouse for all the problems, then you will undoubtedly go into another relationship and repeat the same mistakes that you made the first time. This is another example in which most individuals do not realize that they do not have enough tools to deal with life. They simply blame problems or the lack of being able to solve the problems on their ex-spouse.

ACCEPTANCE OR FORGIVENESS:

I almost did not want to write the word forgiveness, because that may be so far from your mind right now. However, it is a goal that you must reach if you are to be effective as a parent, and a goal you must reach if you are to be successful in future relationships. In other words, it is not an option to consider or not consider. If you are angry with anyone in your past, then you are connected to that person with a 60 foot piece of rope. It is impossible to go very far if you are connected to someone with a 60 foot piece of rope.

A more dramatic way to look at it would be to consider yourself handcuffed to anyone that you have not forgiven. It's pretty hard to have a relationship with anyone in the present if you are still handcuffed to someone in your past. Bloomfield states, "Forgiveness doesn't mean forgetting, nor does it mean whitewashing what has happened. Forgiveness means letting go, moving on, and favoring the positive."[5] Claudia Black, who has done a great deal of work with adult children of alcoholics, says, "Forgiveness is not forgetting, it's remembering and letting go."[6] Rich Buhler, in his book *Pain and Pretending*, reminds us that we don't forgive people for their benefit. We do it for our own benefit.[7]

It is very important for parents to work through the grief cycle for still another reason. Children also need to work through these stages when their parents get divorced. If you have not worked through the stages, then it will be impossible for you to help your children. I know you might now be feeling more guilt, but **don't let guilt keep you from doing what's right**. In other words, begin now to work through the stages. **Remember! It's never too late to do what's right.**

When parents are embroiled in legal battles with their ex-spouses there is a greater tendency to get stuck at the anger/guilt/depression stage of the grief cycle. Parents need to be more accepting of their need to work through the stages in order to become more effective with their children. Professional help may be necessary to help you work through the stages, but a very important step is to realize that for your own well-being and the well-being of your children, you need to work through the stages. As you become healthier, you will be more able to help your youngster.

After working with one particular woman for several months to help her "grieve" her divorce, she became able to help her son. In fact, one of the exercises that I had her do she passed on to her son. She encouraged her son to write a letter to his dad about his anger regarding the divorce, and the fact that he was slighted at his father's wedding. The letter that the boy wrote is included here. (Jennifer is the daughter who was living with her father, and Bryan was the son of the woman he was marrying.)

> Dear Dad,
>   It was not nice of you to take Jennifer from me and mom. Why did you do that for? I hated that!
>   Why did you not include me in the wedding? I did not understand that. That was not nice of you. Why could not I take Bryan's place in the wedding? I felt mad, sitting there at the wedding. because I am your son.
>   Why can't (you) pick me up on time so I could see my sister and see you? **I hate that** Dad. You are not doing your part in the divorce. I am very upset in you because you don't pick me up. I hate it when you do that, I get very, very, very, very mad.
>   I get very sad when I don't get to see my sister. I have no one to play with because you took my sister.
>   Why don't you let Jennifer come over every weekend?
>   Why did you and mom have to fight every hour of the day?
>   Make sure you answer all of these questions.
>   Your Son,
>   *Brett*
>
>   Used with permission

Brett's mother was helping him to deal with his pain and anger regarding his parents' divorce and his dad's remarriage.

Writing a letter to someone is a very effective way to deal with your anger, and an effective way to help your son or daughter. The letter does not have to be sent. In fact, sometimes it may be worse to send it, because the recipient may not accept your anger. Writing it is a way to get the feelings out of your body and away from you, onto a piece of paper. As I discuss in Chapter 10, **Part II** on helping children express their anger, it may take several weeks or months of giving youngsters permission to write their anger, before they actually sit down and do it. I have also found this to be true of adults. Sometimes it takes several weeks or months (depending upon the person's childhood upbringing about feelings and anger), before he feels that it is OK to express his anger.

Remember, it is crucial to your own welfare and the welfare of your children, that you work through the grief cycle. In doing so, you become more effective as a parent, and you become more capable of helping your children do the grief work that they need to do. I have listed several books in the *Suggested Reading* section at the end of this book that may assist you in helping your youngster grieve properly. Accept the need to help them grieve; don't try to pretend that nothing is wrong. Don't be hesitant to bring up the subject because you are afraid it will make your child sad. You may have to help them to cry and express anger, but this is far healthier than pretending that things are OK.

A Spouse Has Died

One of the most stressful events in the life of an adult is the death of a spouse. Obviously, this is the most dramatic event in the life of a child. The death of a spouse and the death of a parent brings on many changes for the family. These changes include: loss of companionship, help in parenting, financial status; possibly a move to a smaller house or apartment, and sometimes a move to a different city, school, or neighborhood; acquiring different friends, etc. As mentioned in **Part II**, Chapter 11 (on stress), all the changes cause an overload to the system, and can result in many behavioral, emotional and physical difficulties. As previously mentioned, the stages of grief as defined by Kubler-Ross include:

1. Denial and Isolation
2. Anger

3. Bargaining

4. Depression

5. Acceptance[8]

Several factors are needed in order to grieve the death of a spouse. Time is definitely one of them. Grieving is definitely a process. It does not happen overnight. You need to give yourself time, to get through the grief cycle. Also, you need to realize that as you work through the stages, something or someone you may run into may cause you to regress to a stage you thought you had already gone through. In fact, it's not unusual to move back to anger/guilt/depression even years after the death of a spouse.

Generally, when you slide back, you won't stay at that place for as long as you did before. Grieving is also an active process. You need to cry and get angry. If you went into a closet for two years, time would have passed, but you would be no better off than you were when you went in. A support group is also very helpful to you when grieving the death of a spouse.

You may also want to enroll your son or daughter in a support group at the same time, since it can be very difficult to help your child grieve when you are experiencing your own grief. It's extremely important for parents to help their children to grieve the death of their father or mother.

Although this section has been written to help explain factors that may interfere with effective parenting, it is equally important for parents to realize the need to help their children deal with the pain associated with the death of a parent. Rich Buhler's book title, *Pain and Pretending* applies in many situations. When a child goes through the pain from the death of a parent, he needs to deal with the pain, express it and get it out, not pretend, or act like everything is OK.

One of the biggest problems that I see when counseling adults is the pretending. They may be experiencing tremendous pain in a marriage, a job, with their children, etc., but they pretend it's not there, and therefore don't take any corrective action. In other words, they had to pretend as children when in pain (if they were not helped to grieve a loss or disappointment), so they may continue to pretend as adults that they really aren't in any pain. In doing so, they will not take any action to correct the problem.

I remember counseling a 70-year-old woman, who was having a great deal of difficulty dealing with the death of her husband, two years earlier. Was it necessary to dig deeper and look into her childhood for possible reasons? Definitely! As a four-year-old child, her mother had died, her father was gone a lot, and she was raised by her grandmother. She was never helped to deal with the loss of her parents. She was never helped to grieve as a child, and therefore it was extremely difficult for her to grieve her husband's death.

We need to ease the pain of our children as they grow up, but easing the pain does not mean that we ignore it and pretend that they aren't hurting. Parents often make the mistake of waiting until the child brings it up before talking about the death of a parent. This is a big mistake.

If a child does not bring it up on his own, then you need to try and draw the feelings out of him. In other words, you need to induce them to grieve. Get them to talk about a favorite time they had with their dad or mom, or look at old pictures, etc. Sure it's painful, but the pain needs to be dealt with. A stitchery that my mother made, which hangs in my office states, "You can't heal a wound by saying it's not there."

In summary, upon the death of a spouse, you may need to get help to deal with your loss, and you need to be able to help your child deal with his/her loss. Additionally, you need to accept that at least for a time, your effectiveness as a parent will not be what either of you would like or expect. Be patient but persistent, as you deal with this tremendous loss.

A Child Does Not Achieve
Or Behave At A Level
You Had Expected

Throughout the life of a child, a parent will need to experience and deal with many major and minor losses. To put this in quantitative terms, I remember explaining to a parent that her child performed within the average range on an intelligence test. She looked shocked, and said, "You mean the highest his IQ could be is 110?" I said "Yes, according to the test I administered. What did you think your son's IQ was?" She said she thought it would be at least 125 to 130. This was a "loss" of 15 to 20 IQ points in her mind. I've talked to many parents whose child had achieved a "D" or "C" average in school. They had expected that their youngster would be at least a "B" or "B plus" student.

I've coached soccer for over 10 years, and have coached quite a few All-Star teams. It's a difficult process to select an All-Star team, and if a child does not make the team, it's another loss that his parents may need to deal with. Perhaps you were hoping that your child would run for an office at school. When they didn't run, or did run and didn't get elected, you had to deal with a loss. Maybe you wanted your child to join the school band or try out for some sports at high school, or join some clubs. We all have expectations of our children, and it's good to have expectations. It's good to encourage our children to reach certain goals, and it's important to help them achieve goals. It's also important to realize that when they fall short of our expectations, we need to deal with that loss. In dealing with any loss, we need to go through the grief cycle. I won't go into great detail about each step, because they are very similar to those I've previously mentioned.

You may be angry at your children for not reaching a goal; you may feel guilty because you "should" have helped them more; or feel that if you hadn't been working, they might have reached their goal. You'll feel depressed about it. All these emotions are real and valid. Don't deny them. Accept that you have to work through a loss. Remember, you will not be as effective as you would like to be if you get stuck in anger/guilt/depression.

It is important to work through the stages to the point of understanding and acceptance. It is only at this point that you will be effective as a parent. It may also be necessary to help your child deal with his loss. Maybe he had been counting on making the All-Star team, or going on the Honor Roll Field Trip. He will be experiencing some pain, and you need to help him deal with his pain. Do not pretend that he isn't in pain. If he doesn't bring it up, you may need to say something like, "I bet you are really disappointed that you didn't get to _____ ." That may get him talking about it. If he says he isn't disappointed say, "Well that's good, but I know I would be disappointed, and if you are upset I can understand that."

Sometimes the loss a parent experiences is much greater than those expressed in the previous paragraphs. Sometimes a youngster has gotten into trouble with the law, or has begun to abuse alcohol or drugs, or has dropped out of school and isn't trying to find a job. The loss may be greater, the need to grieve is the same. Parents need to recognize the grieving process and work through it.

A father said to me, "I've had it with my son. He's not going to school. He doesn't do what we would like him to do. He's getting terrible grades—so I quit. I'm not coming back to counseling anymore."

I was in shock for a few minutes. I didn't know what to say. Finally I said, "I didn't know you could do that. I didn't know you could stop being a parent. I know you made Marriage Vows, but maybe you didn't make any Parenting Vows, such as 'til death do us part.'" This father was obviously in the anger/guilt stage, which was a very normal place for him to be. But he was unwilling, or unable (possibly due to other factors in his childhood), to continue in counseling to work through the grief cycle. That particular situation was also another reminder to me that at that point most parents blame all the problems on the teenager. They fail to realize that maybe they do not have the right tools to raise a teenager.Possibly they have brought some Dragons into their adult lives that are interfering with their roles as parents. Please don't get me wrong. Teenagers do have some responsibility as well. All problem teenagers can't be traced to problem parents. There needs to be a balance. Both parents and teenagers need to accept responsibility for their behavior and for the choices they make.

Often, when I counsel parents of teenagers, a major goal is to help the parents maintain their sanity and self-esteem, while their teenager is in the process of deciding what he wants to do with his life. For additional help in this area, look at the chapter titled "Is Your Life In Balance?"

There are several good books in this area as well. One is *When Parents Cry*[9] by Joy Gage. "It is a book written from the perspective of the parent who has tried everything (with their teenager or young adult) but who is, nonetheless faced with a casualty. It attempts to answer only one question: After the parent has done everything possible for his child, what can the parent do for himself?" The three major areas which this book considers are: 1) causes of disillusionment, 2) coping with casualty, and 3) discovering life "after Johnny." Another helpful book in this area is *The Hurting Parent*[10] by Margie M. Lewis.

Special Circumstances Put You In A Place You Hadn't Expected

Many situations probably could fit in this area. I will describe a few.

I once counseled grandparents who were placed in a situation in which they had to raise their grandchildren. The childrens' parents were alcoholics, and unable to take care of their children. This is a very difficult situation for many reasons. First, let's look at the grandparents dealing with their loss. I am sure they thought they would be retired and through with parenting by this time in their lives. They probably had visualized themselves camping and traveling. They lost some freedom. The grandfather was often in anger, "Why do we have to do this now?" and the grandmother was often in guilt, "Maybe we should have gotten them away from their parents earlier."

All these feelings and emotions are valid and normal. The grandparents need to deal with their loss. The grandfather would too quickly get angry at the two teenagers, and the grandmother would often bend over backwards to give them whatever they wanted. They needed to recognize the grief cycle, and to work through it in order to effectively parent their grandchildren. What makes the situation even more difficult is that it was necessary for the two teenagers to work through the loss of their parents and the loss of a "normal childhood." They then had to deal with the anger they carried due to the unfair treatment they received when they lived with their parents.

Other situations that could fall in this category include:

1. Having to raise the child of a relative who has died, gone to jail, or a rehabilitation program.

2. Losing your job and being out of work for a time.

3. Having to take care of your own parents in your home, because they can no longer take care of themselves.

4. Dealing with an illness, such as Cancer, Depression, or a life-threatening heart condition.

The list could go on, but I am sure you get the point. Any changes in our lives can be seen as losses that have to be dealt with. Recognizing the need to grieve is half the battle. The other half is to actively grieve and reach a point of understanding and acceptance. Remember, grieving is a process. It takes time and effort, but it is worth it and far better in the long run, than is pretending.

A Challenge To You, And A Time To Reflect:

1. If you have been divorced, have you worked through the stages of grief to the point of acceptance?
   Have you forgiven your ex-spouse?
2. If you want to be effective as a parent, do you accept the need to work through the stages of grief?
3. Do you have the necessary tools to work through the stages of grief?
   a. Can you cry?
   b. Can you express anger?
   c. Can you look objectively at your marriage?
   d. Are you willing to look at your childhood and learn how it affected your marriage?
   e. Are you able to look at your marriage and determine what you did wrong?

(If you answered "no" to any of these questions, you may need to work with a pastor or counselor to assist you through the stages. Support groups for divorced adults can also be a great deal of help.)

4. Has your child failed to meet your expectations?
5. Have you *grieved* this loss?

ENDNOTES

1. Kubler-Ross, Elizabeth, *On Death and Dying,* New York: MacMillan Publishing Co., Inc., 1969.
2. Leydorf, Mary, M.D., Paper on stages of grief.
3. Bloomfield, Harold, *Making Peace With Yourself,* New York: Ballantine Books, 1985.
4. Ibid., p. 50.
5. Ibid., p. 53.
6. Black, Claudia, *It's Never Too Late To Have a Happy Childhood,* New York: Ballantine Books, 1989.
7. Buhler, Rich, *Pain and Pretending,* Nashville: Thomas Nelson Publishers, 1988.
8. Kubler-Ross, 1969.
9. Gage, Joy, *When Parents Cry* (retitled *Is There Life After Johnny? Standing Strong Through Your Child's Rebellion*), San Bernardino, California: Here's Life Publisher, 1989.
10. Lewis, Margie M., *The Hurting Parent,* Grand Rapids: Zondervan Publishing House, 1980.

9

Two Case Studies

The purpose of these case studies is to help the reader see how Dragons have impacted real life situations. In some ways, these case studies may be much more complex than your own personal situation. The case studies will also illustrate that there may be more than one Dragon present for parents to deal with. (The names have been changed to protect the individual's identity.)

Case Study Number 1

At the time counseling started for Susan and her family, she was 35-years-old, her husband Bill was 34, and their two sons, Brian and Tim, were 11 and 7 respectively. The problem was that Brian was experiencing academic and behavioral problems at school and at home. During the course of Brian's evaluation it was determined that his intellectual ability was in the low average to borderline range. He appeared to have *Attention Deficit Disorder Without Hyperactivity*. Susan had a great deal of difficulty relating to and disciplining Brian, explaining that, "if only Brian would do the right things, then our family would be perfect."

Initially, it seemed we spent many months stuck in the "educational" aspect of counseling with regards to parenting skills. Yet, in spite of all our discussions about spending time with the children, chore charts, praise, giving them choices, logical consequences, etc., nothing was changing. I am not sure what caused us to dig deeper. It might have been the day that Susan said in counseling, "I say every hateful thing to Brian that I would like to say to my brother George." In fact, Susan stated that she could still not stand her brother and rarely spoke to him or saw him. Susan could not stand her son Brian, and felt very hateful toward him. (I wonder if we could have gotten to this point sooner. Hopefully, this book will help people to at least identify the issues sooner. Each person, I am sure, will differ in his or her willingness and ability to deal with the issues that are uncovered.)

Digging deeper uncovered the following family history, and revealed the issues that needed to be addressed. As previously stated, Susan was 35-years-old at the time counseling began. Susan has three siblings, George, age 32, Kevin, age 27, and Sarah, age 22. As a child, Susan felt very neglected by her father. Much of the time, he was gone with his job. When he was at home he was not involved with the family. He pursued his own interests. Susan cannot remember spending any time talking to her father, and does not remember taking family vacations. Her father never disciplined her, never praised her, and never spent any time playing with her. However, she did notice that her father spent a great deal more time with her younger brother Kevin, and younger sister, Sarah. Susan's parents did not talk to each other about parenting issues, and all the parenting responsibilities were left to her mother. Her father was often very moody and frequently pouted, especially if things did not go his way. (Her father's mother also was a moody person.) Susan never saw her parents show love to each other. Susan remembered that at times her parents blamed her and her siblings if they did not have a good time while the parents were away, especially if they found out that the children had misbehaved for a babysitter. She remembers always doing what her mother said without arguing; however, she also remembers that if she would pout or complain, her mother would frequently give in to her desires. Her father appeared to procrastinate on a lot of chores and other responsibilities, and appeared to dwell in the negative a great amount of the time. He was not sympathetic to her mother's needs, and did not like to just sit and talk about things. Susan remembers once when a family member was taking some time to describe something that had happened to him, Susan's father said, "Just get on with it!" Susan never saw her mother deal with pain. She would just seem to ignore it and keep doing what was needed.

Susan's brother George appeared to take on the role of the "acting-out child" in their dysfunctional family. George lied, told stories, was stubborn, pestered Susan, and appeared to be the "king of the household." He didn't care how he looked and he never shared. Susan had all of these same complaints toward her son Brian. In fact, Susan's mother said recently, "I see so much of George in Brian."

Remember, the family of origin work is not done to put the blame on parents or siblings. It is done to gain understanding as to why you do what you do, to identify irrational beliefs you have picked up, and to recognize resentments that need to be worked through. Susan and I are still trying to find out more about her parents' parents. Her mother's father was an alcoholic, and her mother did everything in her family. Just knowing these few things helps us to know a lot about why they did what they did. But I will encourage Susan to find out more information about her grandparents.

The purpose of this case study is to illustrate the Dragons that Susan needed to deal with in order to apply parenting tools. There are many to deal with, some related to Brian, and many related to her childhood. They include:

1. When Brian was diagnosed as having borderline intellectual ability and Attention Deficit Disorder without Hyperactivity, Susan and her husband needed to deal with this loss, which was discussed in Chapter 8. They had not anticipated their son having these difficulties, and needed to deal with it. They needed to reach Understanding and Acceptance of Brian's problems to be effective as parents.

2. Susan never saw her parents discuss parenting issues. Her mother was the controller, and did everything with the children. Therefore, it was Susan's belief that she should deal with the boys by herself without the help of her husband. Additionally, since she rarely spoke with her father, it was extremely difficult for her to talk with her husband. She would often react like her father. "Just get to the point, don't take so long to talk about things," would often be her reply to Bill. I have encouraged Susan to write letters to her husband about her feelings, and have encouraged Bill to write back. This is a first step toward getting them more comfortable with communication. I strongly encourage many couples to write to each other. It allows one to be more assertive and get all of one's feelings out without interruption, and it allows the receiver of the letter time to think about things before blurting out a response. Bill was also reluctant to write, because he felt comfortable talking about issues. However, since his wife has not been used to this, he needs to use approaches that will be effective in communicating with her.

3. Obviously, a big Dragon is Susan's resentment toward her brother George. She has reassigned her resentment of George to her son Brian, which has made it impossible for her to react to Brian calmly and assertively. Susan has written some angry letters to her brother George, which she has not sent. She is trying to understand the

role that her brother had to take on in their dysfunctional family. Hopefully, this will help her to forgive her brother, and thereby be less angry toward her son, Brian.

4. Another Dragon is her resentment toward her father for not spending time with her, praising her, showing love to her, and spending time with the family. Susan needs to resolve her resentment toward her father so that she does not reassign her negative feelings toward her husband. If she can resolve her resentment toward her father, she will be more able to have a positive relationship with him. If she can learn to be more assertive, she will be able to communicate her needs and feelings to her father, and work toward a more positive relationship with him.

5. The chapter on Codependency also covers many issues relating to Susan's situation. After all, since her grandfather on her mother's side was an alcoholic, Susan, theoretically, is an adult child of an alcoholic. Susan has been too affected by her son's behavior. She gets too upset over his actions, and she has tried to control his behavior and force him to do the right things. It is very hard to get most parents, especially extreme codependents, to look at their own behavior, as opposed to blaming the child for everything. Susan's parents appeared to blame the children, especially George, for the problems the family was having. They did not realize that they themselves did not have enough parenting tools to deal with the children, and they certainly were unaware of the Dragons that they had brought into their family and marriage.

6. Susan has tried to recreate her "at home" feeling in several ways, some consciously, some subconsciously. She has tried to be the controller and do all of the parenting. She has been overly critical of her husband

Bill at times, and frequently finds fault with him, which may be her way to maintain the distance that she felt with her father. Additionally, Bill has brought his own Dragons into the marriage, which will not be discussed in this case study, but the reader should be assured that both parents lacked tools and brought Dragons into the marriage. At times, Susan will encourage her husband to do things for himself, then get angry about it, possibly feeling that he is selfish, like her father appeared to be. Sometimes when the family is getting ready to do something together, a fight over something—anything— will develop. Then, the trip is called off. This may be a way to recreate her "at home" feeling of never doing anything as a family. Susan has also recreated her "at home" feelings by zeroing in on one child (Brian), and blaming him for most of the family problems, which is what her family appeared to do to her brother George.

7. Some beliefs that Susan has had to identify, attack, and eliminate are:

- "Children should just 'go with the flow' and not talk back."

- "Children should do what I say, even if I don't model the same behavior." (Remember Myth #10 about the seatbelt?)

- "Husbands are not sympathetic." (At times her husband would be very sympathetic, but Susan could not or would not accept it. She would get angry, which would cause her husband not to be sympathetic. Thereby, she had recreated her "at home" feeling of the husband not being sympathetic to the wife.)

- "Children make us feel a certain way."

- "Husbands and wives do not spend time together alone without the children."

8. Because of the difficulty in communicating with her husband and his own Dragons, Susan and Bill have not resolved some conflicts during the past 7 to 8 years. The resentments related to these issues need to be dealt with, and solutions need to be determined for some of the conflicts.

9. Susan also has investigated the need for medication to help her with her mood swings and her temper. As of this date, the medication appears to be giving her a longer fuse, and is helping her to remain calmer, to be more able to deal effectively with the Dragons, and to apply the parenting tools. Quite possibly, her father may have had a chemical imbalance, which might have explained some of his moods and behaviors.

10. Susan has also developed some very ineffective ways to deal with pain, having had a very bad model for this as a child, when she was not able to talk about painful things. She may work compulsively, swear, talk rudely, spend money, work in the yard excessively, etc.

It would be impossible to summarize this case study, but one comment I would like to make is that many adults feel powerless. When a person grows up in a dysfunctional family, they are, as a child, really powerless to do anything about that situation. The problem is that many people bring that same feeling of being powerless, into their adult lives, which further complicates their ability to develop new parenting tools and to "slay the Dragons." You are not powerless. You are an adult. You can do something about your situation, if you stay on the road to recovery, or get back on it when you fall off.

Another observation from this case study, is that a parent may definitely have more than one Dragon to deal with. Dragons that are brought from childhood into adult life may not make themselves known until well into the marriage or the role of parenting. When Dragons don't appear immediately in a marriage, which they rarely do, there is an even greater tendency to blame a child or spouse, rather than recognize the presence of Dragons.

Case Study Number 2

This case study is similar to the first one in several ways. A parent has brought Dragons into his role as a parent which have gotten in the way of applying the parenting tools effectively and consistently. In addition, an important Dragon that this case study discusses is the importance of interpreting our childrens' behavior problems accurately, if we wish to deal with them calmly and effectively. Parents interpret the behaviors of their children from their own viewpoints of why children misbehave, which they developed in their own childhood.

Jim and Pam entered counseling because they had been experiencing marital problems and problems with disciplining their two children. Additionally, Jim suffered some physical problems, having had an ulcer for many years.

Jim grew up in a family where he was unable to express his feelings. He was also frequently compared to a twin brother, who always seemed to do things a little better than Jim. His dad was overly coercive, always telling Jim and his brother what to do and when to do it. It always appeared to Jim that things he did could always be done a little bit better. It is little wonder that Jim has suffered with ulcers. He is not able to express his feelings as an adult, and always feels that he could do things a little bit better. All of these factors have contributed to Jim's low self-esteem, which is one of the Dragons that he has had to deal with. Jim has also had to work hard to learn to allow his two children to express their feelings, and to learn to praise their small efforts at things, rather than wait until they do something "perfectly." Jim's father was an alcoholic. Discussing this in counseling has helped Jim to understand and to forgive his father. In doing so, Jim has been able to speak more assertively with his father, and their communication has improved a great deal.

The main reason that I have presented this case study is to illustrate the importance of accurately determining why a child misbehaves. The following was written by Jim's wife:

"When our daughter, Suzie, was a baby and a small toddler, we always knew that she was an "active," "difficult," and "strong-willed" child. When Suzie was one-year-old, we were invited to a birthday party at a close friend's house. There were four other families, each with two children. Since we were the first to arrive, Jim and I got busy helping out, and meeting the other couples. Suzie was very fussy, and as the afternoon went along she kept disappearing. This, combined with meeting new people, left all of us pretty tired and irritable on the way home and into the evening. We kind of made a mutual decision that to interact with other young families was more work than it was worth. Suzie remained the apple of our eye throughout the next year, but we decided that she really needed a sibling. When Suzie was approaching two years of age, her brother was born.

One night, as we were putting the kids to bed, Suzie decided that she didn't want to put her pajamas on. She started to fidget and give Jim a difficult time. Jim gave her a spanking and she started screaming at him. At this time in our lives, we believed that parents *speak* and and children *obey*. The next forty-five minutes was a battle of wills, where Suzie would spit and Jim would spank, and Suzie would scream and I would spank. Finally Suzie passed out and we tried to figure out what had happened. We consulted our family doctor, and our family, and everyone agreed that a 2½-year-old needed to learn that the parents had the authority.

Around the same time frame in Suzie's life, there was another similar incident. We had gone to a school garage sale in Ventura with Suzie and our son, Todd. It was the same nursery school that Suzie would be attending in the Fall. We went with the idea that we wanted Suzie to see the school during a non-threatening situation. We got there and then let her explore all of the open areas, where she picked out a few sale items. We went to go home and then it happened. Suzie refused to get into her car seat. I warned her twice with the threat of a spanking at warning number three. At warning number three, Jim spanked her. Suzie started screaming and spitting and Jim returned a slap on the leg for each infraction of the "no spitting" rule. I was very supportive of Jim, because we had planned the unified front approach when we had planned for children. The situation deteriorated to a hysterical child and two frantic parents. We didn't feel that we should start the car until the car seat was occupied. We both felt that we should stand our ground. Finally out of exasperation, Jim said, "I will be back with her." He took her to a grassy spot and told her that they would stay there until she decided to get into her car seat. It took Suzie about thirty minutes to calm down and then we went home. (You will read later in this case study that this was one of the best things Jim could have done.) Jim and I talked about the episode on the way home and we were both physically and mentally exhausted and disappointed that we had to strike Suzie again.

The next large problem that surfaced with Suzie was when she was about four. She started a new pre-school, one that better suited our work schedules. It was larger than her previous nursery school and she was very uncomfortable. I thought the school was good because there were so many things for the children to do and the director was really educated in the pre-school learning processes. Suzie's teachers were bright and cheerful and the kids were all from good families.

Suzie always cried when I left her and the teachers always took her away and distracted her. When I picked her up in the afternoon or at lunch, I always got the same comforting words that she had "settled" right down after I left. At the same time that I was getting this message that everything was OK, Suzie's teachers were asking, "Does she get enough sleep at night?" "Does she eat a healthy breakfast?" "Is there a family problem that we should know about?" "Does she have a learning disability?" "Can Suzie be *tactilely defensive*?"

After the initial shock of someone suggesting a less than perfect child, my husband and I started using different techniques that we had learned from counseling. We started using statements like, "I can understand . . . ," instead of "one, two, three, boom!"

Both Pam and Jim had to work through the grief cycle at a different rate. It seemed to take Jim a little longer, and happened only after several different conversations with professionals that had worked with Suzie.

Pam and Jim had begun to add tools to their parenting tool kit. They began to show her more unconditional love, with eye contact, physical contact, and focused attention. They also used a school-to-home communication system which is discussed in **Part II** to work more closely with the school personnel and to reward Suzie's appropriate behaviors. They also learned to give her choices in many situations where they could, instead of demanding certain behaviors. Because of both of the parents' Dragons, they tended to want to control Suzie and force her to behave correctly.

Jim and Pam also became more open to investigating other possible explanations of their daughter's behaviors. They had labeled her a "strong-willed" child, and a "difficult child." After consulting with several different professionals, it was determined that Suzie did in fact have a condition described as "tactile defensiveness." The following comments were taken from a book entitled *Sensory Integration and the Child.*[1] "Tactile defensiveness is a subtle, yet serious neural disorder. The neural disorder that causes a child to be tactilely defensive does not necessarily hinder learning, but the discomfort and behavioral reactions caused by this disorder do interfere with the learning process. Very often the child is emotionally insecure.

Tactile defensiveness is the tendency to react negatively and emotionally to touch sensations. The reaction occurs only under certain conditions. He (the tactile defensive child) is overly sensitive to stimuli that other people would hardly feel. Relatives and friends may be offended when he shrugs off their hugs and kisses, they may assume that he dislikes them, when actually his rejection is not personal. Even a friendly arm around the shoulders may feel uncomfortable. Games like tag may bring him agony. Being touched from behind or when one cannot anticipate the touch is especially threatening, and so making the tactilely defensive child wait in line with other children is just inviting an incident. Even washing his face may be an ordeal for both parent and child. Many tactile defensive children cannot tolerate having their hair washed or cut."

There are many other characteristics of tactile defensive youngsters. The main purpose of this case study has been to demonstrate how important it is for parents to correctly determine the reasons that a youngster may be misbehaving. To simply say that a child is "strong-willed," or a "difficult child," only causes a parent to become angry and frustrated, and does not necessarily point toward the correct interventions to take.

For example, in the book *Sensory Integration and the Child*, the authors state, "If your child does lose his temper or self-control, punishment will only lower his self-concept even further. Instead of punishment, the child needs something that will help him regain his composure. A quiet place such as his own room, away from the stress will help him more than anything else. When the brain becomes disorganized, don't think punishment. Instead, think of controlling the sensory input from the environment to help organize the brain." "Rewarding good behavior and taking away privileges (such as watching television) for inappropriate behavior is a basic principle of discipline." (And is definitely OK to do.) Expectations are also important. Parents need to make sure that their expectations of their child are within the capacities of his particular nervous system. Many other suggestions are available for parents of tactilely defensive children in the book that has been mentioned.

It is extremely important, as can be seen by this case study, for parents to accurately determine the reasons for their child's misbehavior. Do not jump to conclusions. Generally, parents will interpret a child's motives in a very negative way, which then causes the parent to react with more anger. Parents may think, "He's acting this way to make me mad." Jim and Pam really began to make changes in the way they dealt with their daughter. They have added many additional tools to their parenting tool kit, and have learned to interpret her misbehaviors in an entirely different manner. They have also been able to discuss her symptoms and behaviors with Suzie, so that her self-esteem will not suffer. They have learned to make changes in her environment, or deal with "A," the antecedents to her misbehavior, instead of simply concentrating on her misbehaviors, "B," and then thinking of a consequence, "C." They have also been made aware that physical spanking will simply make the problem worse, rather than serve as a deterrent.

ENDNOTES

1. Ayres, A. Jean, *Sensory Integration and The Child*, Western Psychological Services, 1979.

Part II — Tools

Introduction To Part II

Adults enter their role as parents without all the necessary tools to complete the job successfully. Realizing that you may need to add tools to your parenting tool kit is a major step to take. **Part II** of this book deals with specific parenting strategies or tools. Just as a good carpenter needs the proper tools to build a house, parents need the proper tools to help children develop into healthy adults. Do not assume that you already have the necessary tools as many parents often do. Be receptive, as you read this section, to adding some new tools to your parenting tool kit. **Part II** is divided into several sections.

A Parenting Quiz begins this section in order to get you thinking about proper parenting strategies. Take the quiz, then read the chapter, and change any answers as you read. The answers to the quiz are given at the end of **Part II**.

Some authors refer to the ABC's of parenting. The B stands for the child's behavior. C stands for consequences or what a parent should do when the youngster misbehaves. Too much concentration is spent on C, the consequences, and not enough emphasis on A, the antecedents, or what preceeds the behavior. The format that I have used in this section on tools is to get the parent to first look at A, or what kind of things he should be doing that might tend to cut down on misbehaviors.

The following situation, seen in a cartoon, illustrates this concept perfectly:

> Upon being punished for using his father's tools, a boy said, "If I had my own tools, I wouldn't always be losing yours!" Rather than always looking at what to do after a child misbehaves, parents need to consider the situation/s that may be preceeding the misbehavior; the Antecedents.

Chapter 10 is entitled "Creating a Positive Home Environment." A key ingredient in healthy parent-child relationships is having a positive home climate. The importance of parental teamwork is discussed in this chapter. Additionally, the concepts of modeling, showing unconditional love, accepting feelings, praise, resolving conflicts, the effective use of rewards, and chore charts are reviewed.

Chapter 11 is entitled "Self-Esteem and Stress." Having a high self-esteem and possessing the ability to deal appropriately with stress are essential for all youngsters. Techniques for improving your child's self-esteem are discussed. Parents will also learn how to deal with stress effectively, and how to teach their children to deal with stress. Parents will be unable to effectively utilize the parenting tools if they are unable to deal with their own stressors effectively.

Chapter 12 is entitled "Techniques For Dealing With Inappropriate Behavior." In this chapter, punishment is defined. All appropriate strategies for responding to inappropriate behaviors are discussed. A system is also described to help parents and school personnel work together effectively in the event that a youngster is experiencing school problems.

Parenting Quiz

Select the correct answer by circling the letter which corresponds to the most appropriate response to the situation described. Sorry! Regardless of how you do on the quiz, you have to keep your children.

1. Your four-year-old comes running into the house after playing with several older neighborhood kids and yells a profane word. It's the first time you've heard him use the word. The best thing to do is:

   A. Wash his mouth out with soap.

   B. Ignore it.

   C. Take him aside and explain why you don't approve of that word.

   D. Confine the child to his room for 30 minutes.

2. You've caught your two-year-old in the middle of the street in front of your home. The best thing to do is:

    A. Take the child into the house and explain the dangers of the street.

    B. Tell your husband when he gets home to talk to your child.

    C. Spank your child while still in the middle of the street.

    D. Get the child out of the street, then spank him.

3. Johnny, age 6, and Bobby, age 8, who are brothers, are fighting in the living room. The best thing to do is:

    A. Ignore it.

    B. Stop the fight and try to find out who started it.

    C. Send each of them to a different place in the house to sit for 5 minutes.

    D. Tell them to wait until their dad gets home— then they will get punished.

4. The worst time of the day for children and their parents is:

    A. The first hour in the morning.

    B. The hour before dinner.

    C. The hour after dinner.

    D. The hour just before bedtime.

    E. Sorry! You cannot pick all of the above.

5. Your first-grader says she hates school. You should:

    A. Tell her she shouldn't hate school.

    B. Ignore her in hopes she'll forget it.

    C. Let her stay home and watch TV that day.

    D. Say to her, "You really don't like school, do you?"

6. Your two children are coloring quietly in the living room. You should probably:

    A. Ignore them so they'll keep coloring quietly.

    B. Tell your husband when he gets home how well they behaved.

    C. Yell into the room and tell them that they are being good.

    D. Go in and tell them that you like the way they are coloring quietly.

7. Your kindergartner does not get ready for school on time. The thing to do is:

    A. Let him go to school partially dressed.

    B. Don't feed him breakfast if he doesn't get dressed in time.

    C. Keep him home from school that day.

    D. Set up a chart so that the child can earn rewards for the appropriate behavior.

8. Giving your children rewards for doing well in school and for doing their chores:

    A. Shouldn't be necessary.

    B. Is a bribe, thus is a bad thing to do.

    C. Is OK to do.

    D. Is OK to do if the reward is money only.

9. Which of the following can never be a reward:

    A. Praise.

    B. Candy.

    C. Money.

    D. Spanking.

    E. None of the above.

10. Your 7-year-old complains every night about going to bed, and it takes you 30 to 45 minutes each night to get him to bed. The thing that would probably not help resolve this would be:

    A. Reading to him before bedtime.

    B. Setting a timer for 10 to 15 minutes and let him know that when the timer goes off, he will go to bed.

    C. Wrestling with him before bedtime to tire him out.

    D. Eliminating his nap.

11. Johnny has always done well in math, but has started bringing home incomplete math papers and low grades. You should:

    A. Confine Johnny to his room every night for two hours.

    B. Wait another month and see what happens.

    C. Tell him not to worry about it—the teacher probably doesn't know how to teach math.

    D. Call his teacher and set up an appointment to discuss it, possibly along with the school counselor.

12. Suzie, age 8, refuses to eat her entire dinner each night. The thing that would probably not help this situation is:

    A. Reducing the size of the dinner portions.

    B. Making her stay at the table until she is finished.

    C. Allowing her to go to bed hungry.

    D. Making sure she does not snack before dinner.

10

Creating A Positive Home Environment

This chapter will cover a variety of strategies or concepts that are necessary for parents to utilize in order to create a positive home climate. These strategies also need to be applied before parents consider what punishment to utilize for a child's misbehavior. Applying the following strategies will significantly reduce the incidences of discipline problems. Parents are often blamed for the actions of their children, but few ever receive any formal training in how to be a parent. Therefore, don't feel bad if you need to read this to learn what to do. After all, you probably studied your computer manual or your driver's license test book for several hours or even days, to prepare to use the computer, or to drive. Surely people should devote time to learning to be a good parent.

In a cartoon that I once saw, a young girl asked her mother
how long she had to go to school to learn to be a mother.
The mother replied, "You don't have to go to school." Then
the girl asked, "Well, how did you pass your test for your
Mothering license?" The mother said, "That's cute, but
nobody's required to have a license to be a mother." The
young girl left, with a puzzled look on her face and replied,
"That's not cute, that's scary!"

A speaker that I once heard said, "There is no success outside
the home that will make up for a failure within the home."
I believe that if more parents could accept this belief, much
more time, effort, and studying would go into being the very
best parent that one could be.

Included in this chapter are the following:

- Parental Agreement and Teamwork
- Modeling Appropriate Behavior
- Demonstrating Unconditional Love
- Accepting Feelings, Encouraging Communication,
  and Teaching Your Children to Express
  Anger Appropriately
- Resolving Conflicts
- Rewards for Appropriate Behaviors
- Chore Charts
- Developing a De-Parenting Plan

Parental Agreement And Teamwork

A model of counseling that I have found to be very useful
in looking at parental agreement and teamwork in parenting
is *Transactional Analysis*. I have already discussed this concept
earlier, but let me briefly review it, since it applies to this
topic. According to Transactional Analysis, a person can be
divided into three parts, the Parent (P), the Adult (A), and
the Child (C). The Parent part of our personality consists of

our beliefs, "shoulds," values, or "tapes." The term "tapes" is often used because these are often automatic thoughts or statements that we make without much thought. We simply replay a message we heard or learned as a child from our parents. The Adult part of our personality is the unemotional component, or the facts. The Child part is the emotional part, or the feeling part of our personality. When looking at a couple and the idea of parental agreement and teamwork, the following diagram could be utilized.

MOTHER   FATHER

PARENT   Beliefs   Beliefs   PARENT
                Values   Values
                Tapes   Tapes

ADULT   ADULT

CHILD   CHILD

Each person in a marriage brings their beliefs about parenting from the family they came from. Sometimes a person will want to do exactly what their parents did because they feel they turned out OK. In this way, they may be trying to recreate their "at home" feeling, which was discussed in Chapter 2. Sometimes people make vows as children that they will never do something which their parents did to them. Vows were covered in Chapter 3. In other words, the Parent part of the personality may want to duplicate what their own parents did, while the Child part may "take over," and want to do something completely different.

Let's look at this individually and as a couple. You need to decide how to parent your children out of your Adult. That is, you need to study parenting books or consult with an expert, and determine what is best according to proven theories of child rearing, and not base your approach solely on what your parents did or did not do for you. Looking at things from the standpoint of a couple, it should come as little surprise to parents that they are bound to disagree on some problems and strategies to discipline their children. Parents will often disagree on: (1) what constitutes a problem, and (2) what action to take if they identify something as a problem. What parents need to do is to get into the Adult part of their personality, and objectively determine what is a problem, and what to do about it. If they are unable to do this on their own, then it may be necessary to obtain the help of an expert.

For example, talk to a doctor or nutritionist if you disagree about eating issues, or a pediatrician and child counselor if you need help determining what is normal for children to do at various ages, or how to deal with specific behavior problems. It is imperative for your child's sake that you work toward resolving or reaching a compromise regarding your different parenting approaches. When parents do not agree on what constitutes a problem and what course of action to take, the child becomes very confused. Later in this section, I will discuss resolving conflicts, so please refer to that section for additional information regarding this process. Many times parents argue over differences in beliefs based on their own childhood experiences, rather than deal with the situation unemotionally and factually.

When problems arise, it is best for parents to have a strategy meeting to discuss the situation, and a course of action should be agreed upon. Too often, parents dwell on who is right or wrong, rather that coming up with a course of action that they can both agree upon. Discussing what happened in your family of origin will help you to better understand each other. This should help you a great deal in realizing where each person is coming from, and will help lead toward a better resolve of the problem.

Several examples may help with the above points. Our son Matt was pretty rowdy and rambunctious when he was about 5-years-old. My wife Pam said we had a problem, and that we needed to do something about it. I didn't think so. I just said that he was being "all boy." Needless to say, we couldn't come up with any strategy to deal with his behavior because we did not both see it as a problem. Once parents identify something as a problem, then they need to decide on the correct course of action to resolve that problem. Part II of this book should help you to figure out the appropriate tools to utilize.

Another example with Matt will help illustrate why it is important to talk about your own childhood and dig deeper. Matt and 4 or 5 of his friends frequently liked to move all the furniture of our newly decorated family room next to the walls and play indoor soccer. Needless to say, after ten minutes, the room smelled and looked like a gym. Pam and I were at odds over how often they should be allowed to do this. Neither Pam nor I got to play in our living rooms as children. My tendency was to not want the boys to play in the room at all, while Pam allowed them to do it anytime they wanted, because she felt bad that she could not do so in her house while growing up. We were much more able to come up with a compromise once we discussed each other's childhood experiences.

A very common occurrence between two parents is that one of them may tend to be very strict with discipline. Often when this happens, the other parent becomes too lenient in an effort to counterbalance the strict parent. Parents need to develop a willingness to reach a middle ground on many issues, and to be willing to reach a compromise in areas of disagreement.

DIGGING DEEPER

Parents will learn a great deal about each other and why each one believes in certain things, if they can discuss with each other what they each experienced as a child. Consider discussing the following questions:

1. Did you have to do chores?
2. Did both parents get involved with parenting?
3. Were you spanked as a child?
4. Were you given an allowance for work done?
5. Did your parents yell and scream a lot?

The list could go on. When you are having a disagreement, try to discuss what happened in your family when the situation you are currently looking at arose. Chapter 5 on Frozen Needs may also help you and your spouse to understand why you might struggle so much to agree on what to give to your children.

Frequently, by necessity or default, one parent may have assumed all of the parenting responsibility when you were a child. If this happens to you, then you may not feel it is necessary to consult with your spouse about your children, or you may defer all parenting to your spouse. Thus, it is important to discuss what role each of your parents took in the parenting process to see if you have been consciously or subconsciously trying to recreate your "at home" feeling (Chapter 2).

Model Appropriate Behavior

It seems very obvious to me, as well as most parents, that if we want our children to do or not do certain things, we must set an appropriate example. We need to be models of the behaviors we would like our children to have. I never cease to be amazed at the number of parents who come to me and ask me to change a certain behavior in their child, or give them the tools to change a behavior that they are unable or unwilling to change in their own personality.

What behaviors do you need to change in order to be a good model for your children? _____ .

When my son Matt was about 5 years old, we stopped at a shopping center to do some errands, and then we crossed the street to check out a new hobby store. The quickest way was to just grab his hand and start walking across four lanes of traffic. About halfway across, Matt said, "Shouldn't we go up to the intersection and cross there?" Another time, I was about to take a short cut and go up a road marked, "ONE WAY." I didn't think Robyn could read at the time so I felt safe, but she said, "Doesn't that say One Way?" I was able to quickly turn the wheel and go the right way. Remember, your actions speak louder than your words.

To go into more detail about the "seatbelt." A mother that I was counseling said that her 13-year-old son was very rude and sarcastic to her when she told him to put his seat belt on. When I asked the mother (an embarassing question) "Do you wear your seat belt?" She sheepishly replied, "No, but shouldn't my son realize that he needs to wear his seat belt?" The boy was also modeling his mother's sarcastic tone of voice, since she frequently responded to him in that fashion.

A teenager standing by the kitchen counter complained (in a cartoon strip), "My parents are against me using drugs, but this is their collection," as she looked at a wine bottle, coffee, and diet pills.

I could give you countless examples to encourage you to be a good model for your children, but I'll limit it to a few areas, just to get you thinking:

1. Do you use appropriate language, not profanity?
2. Do you get jobs done ahead of time, or do you wait until the last minute?
3. Do you express your anger appropriately, rather than yell, scream, slam doors, or pout when you don't get what you want?
4. Do you have chores to do around the house?
5. Do you do your chores around the house in a timely manner?
6. Do you show consideration to your spouse and call him or her if you are going to be late coming home?
7. Do you write thank-you notes for gifts you receive?
8. Do you show concern for the welfare of the less privileged or for people in need?
9. Do you wear slippers in the morning?
10. When you make a mistake on something you are working on, do you throw it away and start over to make sure it's perfect, or do you accept minor flaws and express to your children that no one can be perfect? (Perfectionism is a very common problem for parents to deal with in themselves and in their children.)

For Better Or For Worse by Lynn Johnston

For Better Or For Worse Copyright 1982, 1983, 1986, 1988 Lynn Johnston,
Reprinted with permission of Universal Press Syndicate.

Children and teenagers definitely learn a lot of their behavior
by watching their parents. What behavior are you modeling
for your children and teenagers?

THE FAMILY CIRCUS by Bil Keane

"Do you want to catch cold, young man? How many times have I told you not to run around without your slippers?"

Our actions speak louder than our words. Be sure that you are modeling appropriate behaviors for your children and teens.

Someone once said, "Out of the mouths of babes come things parents shouldn't have said." How true this is and how very important it is for parents to be good role models for their children and teenagers.

I realize that by the examples I've given, you'll detect some of my values concerning what's appropriate and what is not, but I'm sure you'll be able to choose some of these, along with areas where you need to make changes in your behavior. I guess that's enough to get you feeling guilty about your behavior. But remember, don't let guilt keep you from doing what's right, even if that means changing your own behavior.

Another important concept about modeling appropriate behavior, is that parents should frequently verbalize what they are modeling. Don't assume that your child will always notice some admirable trait that you are demonstrating. Verbalize it. One day when my daughter Chrissy was going to help me fix something around the house, I told her before we started that it may take a while to do it, but we would stick to it until we got it done. If you are doing a project that is due in several weeks, let your children know that you have started work on it ahead of time. If you put money away for something special like a future vacation, let your children know that too.

DIGGING DEEPER

When looking at what you are modeling for your children, you simply need to look back at your parents and consider what they modeled for you. You may have no idea what to model for your children if it was not modeled for you. You may need to go to school to learn what behaviors are best to model. This is especially true if a parent was not involved in your life, or if you lived with a single parent and did not observe two parents work on problems together. In reality, most of us know whether or not our behavior is an appropriate model for our children. What we need to realize and accept is the need to be a good model. We need to overcome the belief that children should do what we say, not what we do.

Demonstrating Unconditional Love To Your Child

John McKay, the great football coach at the University of Southern California was asked in an interview on television to comment on the pride he must have felt for his own son's accomplishments on the football field. His son was one of the stars of the USC team. John McKay's answer was most impressive. "Yes, I'm pleased that John had a good season last year. He does a good job and I am proud of him. But I would be just as proud if he had never played the game at all." Coach McKay was saying, in effect, that John's football talent was recognized and appreciated, but his human worth did not depend on his ability to play football. (From Dobson's book *Hide or Seek*.)[1]

Kyle Rote Jr., an excellent soccer player, once stated, "When I was growing up, I would come home from a Little League baseball game, and my parents would never ask, "How many hits did you get?" or "Did you win?" or anything like that. It was always, "Did you have a good time?" or "Are you OK?" I grew up knowing that my parents' love for me was unconditional, not based on how I performed. And that, to me, is the critical goal for parents—to make sure that our young people are loved unconditionally and understand that winning has nothing to do with scores—but rather with performing to the maximum of their ability."

THE FAMILY CIRCUS by Bil Keane

"Have you hugged your kid today?"

Physical contact is one of the best ways to fill a child's emotional needs. Teenagers also need physical contact. In the above case it can also be OK to put it off until after the bath.

These are two good examples of the most important thing we can and should give our children—the feeling that they are worthwhile no matter what.

A question I have often asked parents whom I have lectured is—how many of them love their children. Generally everyone raises his hand, unless of course he has had a particularly trying day. Then they may hesitate a little. I share with them that I realize that they love their children, but I frequently counsel children who do not feel loved. Why isn't the parent's love reaching their children? It's because the parents are not communicating love to their youngster in the right way.

By far, the best book available which discusses the need for love and "how to's" about showing love to our children is Ross Campbell's book, *How To Really Love Your Child*.[2] I strongly encourage each parent to have this book in their library and therefore will discuss several key aspects of the book.

According to Campbell, the greatest influence on a child is his parents. The second greatest influence is congenital temperament. It's important to realize both of these factors. The role of parents is extremely important, but congenital temperament, what our children are born with, is also a large contributing factor to their personality. Understanding the many facets of temperament will also help you to more unconditionally love your child.

Campbell lists nine different aspects of congenital temperament:

- activity level
- rhythmicity
- approach or withdrawal tendencies
- adaptability
- intensity of reaction
- threshold of responsiveness
- quality of mood
- distractibility
- attention span
- persistence[3]

Parents are often amazed to see so many different aspects of temperament. Mothers often realize right at birth that the child is different from an older sibling. It's very important to realize the extent of congenital temperament to help us understand our children, and hopefully knowing this will help us to better show unconditional love.

For Better Or For Worse by Lynn Johnston

For Better Or For Worse Copyright 1982, 1983, 1986, 1988 Lynn Johnston,
Reprinted with permission of Universal Press Syndicate.

Each parent needs to study their child and understand their unique temperament, when determining the appropriate strategies to use. Parents should not compare themselves to others as each child is different.

For Better Or For Worse by Lynn Johnston

Parents definitely need to consider a child's temperament
when deciding on how to deal with inappropriate behavior.
This child feels bad enough without the father having to
continue lecturing.

For Better Or For Worse by Lynn Johnston

Often children need their emotional tank filled, when we feel
least like doing it.

Another extremely important concept regarding temperament is the "Goodness of Fit" concept. An example will best illustrate the point. One day while I was playing tennis with my oldest daughter, Robyn, she got upset that I was hitting the ball to the sides of the court and that she had to run to hit the balls. I was getting upset that she wasn't more willing to run hard. My son, Matt, on the next court playing with a friend, was running into the fence to hit balls, and tumbling on the court after hitting one. I could identify with Matt, because my temperament is much like his, while Robyn and I weren't getting along. In fact, she said after we were through that she never wanted to play with me again. I told her that I understood, and that I would ask her next time if she wanted me to hit the ball to her, or require her to run more. I would also realize that it's not a matter of right or wrong, but a difference in temperament.

If you are not a morning person but your child is, then the "fit" is not good. If you are a "go-getter" and your child takes his time, then the "fit" is not good. Keeping this in mind will help you to stay calmer, and help you to be more understanding of individual differences.

In what ways is your temperament alike and in what ways is your temperament different from your child's? The difference in temperament can be the source of a lot of disharmony. It's important to understand the effects of different temperaments. It is also important not to give up on a child if a particular temperament trait of his consistently gets him into some difficulty. It's still important to develop a strategy to help him deal with it more effectively. However, a strategy born out of anger and resentment will not be effective.

Campbell introduces the concept of an *emotional tank* in his book. Each child has an emotional tank, and if that tank is full, you can expect fairly good behavior. When the tank begins to go dry, the misbehaviors usually increase. To fill the tank and demonstrate unconditional love, Campbell says that parents need to show love through:

1. *Eye Contact*

   Look at your child when you are talking to him, especially when you are listening to him. Don't force him to always look at you, but be sure to make an effort to give eye contact. One teenager told me that he felt much better when his parents came into his room and kneeled down by his bed to say good-night, as opposed to standing by the door and saying good-night.

2. *Physical Contact*

   All children need appropriate physical contact from their parents. Some children are more comfortable with this than others, but parents need to find ways to touch their children through hugs, kisses, wrestling, high fives, combing their hair, etc.

   There was a study done during which a librarian touched some people on the hand as they checked out a book, while with some people the librarian avoided physical contact. When the people left the library, they were asked how they felt about the library. Sure enough, the people who had been touched felt that the library was a warm and comfortable place to be, while the others felt it was a very cold place. This really illustrates the importance of touch. There is a lot of truth to the saying, "hugs, not drugs."

   A cartoon that I once saw depicted a boy in the corner for time-out saying to his mom, "Mommy, I need a hug." Although "time-out" is a very good strategy sometimes what a youngster needs more is a hug in order to fill their emotional tank.

3. *Focused Attention*

This is the most powerful way to show unconditional love. Spending time with your child is extremely important. This can mean an all-day fishing or shopping trip, or reading a bedtime story. You also need to realize that children will not always show appreciation to you for the time you spend with them in the way that you might like. A favorite story of mine comes from a book by Charlie Shedd where he described a situation where a father and his son spent the whole day together. At the end of the day, the father wrote in his diary that not much happened, that it was a "so-so" day. The son wrote in his diary that it was the best day of his life, but he did not express this directly to his father. So, don't expect a big show of appreciation from your youngster.

I once saw a very convicting cartoon where a small boy said to his father, "When I grow up, I'm going to be successful and not have much time to spend with my kids too!" If this statement does not convict you to spend time with your children and teens then I'm not sure anything will.

For Better Or For Worse by Lynn Johnston

Spending time with a child is one of the most effective ways to meet their emotional needs. Remember to be patient and communicate love in their language, i.e. if they want to ask questions, answer them. Do not be in a hurry to simply finish the book.

Which of these three ways (Eye Contact, Physical Contact, and Focused Attention) of showing love did your parents exhibit toward you? _____ .

Which of the three ways to show love do you need to exhibit more? _____ .

How do you plan to do this? Set a goal. _____
_____ .

Some parents often feel guilty when reading a book about what they should be doing with their child, especially if they haven't been doing it very well up to that point. A little guilt is OK, and maybe even necessary, to get us to change our behavior. Just don't let guilt keep you from doing what's right. It will take a concentrated effort to change your behavior toward your child, so set a goal now and go for it. Monitor your youngster's behavior. I think you will be amazed at the positive changes you will see due to your efforts to keep their emotional tank full.

Another important concept to consider when trying to show love to your children, is to get tuned in to their "language of love." An example will best illustrate this concept. One year, when Chrissy, our youngest daughter, was in the fifth grade, she kept asking me to go to a *Taco Bell* restaurant and get 4 tacos, 2 burritos, and 4 cokes, and bring them to her school, so that she and three of her friends could have lunch together. I told her that I wouldn't do that, but that I would take her to Taco Bell. We had a good time going to Taco Bell, and we still go occasionally, but I was really angry with myself, because Chrissy had been trying to tell me what she would like from me, and I was ignoring her. When I finally realized this, the school year was over, and I had to wait all summer before I could show her love in her "language of love," and not my own. I still remember her and her three friends standing by the curb at the school, cheering for me as I drove up with their lunch. I am not saying that you should give your youngsters whatever they ask for. I am asking you to get tuned in to what their language of love is, and communicate your love to them in a language they can see and accept. Often you may spend the same amount of time and money, but you will be communicating in a fashion that is much more meaningful to the youngster.

Are you tuned in to your child's language of love? You might figure it out by just noticing what they like to do, or you might be so bold as to ask them. The direct approach is always worth a try.

I also encourage the reader to get Campbell's book, *How To Really Love Your Teenager*,[4] since it not only considers many of the above stated points, but also gives some special suggestions for dealing with teenagers. The book also discusses teenage anger, depression, and letting go.

DIGGING DEEPER

In today's society, most parents realize the need to show unconditional love to their children. However, many parents do not feel that they received unconditional love from *their* parents. Therefore, it may be difficult at first to realize the need to show love to your children—no matter what they do. In other words, do not withhold love from your child because he misbehaves.

It will also be beneficial for you to consider which of the three (eye contact, physical contact, and focused attention) you received and did not receive as a child. If you did not receive one of these, it may be very difficult and uncomfortable to begin to do it with your child.

Accepting Feelings, Encouraging Communication And Teaching Your Children To Express Anger Appropriately

Often in counseling, I'll ask parents if they accept their children's feelings. Before they answer, I'll warn them that it's a more difficult question than they think. Accepting children's feelings and encouraging them to express their feelings is very important towards helping them to set a positive climate in the home, and a very important ingredient toward reducing inappropriate behaviors. When feelings are not expressed verbally, they will probably be expressed through a youngster's behavior. When counseling with children, I often describe feelings as little animals running around inside them. If they don't get out, they'll multiply and make you feel uncomfortable. When your child says, "I hate you!" what is your response? Do you say, "You shouldn't hate me, because I am your parent?" Comments like that do not indicate acceptance of your child's feelings, and therefore do not let the feelings out. When your child says that you love his brother or sister more than him, is your response, "No, that's not true, we love you both the same?" Our first response needs to be acceptance of the child's feelings, so we can explore reasons for the feelings, and then develop a strategy to deal with the feelings if it appears necessary to do so. Sometimes just listening to his feelings and accepting them is enough, without the need for any further action on your part. Comments or responses that indicate acceptance of feelings in the two examples above would be: "Boy! I can tell that you are really mad or angry at me." and "It seems like we don't love you as much as your brother/sister." With these responses, you have accepted the feelings. You can now move to the next step of asking him what has led him to these feelings, and then determine if your behavior as a parent needs to change.

Remember, feelings are neither right or wrong, they are just there.

One of the best books on communication is one by Thomas Gordon entitled, *Parent Effectiveness Training.*[5] I encourage you to consult this book if you struggle in the area of effective listening.

Another important facet of accepting feelings is not only accepting your child's anger, but also teaching your child to express anger in appropriate and effective ways. Parents need to accept more completely that it's their job to teach their children how to express anger appropriately. In fact, I believe that this is one of the most important things that parents can and should teach their children. One of the best discussions of anger is in Ross Campbell's book, *How To Really Love Your Teenager.*[6] Campbell discusses an *anger ladder*, which I will briefly review, but I strongly encourage the reader to obtain Campbell's book.

I generally discuss the anger ladder, described by Campbell, by using the following diagram:

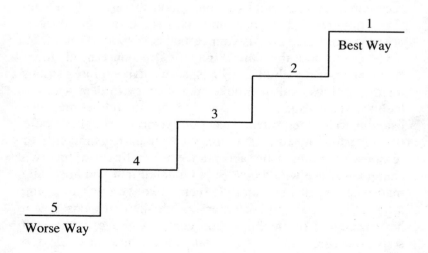

The best way to deal with anger is at the top of the ladder, while the worst way is at the bottom. Let's use an example: Let's say that your son or daughter is mad at their mother because they feel their chores are unfair. The best way to deal with the anger (position number **1**) would be for the child to tell the mother that he is angry about the chores, and for the mother and the child to resolve the problem. If the mother says, "Tough, you have to do chores," or they do not resolve the problem, the tendency is to push the child down the anger ladder to the next step. The child may yell at the mother, "I hate you." This is position number **2**. If mom were to say, "You can't yell at me like that," the child may slip down to position number **3**. The child may slam a door, or kick the cat, or take his anger out on a sibling.

Generally, parents will not accept these displays of anger, and will stifle the youngster in some way, pushing them down to position number **4**, where he may simply go to his room and keep his anger in and let his stomach handle it and possibly pretend that he is no longer angry. Many adults as children had to pretend that they were not angry, because few parents allowed children to express their anger 20 or 30 years ago.

Consequently, parents generally need a great deal of help to become good listeners, and to learn to accept their child's anger. At position number **4**, I can imagine what a child must be thinking: "I told you calmly that I was angry and that didn't work, I yelled at you and that didn't work, I slammed the door and you still didn't listen to me, I kicked the cat and hit my brother, but you still haven't heard me." Youngsters then often slip to position number **5** of the anger ladder; the passive aggressive approach. One definition of passive aggressive that fits many situations is that the youngster makes someone angry by their behavior (usually the parent or a teacher or other authority figure), while they actually hurt themselves without realizing it. Some passive aggressive behaviors are: procrastinating on chores, taking a long time to get ready when the parents are waiting to take him to school, getting D's and F's in school, getting speeding tickets, shoplifting, and abusing drugs or alcohol.

I personally believe that there are many inappropriate behaviors that youngsters display that may be directly related to the fact that they are angry about something, and unable to express it in appropriate ways. Therefore, when counseling parents about a youngster's misbehavior, I will always investigate with the parents how the family deals with anger.

We began discussing the anger ladder in our home about five years ago. I still remember the first night we talked about it. Our children actually thought it was better to slam a door when they were angry than to tell us what they were angry about. Obviously, we were not doing a very good job of helping our children to express their anger at that time. We have made a conscious effort to accept our children's anger and feelings, and to give them ideas on how to express their anger appropriately. Our efforts have definitely paid off, so I will share several successful situations with you. In one, our son Matt met with his 8th grade physical education teacher because he felt he had earned a higher grade in the class. He discussed his grade with the teacher and found out what he needed to do the next quarter to improve his grade. In another situation, Matt wrote a letter to a friend who had backed out of a camping trip at the last minute. Matt told him politely that he was angry, the friend considered the letter, then changed his mind and went on the trip. Matt has learned to express his anger in a positive way to the appropriate party.

Robyn received a low grade on a paper in her junior year of high school, and was very frustrated and disappointed. We helped her to write a letter to the teacher, which she eventually gave to the teacher at the end of class one day. Several days later, she met with the teacher and discussed her feelings. Robyn got her grade raised two points, which was not as important as directing her anger at the person she was angry with, and doing so in a polite, courteous manner. Many students, when they are angry at the teacher, start coming to class late, or fail to turn in assignments. This is the passive aggressive way to deal with anger. They make the teacher and their parents angry, but hurt themselves.

Parents need to accept their responsibility to teach their children how to express anger. Another excellent book regarding this is Ross Campbell's book, *Your Child and Drugs*.[7] Campbell points out that about 75% of children will blast you with their anger, and you have to help them channel it in the right direction. The other 25% will tend to keep their anger in, and you will have to continually encourage them to express their anger. With some children, you may need to frequently say to them, "Is there anything that I have done lately that makes you angry?" then bite your tongue and accept their anger. Don't try to explain to them why they shouldn't feel that way or be angry, which will be your natural reaction. Remember, feelings are neither right or wrong, they are just there.

Another way to teach your children appropriate ways to deal with anger is to calmly impose penalties, when they express their anger inappropriately. If they swear or yell at you, you may want to impose a fine system (ie., 25 cents for each word), use the "X" chart that will be discussed later, or place them on restriction. If they slam their door and break something, then they should be required to pay for it. Fighting with a sibling could result in a time-out for each youngster.

Thus, teaching children how to express their anger effectively involves several components:

1. Accepting as a top priority your need to teach your children to express their anger appropriately and effectively.

2. Creating a climate in your home where children can feel safe to express their anger by saying they are angry.

3. Being a good model to your children of how to express anger effectively.

4. Being willing to really listen to your child and work toward resolving conflicts. (See the next section for more information on resolving conflicts.)

5. Imposing negative consequences when your children express their anger inappropriately. If you just impose penalties without doing the first four suggestions, you will definitely drive your youngsters to the bottom of the anger ladder, which you do not want to do.

DIGGING DEEPER

It is very important to consider your own childhood and how you and your siblings were allowed to express anger. If you were not allowed to express your anger verbally, it may be very difficult for you to accept this concept, and difficult at first to become a good listener. If your parents did not work with you to resolve conflicts, then this too may be a strange, and at first uncomfortable concept to think about.

The chapter in Part I on Codependency and parenting will also help you to understand why you may have difficulty in this area. Codependents often are too affected by their child's behavior, may take the anger too personally, and are therefore unable to calmly deal with the issues.

Resolving Conflicts

A key concept involving the anger ladder is that at the top of the anger ladder, the best way to deal with a conflict is to talk calmly to the person you are angry with and resolve the conflict. If children express their anger, and parents accept the anger without resolving the issue, then the tendency is for the child to slip down the anger ladder. It is especially important as children grow up that parents develop an attitude of resolving conflicts, and to some degree, it can begin at an early age. The following diagram is one that I use frequently when counseling married couples and parents of teenagers.

It comes from a book by Norm Wright[8] on marriage counseling. It depicts five different ways to deal with a conflict.

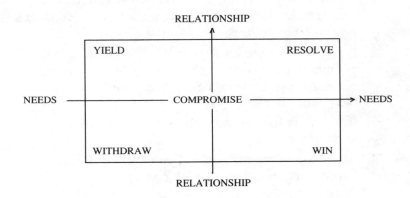

This will explain the diagram. The five ways to deal with a conflict are to:

1. *Yield*—Give in to the other person/s.

2. *Withdraw*—Not talk about the problem.

3. *Compromise*—Discuss the issue and reach an agreement where both parties give in a little and each wins.

4. *Resolve*—A resolve is similar to a compromise, however it is usually a better solution, because more talking has taken place, and the solution may consider each person's needs more than the compromise would.

5. *Win*—Fight to get it your way.

For example, if you want your teenager to be in bed by 10:00 PM and he wants to stay up to 12:00 PM, a compromise would be 11:00 PM. A resolve would require more discussion and might end up with him going to bed at 10:00 some nights and 12:00 some other nights when he might want to watch something special on television.

The five approaches are shown in the rectangle for a particular reason:

1. If you Yield or Withdraw (those two are on the left side of the rectangle), then your needs or your teenager's needs do not get met.

2. If you Resolve the conflict or Win, then your needs get met (these two are on the right side). However, one cannot just look at needs. What will happen to the relationship?

3. If you Withdraw or Win, not much good will happen to the relationship.

4. At the top of the rectangle, if you Yield or Resolve the conflict, that shows a high concern for the relationship.

5. It is OK at times to Yield to help the relationship, but if you Yield all the time, then your needs do not get met, and you will become very resentful.

Thus, the goal is to work toward a resolve or compromise whenever possible. Parents yielding to their child's wishes may help their relationship with their child, but may put them into a situation that they are not yet prepared to handle.

How do you and your children deal with conflicts? In my opinion, we would be "dead in the water" as parents, if we had not developed an attitude of resolving conflicts with our children, or attempted to reach compromises. Furthermore, the only way teenagers will learn how to reach compromises or resolve problems in their future relationships is if the parents are modeling this process with them. Do you have an attitude of wanting to work things out with your teenager so that you both feel good about the solution, or do you want to win?

Thomas Gordon, the author of *Parent Effectiveness Training*,[9] once defined three parent/child situations:

- Child causes the parent a problem.
- Child has a problem.
- Child and parent have a conflict.

In the first situation, child causes the parent a problem, the parent needs to take action. Utilize time-out, a chore chart, or the "X" chart system at home. In the second situation, when the child has a problem, the parent needs to be a good listener. Parents are always amazed at how helpful they can be to their child if they simply listen. When your child loses an election at school, or breaks up with a special friend, all you can really do is be a good listener. In the third situation, when both parent and child have a conflict, it is time to negotiate a compromise or resolve the conflict.

Several examples should help. When Robyn was about eight years old, she would circle the days she would buy her lunch at school on the school lunch menu, and then my wife Pam would not fix her lunch that day. Occasionally, Robyn would change her mind on a morning when she was to buy her lunch and expect Pam to make a lunch at the last minute. Obviously, they had a conflict. Pam thought of a great compromise. She let Robyn change her mind and take her lunch, as long as Robyn made her lunch that day herself. Everyone wins. When Robyn was 16, a friend of hers wanted to drive a group of girls to an amusement park that was 2 hours away across one of the worst roads in California. We could have won and said no, or yielded and let her go, which may have put her life in jeopardy.

The compromise was that the girl's mother took them to the park, and I picked them up at midnight. Everyone wins. A key to resolving conflicts is developing an attitude of "how can we work this out so we both feel good about it." Remember, you are the parents, and you don't have to come up with a compromise or resolve on every issue. That would be impossible, and not very wise.

There are some situations where, as a parent, you state the rules or make a decision and it may appear that you have won and your child has lost. That's part of being a parent. Just don't overlook the opportunities where you could help generate a win-win. Sometimes, children are much more adept at this than us parents. I remember Robyn coming to us to say that she did not like doing the dishes at night after dinner. She said that she would be willing to clean a bathroom, instead of doing the dishes. She proposed a compromise or resolve, and believe me, it required less hassle to get her to do the bathroom than it did to try and continue to get her to do the dishes.

DIGGING DEEPER

One of the main reasons that parents have difficulty with the concept of resolving conflicts with their teenagers is because they, themselves, were not taught this as teens. Parents may have difficulty resolving conflicts with their spouse, let alone realizing that they should strive toward resolutions with their teenagers. Were you able to speak up and express yourself to your parents? Were your parents willing to negotiate compromises with you or were you told to obey "or else?" Remember, that was 20 or 30 years ago. Today, children are less willing to tolerate power and authority. I always laugh when I write this or say it, because parents and all adults are less willing to bow down to the authority figures as well. As I type this, the school teachers in our city are trying to hammer out a contract agreement with our school board, and the talk of a strike has come up. So you see, it just isn't teenagers that do not tolerate power and authority. All adults question authority more than they did 20 or 30 years ago.

If you have difficulty in trying to reach a compromise with your child, two previous chapters may be particularly helpful: Chapter 1 on Codependency—codependents frequently want and need to be in control, and often feel that there is only one way to do something, and Chapter 2 on Recreating Your "At Home" Feeling—you may be simply repeating a pattern that you observed in your parents.

Rewards or Approval For Appropriate Behavior

An essential ingredient in setting a positive home climate, and helping to prevent discipline problems, is rewarding or showing approval for appropriate behavior. I have struggled with getting started on this section, and I think the reason has been that I was not sure how to convince you of the need for positive reinforcement, rewards, and approval for appropriate behavior. Then I thought of a joke that I have told for many years at my seminars: "Do you know how many school principals it takes to change a light bulb? It takes seven; one to hold the light bulb, and six to turn the ladder. Do you know how many psychologists it takes to change a light bulb? Only one, but the light bulb has to want to change." Do you want to change and have a more positive relationship with your children? If so, it should not be necessary to convince you of the need for positive reinforcement, but I will give you some justification for the importance of it. More importantly, I will give you some very practical ideas on how to use positive reinforcement in your family.

According to social learning theory, most behavior is learned from the environment, and as a result, subject to the laws of learning. I previously discussed the ABC's of parenting. *A* stands for the antecendents, *B* for the behavior, and *C* stands for the consequences that follow the behavior.

A (antecedents) $\longrightarrow$ *B* (behavior) $\longrightarrow$ *C* (consequences)

Learning occurs primarily in two ways either through modeling the behavior of another person, or through the effects of reward. Modeling, the process of learning through observation and imitation of other people, has been discussed in a previous section. The second manner in which behavior is learned is through the effects of rewards. A reward is anything likely to increase the probability of a particular behavior occurring again.

Rewards can be divided into three different groups. It is important to realize the different types of rewards, and to learn that when rewarding children, parents generally progress from the first type of reward, tangible rewards, to intangible or social rewards, and ultimately hope that the child's reward is more intrinsic, that is, that it comes from within. Before discussing each type and giving you specific ideas, I need to emphasize that the progression of rewards is not always clear-cut and lock-step. It's very important for parents to praise their children when giving them tangible rewards. That is, to pair a tangible reward with a social reward. This is one way in which the tangible rewards become less important, and social rewards become more important. This will eventually lead to something being intrinsically rewarding to a child. Several important principles of rewards are important to remember:

1. *Different strokes for different folks!*

    Parents need to know their child, and offer rewards that are meaningful to him or her. Dinosaur stickers may be fine for one child, but happy face stickers may be needed for another. Money may be important to some children, whereas for others activities may be a more powerful reward.

2. *Catch your child being good.*

    This phrase has been around a long time, but it's very important. Misbehavior tends to attract a parent's attention more readily than good behavior, so it's important for parents to pay closer attention to appropriate behaviors and reward their child.

3. *Rewards are actions or things which follow a behavior, and serve to strengthen it.*

Is spanking a reward or a punishment? This question was on the quiz listed earlier in this section. You cannot determine if something is a reward or punishment by what the parent thinks it is. You can only determine if something is a reward or punishment by what happens to the behavior. If your son or daughter draws a picture on your wall with crayons, and you spank the child's hand (physical punishment), or have the child clean it up (logical consequences), and the next day the child draws a bigger picture, then you must have *rewarded* the initial drawing, because the behavior increased. It did not decrease. Physical punishment can be a reward to some children, especially if they are not getting other types of attention.

There are three types of rewards that you can begin to apply immediately in your family:

- Tangible rewards
- Social rewards
- Intrinsic rewards

Tangible Rewards

Tangible rewards are things which can be eaten, played with, held, touched, etc. Activities are another example of a tangible reward. Here are some very practical ideas using tangible rewards.

Marbles In The Jar Technique

One of the most effective techniques that I have suggested to parents over the years has been the *Marbles in the Jar Technique* that I learned at a workshop by Lee Canter[10] on Assertive discipline. You will be amazed at how the climate in your home will change in a positive manner after utilizing this technique for several days and weeks. It's simple, but I'll also explain how parents can blow it. All you need is a small jar and some marbles. If you are afraid the kids will play with the marbles, or be too tempted by them, you can use the plastic "peanuts" that are used in packaging. We used these in our family for about 5 to 7 years. Here are the steps to take to get started.

1. Explain to your children that you will catch them being good, praise them verbally (social reward) for what you see them do, then put some marbles in the jar as an additional reinforcer. You might say, "Gee Matt, I liked the way you helped your sister get her shoes on. Let's put five marbles in the jar." Be generous. Give 4 to 6 marbles each time. One mother called me a week or so after I had suggested this technique at a seminar. She was proud that she had started the idea and shared that her son had earned a marble that week. I praised her for starting the new idea, but encouraged her to be more generous. Sometimes we think the marbles are ten dollar gold nuggets. One good thing about this technique is that you don't need a fancy chore chart, in which you have had to think through all the behaviors you wanted of your child. You can select the activities to reinforce as it seems necessary. I remember when our children were younger, we'd call them, and they wouldn't come very quickly. So, the next time we called Chrissy and she came right away, we said, "Thanks a lot Chrissy, for coming as soon as we called you. Let's go put 5 marbles in the jar." It doesn't take very long before children realize what's important to you.

2. Explain to your child that when the jar gets full, you will do something fun as a family. When we first filled our jar at home, we took our three children to Disneyland. That may seem pretty extravagant, but we were planning to go to Disneyland anyway. We had to work hard to make sure we filled the jar by the weekend we had planned

to go. It was a great way to kick off the idea. Believe me, we didn't go to Disneyland every time the jar got filled. The younger your children are, the sooner the jar needs to get filled. If your children are less than about 6 years old, you should get the jar filled within a week. For older children, you can take 10 days to two weeks to get the jar filled. Parents may also want to get some ideas from their children on what activities they might like to do when the jar gets filled. Early in my private practice I didn't have an office. I made house calls. You really learn a lot by going to people's houses. One boy about 6-years-old showed me the jar they were using for the marbles. The jar was a reasonable size, but instead of marbles they were using small peas. I estimated that it would take three months to fill the jar. Kiddingly, I told the boy to put some water in the jar at night, to cause the peas to swell up and the jar to be filled quickly. (I have already discussed several ways this idea can be used incorrectly, or not as effectively.) One way is to be too stingy with the marbles, the second is to have too big a jar or to use small marbles, which would take too long to fill the jar.

Remember to have one jar for the entire family. If you have separate jars for each child, it may promote excessive sibling rivalry. Having one jar also puts the focus on the family getting along together, and doing something fun as a family when the jar gets filled. Having the jar visible is also a great reminder for parents to be positive, and to remind them to catch their child being good in order to get the jar filled. Don't be afraid to keep the idea going for several months to a year or more. As children get older you can take longer to fill the jar, but continue the idea, changing the focus when necessary, to get your children to do different tasks or exhibit a certain behavior.

Recently, after attending one of my seminars on parenting, a parent wrote, "After the first session, I began a marble jar and made an effort to spend more time with my son and made a conscious effort to listen to his language of love. From time to time I could hear him playing with the marbles. Then one evening my son walked into the kitchen with a marble jar and said, 'Look how many marbles you got, Mom!' When I asked him why I got the marbles, he said it was because I was nice to him, played catch with him, let him choose jello for dinner . . . " What a great story! The family atmosphere was much more positive, and the boy was learning to praise his mom.

The Marbles In the Jar Technique involves praise, tangible rewards (in hearing and seeing the marbles), and a positive activity reward, in addition to being an excellent visual reminder to parents to praise their child.

Fill In The Spaces On A Picture

This is a very simple positive reinforcement system. If your child would like a ball, just draw a picture of a ball, then divide it into a number of spaces. When your child performs a certain behavior or task you have discussed, color in one or more spaces on the picture. When the entire picture is colored in, you and your child can go and buy the ball. Obviously, this could apply to anything that your child might like to work for. The younger the child, the sooner he should reach the goal, just like the *Marbles In the Jar* technique.

Hershey Kiss Faces

I am not a strong believer in using food or candy as a reinforcer, but this technique was utilized by a mother who attended one of my meetings about ten years ago. Before sharing the idea with you, let me first say that it is vital to use reinforcers that are important to your children. If candy or food is very important to them, it could be utilized as a reinforcer, as long as you are aware of the need to move from the tangible reinforcer (food), to social reinforcers (praise), to intrinsic motivation. This mother cut some happy face circles out of colored paper, then glued a candy kiss to the middle of the face. When her boys did something nice, she gave them the happy face. Her letter to me should explain the rest of the idea. "The Hershey Kiss faces I use at home since taking your class. The boys get a 'sweet thing' when they are especially kind to or considerate of another person. Twenty faces they can 'trade in' for a movie or a trip to the beach. It has worked so well that last week when John helped Clint find his missing shoe, Clint got two of his faces and gave them to John. Never thought I'd live to see the day!" She caught the boys doing something good and rewarded them with verbal praise as she gave them the Hershey Kiss faces. So they received social praise, an immediate tangible reinforcer (candy), and they could save up the faces for a long term activity reinforcer. She had learned "well" the principles discussed in the class. After several weeks, she should have continued with the faces without the candy kisses, then gradually faded out the faces for certain behavior and switched to new desired behavior.

Three Quarters At Bedtime

This is another practical idea that worked really well in our family. Parents often experience difficulties in getting their children to sleep without many trips back into the bedroom for another kiss or drink of water. When two of our children were sharing a bedroom, we constantly had to go back into the room at bedtime. We gave them each three quarters on their night stand, and each time we had to come back into the room, we'd take one of the quarters. Whatever quarters were left in the morning they could keep. I think this was prior to another trip to Disneyland, because they were very motivated to earn money, and were very shortly going to bed without much of a problem. We faded out the system after several weeks and after the trip to Disneyland was over. We used a strong reinforcer, backed it up with verbal praise, faded out the tangible reward (money), and continued the intangible reward or verbal praise.

Social Rewards

Social rewards are those that come directly from another person. They include such things as words of praise, facial expressions, physical nearness, and physical contact. One of the best books available for parents to help them really understand the proper way to praise is *Effective Parents, Responsible Children* by Robert Eimers and Robert Aitchison, Ph.D.[11] I strongly encourage you to add this book to your parenting library. The book also discusses the proper way to utilize the negative consequences of ignoring, mild social punishment, and time-out, which will be discussed later in this book.

The seven components of effective praise presented by the author are:

1. Look at the child.
2. Move close to your child.
3. Smile.
4. Say lots of nice things to your child.
5. Praise the behavior, not the child.
6. Be physically affectionate.
7. Reward the behavior as soon as you observe it.[12]

As you strive to incorporate all of the above when you praise, you will be amazed at how much more effective your praise will be. Remember, whenever you use a token or tangible reinforcer, you pair it with verbal praise.

Intrinsic Rewards

Intrinsic rewards are those in which the actual performing of the task provides the reward. A goal of parenting is that children and teenagers will become rewarded through pride in an achievement, learning for knowledge itself, curiosity, feelings of mastery of subject matter, etc. Parents often feel that children and teenagers should possess the attribute of being intrinsically rewarded for what they do. Children will gradually possess this trait. They will become rewarded by performing a task or doing well in school, without needing a tangible or social reward all the time, but this does not happen overnight. If parents properly use tangible rewards, pairing them with social rewards and gradually fading out the more tangible rewards, then children will become more rewarded intrinsically. However, even adults need tangible and social rewards to keep working at an effective pace. How long would you work for a boss that did not pay you? How long would you work for a boss that did not praise you?

An example using different reinforcers may help you to understand the principles of rewards and different types of reinforcers, as well as the progression from tangible to intangible to intrinsic rewards. When our son, Matt, was about 6 or 7-years-old, reading was really a struggle for him. Obviously, reading was not one of his favorite things to do at home so there was always a struggle to get him to read. We finally realized the need to use stronger reinforcers to get him to read. We simply divided a piece of paper into about 9 squares and said, "for every page you read, we'll color in a square. When all the squares are colored in, you can have a piece of sugarless gum." He began to read, and with each page read, we'd not only color in a square (short term, tangible reward), or have him do it, but we'd really praise his efforts (intangible reward), along with more praise. Before long, we had stretched it out that he would get a pack of gum when he completed a book. I remember being in Matt's fourth grade classroom for an open house and noticing paper rocket ships on the wall with a student's name on each ship. They were all headed toward the moon, and got closer with each book they read. Tangible rewards were the rocket ships, as well as visually seeing progress to the moon. Matt is currently in the eleventh grade, and is very interested in pets. In fact, he has a goat, two chickens, two ducks, about five rabbits (depending on which ones have mated recently), a parakeet, and a dog. Obviously, he is very interested in pets, and reads a lot about them. Reading has become intrinsically rewarding. He enjoys reading for what he gets out of it, not what we give him for it.

A goal in parenting is to help our children become more intrinsically rewarded. This will happen if we use reinforcers in the right manner, and realize that it takes time for this to happen. It does not happen overnight. Parents often think that by the time a child is about 8 or 9, they shouldn't have to reward them for appropriate behaviors, but rewards need to continue as we move them from tangible to social to intrinsic motivation.

Putting It Into Action

What behavior do you need to start rewarding your children more often for performing? _____ .
What activities would be rewarding to your children? _____
_____ .
Which component of praise do you need to work at? _____
_____ .

DIGGING DEEPER

It's fairly easy to figure out why most parents have difficulty praising their children, but it needs to be discussed.

1. Did your parents praise you?
2. Did they reward you for a job well done, or just expect that you should do the "right" thing?
3. Did you hear critical comments more than positive comments?

As you answer these questions, you become aware of why it may have been difficult for you to praise your children.

When we come from a critical background we tend to be more critical with our children. That's why the Marbles In the Jar technique can be a helpful reminder to parents to become more positive.

Several Dragon chapters might also help you to better understand why you may have difficulty using positive reinforcement effectively and consistently. You may simply be "Recreating Your 'At Home' Feeling" (Chapter 2) of not getting praise, so you do not realize the importance of giving it to your children. You may have the "Irrational Belief" (Chapter 6) that one should not have to praise the child, and that youngsters should just do what they are told. You may also have some "Unresolved Resentment" (Chapter 7), and may be reassigning anger to a child, and thus are unable to see any positives.

THE FAMILY CIRCUS by Bil Keane

"Just a minute, Tess . . ."

This is a great example of a bribe. The mother is rewarding inappropriate behavior (yelling and fighting while she is on the phone), hoping to get good behavior. Many parents struggle with whether or not they are using rewards or bribes. Most often they are using rewards, but doubt themselves and then cut back on rewards, which can be a mistake.

SALLY FORTH by Greg Howard

Reprinted with permission of North American Syndicate, Inc.

This can definitely be a problem that some parents get into, "nagging by note." Codependents can especially get into nagging and reminding, instead of simply stating the rule and the consequence, then following through calmly.

SALLY FORTH by Greg Howard

Reprinted with permission of North American Syndicate, Inc.

Parents should institute an allowance system at some point to help children learn "fiscal responsibility," but parents also have a right and responsibility to monitor where the money is spent and set some limits on how it is spent.

Chores, Children, And Character
—They Go Together—
How Do You Make It Work?

"Excusing children of responsibilities is a child abuse that doesn't show up until adulthood."

Howard Hendricks once said, "If you do anything for your child that they can do for themselves then you are making them a marital cripple."

Hopefully, these two quotes are enough to get you interested and motivated to consider the importance of chores for children and teenagers.

It is extremely important for parents to require children to complete chores around the house. Some parents refuse to do this because "it's too much work," or "there are too many hassles," or "it's easier to do it myself." Some parents had to do lots of chores as a child, so they may have decided that their children won't have to go through what they went through. Regardless of the reasoning or rationale, it's a grave mistake to excuse children of chore responsibilities. As stated above "it's a child abuse that doesn't show up until adulthood."

Having children complete chores is not just a way to get cheap labor. Being required to complete chores is a most productive way of teaching responsibility and accountability to children. Inevitably, when you talk to a child who is not following through with homework or classwork, you'll find a student who is not being held accountable for chores at home. Accomplishing chores on a regular basis instills a sense of accomplishment in a child, and can very much enhance self-esteem.

Attaching an allowance to the completion of chores is also very important for several reasons. Children feel that they have some control in their lives and are able to "make things happen," if they can earn some money for their wants and needs. They will also learn about money, and hopefully learn the need to save, sometimes for long-term goals. Allowing children to make choices about what they'll spend their allowance on will build decision making skills.

Parents need to allow their children to make decisions about how they'll spend their money, even if they are positive the items the children want will not last, or won't work as advertised. This is one of the best ways for children to learn, and has a much greater impact on a youngster than the decisions made for them. Parents have the right to give some guidelines as to how the money will be spent. For example, you might specify that a certain portion has to go to church, Scout dues, Brownie dues, savings, etc. As children get older and their allowances increase, they should be required to assume more of their expenses. For example, a teenager might be required to buy birthday presents out of his allowance, or snacks, hobby supplies, etc.

In the book *Back In Control*[13] Gregory Bodenhamer states that parents get out of control if: (1) Rules are unclear, and/or (2) Follow through is inconsistent. These are two very important points to consider that apply in all areas of child management. They are especially important when setting up an effective system to get your children to complete chores without yelling and spanking.

> One day while I was working out in our front yard, I overheard a neighborhood boy say to his friend, "Yea, that's my mom calling me, but it's only the third time." He had his mother's number. Many parents give too many warnings to their children and teens. Parents need to set the rule and the consequences, then follow through consistently, not rant and rave.

THE FAMILY CIRCUS by Bil Keane

"I figured out a system for getting along with my mom. She tells me what to do and I do it."

Sorry parents, this is wishful thinking. This will not happen unless your child's temperament is very easy going.

Steps To Take And Points To Consider In Setting Up Chores

1. *Start early*

   Three-year-olds can be taught to set the table, empty waste baskets, etc. Chores can also include personal hygiene, such as brushing their teeth, taking a bath, etc. Just remember, the younger the child, the smaller the list of chores, and you'll also need to accept lesser quality work than from an older child. The reward may simply be stickers, or the marbles in the jar, rather than an allowance system.

2. *Don't discourage volunteers*

   When children express an interest in certain jobs, honor these interests whenever possible. If they are doing something that they prefer, you experience less difficulty in getting them to do it.

3. *Brainstorm a list of all possible chores.*

   These are ones that can be done by all family members. Take turns choosing chores, so everyone gets a chance to select preferred chores.

4. *Spell out each chore in writing, and teach your child how to do the chore.*

   Parents frequently forget this step. Make sure that it's clear to all what is expected, when it is expected, and who is responsible.

5. *Rotate the tasks.*

   Do this every other day or every week depending on the chores and the interest of all family members.

6. *Create and display a chart.*

   One client that came to see me said I was known as the "Chart Man." I am not sure that I want to be known for that alone. I do think that it is very important, to make sure that the rules are clear, the chores are spelled out, it is clear who is responsible, and the chart can be used to record the chore having been completed. Figures 1 & 2 are examples of different chore charts. Parents can help younger children to mark off the chores when completed, while older children can do this on their own. In our family, we always had a clear plastic sheet over the chore chart, so we could mark it with a felt tip pen each week, and erase the marks at the end of the week, reusing the same chart.

FIGURE 1

MATT

75 cents plus one cent for each 😊
Matt pays 25 cents to Sunday School
and Indian Guide dues.

	MON.	TUES.	WED.	THUR.	FRI.	SAT.	SUN.
Make Bed	😊 😊						
Rinse Break-fast Dishes	😊						
Comb Hair, Brush Teeth							
Empty Wastebaskets	😦						
Set Dinner Table	✕		✕		✕		✕
Feed & Water Whiskers							

FIGURE 2

	Mon.	Tues.	Wed.	Thur.	Fri.	Sat.	Sun.
Helping Mom & Dad							
Washing Face ☺							
Picking Up Toys							
Brushing Teeth							
Getting Dressed by Yourself							
Combing Your Hair							

7. *Reward the completion of chores.*

Rewards for chores can vary a great deal. Verbal praise should be given to children and teenagers on a regular basis for the completion of chores. Remember to be specific with your praise. Don't say, "you were a good boy/girl today," but say "I really like the way you brushed your teeth without being reminded." Praise is a non-tangible reward.

Tangible rewards are also effective in getting children to follow through with their responsibilities. Sometimes with younger children, a star or happy face or other stickers are sufficient, and are actually more significant to a young child than money. Remember, "Different strokes for different folks!" You need to get tuned-in to what is reinforcing to your child.

As children get older, I recommend tying a portion of their allowance to the completion of chores. As you'll note on Figure 1 (chore chart), we gave our son Matt 75 cents no matter what he did, plus 1 cent for each happy face he earned. He received two happy faces if he did the chores without being reminded, one if he did it after being reminded, and no happy faces if he did not complete the chore. The base rate and amount per chore as the child gets older should increase, as would the number of items that they themselves become more responsible for purchasing.

8. *Consider a "When-Then" Policy.*

Sometimes establishing a when-then policy, or a daily consequence regarding chore completion, will help parents to get their children on task sooner. For example, if your child has five chores to do each day, you could say "If you finish at least four of the chores (or all five) by 6:00 PM, you can watch TV tonight, or stay up later." If the chores are not completed, the child does not get to do either of these activities. With this system you will be holding your child accountable on a daily basis, and hopefully if he doesn't do chores well on the first day, he'll be more responsible the second day. Remember to be calm when you enforce the daily consequences, otherwise the restrictions lose their impact. This is an example of high control, which is discussed in the next section on developing a De-Parenting Plan.

For Better Or For Worse by Lynn Johnston

For Better Or For Worse Copyright 1982, 1983, 1986, 1988 Lynn Johnston,
Reprinted with permission of Universal Press Syndicate.

It's very important for you to get in the habit of allowing your youngsters to make decisions or choices. When you do however, you have to accept their choice. Otherwise do not give them the choice or change the choices.

9. *Be consistent and follow through consistently.*

Each day you need to help children follow through with marking the chore chart, until the responsibility for that is turned over to the youngster. When it is time to review and pay the weekly allowance, be sure you follow through each week and pay. One major reason that parents say their chore chart didn't work is that their child became discouraged when he or she didn't get paid.

One couple said they knew they weren't consistent when following through. They said it as though they were saying, "We won't be consistent, so what else can we do?" Sorry folks—if you aren't consistent, you won't be effective.

Remember too, that rules or chores listed do not change anyone's behavior. What changes a person's behavior are the consequences; rewards for appropriate behavior and negative consequences for inappropriate behavior. Many parents became discouraged when the chore list didn't change their child's behavior. Rules do not change the behavior of adults either. Speed limit signs do not slow us down as much as the threat of a ticket and fine slow us down.

10. *Continue the chore charts indefinitely.*

Remember the importance of having clearly defined rules or expectations. What better way to make sure that the rules or expectations are clear than to continue to display a chore chart? Obviously, the chart can be changed as youngsters get older to a list of different things they can do. Continue to have the list for teenagers, just remember to revise and update periodically.

Another change with teenagers is to back off on the control, or stated another way, give them a greater say in when they'll complete the chores. Having chores that can be done anytime during the week can be a good way to work with teenagers. Then you could tell them that they must complete their chores anytime before Friday at 6 p.m. This gives them some control over their lives, and will cause fewer conflicts between the two of you. Chores that could be done anytime would include things like washing the car, mowing the lawn, vacuuming the house, cleaning a bathroom, ironing five shirts for Dad, etc.

Remember, you need a consequence when the chores are completed such as an allowance or special privileges, and you need a consequence if your teenager chooses not to complete the chores by Friday at 6 p.m. These could be doing the chores on Saturday without getting paid, or getting grounded Friday night, or losing car privileges, etc. You want to avoid nagging and bugging your teenager. Set the rules and the consequences, then follow through calmly, like a good traffic cop.

Questions Parents Frequently Ask About Chores

1. *"Do I have to pay my children for everything they do?"*

   Definitely not! Kids need to pitch in and do some jobs because they are part of the family. Once when one of my children asked what they'd get for an additional job I gave them, I calmly replied, "Dinner." Don't expect children not to ask for something for the work they do, just calmly reply, "Some things you do just because you are part of the family." Parents are often unrealistic by expecting children to not ask each time.

2. *"What if my kids don't seem to care about an allowance?"*

   There may be several reasons for this. If grandma or grandpa gives your kids money each week just because they love them, then your kids probably won't be motivated to work for their allowance. You may need to discuss this issue with grandma and grandpa, and ask them to show their love in another way, or make special privileges be the reward they work for, such as having a friend spend the night, using the family car, etc.

A weekly allowance may seem too far away for a youngster on Monday. This is one reason why the when-then policy might be effective. It holds the youngster accountable on a daily, not weekly basis, and the consequence is an activity that may be more appealing to the youngster, i.e., staying up later, or watching TV.

3. *"What if my child consistently makes the wrong choice and chooses to not do his or her chores?"*

It would be good to discuss with the child the reason for their behavior if they have any insight. Is it time to rotate chores? Eliminate certain chores? This question really stumped me the first time I heard it, but the answer is fairly obvious. You do what society at large has done. Penalties for drunk driving have gone up drastically in the past few years because people were consistently making the wrong choices, i.e., deciding to drive while intoxicated. If your child makes the wrong choices and decides to not do the chores because he is lazy, or because he does not need the money that week, then change the choice. State that if the chores aren't done, he can't play with friends the next day, etc. In other words, change the negative consequences. Another approach: If he decides to skip a certain chore because he'll only get a quarter for it, you can set up a fine system, and fine him one dollar when he chooses to skip the chores.

THE FAMILY CIRCUS by Bil Keane

"But, a little while ago you said you weren't gonna ask me to clean up my room again."

Parents often give very unclear messages to their children. It's important that rules and expectations are clear, and consequences to misbehavior are known by the child in advance of any infractions, when possible.

Developing A De-Parenting Plan

Before discussing the importance of developing a de-parenting plan, it is helpful to look at inappropriate parenting styles and mistakes parents frequently make. You may identify yourself in one or more of the inappropriate parenting approaches, and hopefully learn how to change your approach.

Three different approaches to parenting could be labelled as *Authoritarian, Permissive,* and *Authoritative.*

A letter to Dr. Joyce Brothers,[14] and her response in the December 5, 1989, Los Angeles Times, could best summarize these types of parenting styles.

> "Dear Dr. Brothers: My father-in-law is an old-time military man and a believer in firm discipline—the 'do-what-you're-told-because-you're-told' type. My husband is of the 'laid-back-who-cares' style and I'm in between. We have two children and I'm constantly trying to figure out what type of discipline is best." Signed A.L.
>
> Dr. Brothers' response was as follows: "Dear A.L.: There's a difference between authoritarian and authoritative discipline. Authoritarian discipline, such as that of your father-in-law, doesn't stimulate or prepare the youngster to be able to think on his own, while the authoritative discipline, that which lets the child know what is expected and explains why this is correct behavior, teaches the child how to think and make good decisions when the parents aren't around.
>
> "Authoritative parenting requires more effort than the traditional do-as-I-say discipline, but the results eventually pay off.
>
> "Psychologist Diana Baumrind and colleagues at University of California at Berkeley tracked children from preschool to high school to see what effects their parents' discipline style had on their characters. Both youngsters of authoritarian and permissive parents had low self-esteem. Those of permissive parents were immature, had

a hard time getting along with peers, tended to be pro-
miscuous and had the heaviest drug use. Children raised
by authoritarian parents were also immature and scored
the poorest on verbal and math achievement. Children
with authoritative parents were outstandingly well-ad-
justed, mature, happy, motivated and independent." J.B.

Another term for authoritative could be "democratic." That
may help you in differentiating the three parenting styles.
Research studies show that the most effective, healthiest
approach is the democratic, or authoritative approach. The
parenting strategies discussed in this book are definitely more
democratic approaches. Discussing situations with children,
offering choices, calmly following through with actions based
on their choices, allowing children to express anger, and being
willing to resolve conflicts with children are some examples
of a democratic approach.

It also appears from the letter, that the father in this case
was trying to swing to the complete opposite approach of
his father. His father was more of a dictator (authoritarian),
so he decided (consciously or subconsciously) to be more
permissive, probably because he did not want to be like his
father. His father had made one mistake, and this man was
making another one. Permissive parents often allow their
children to do whatever they want, then begin to resent their
children because they cannot stand their behavior. Children
need and want limits, even though they will constantly test
them. When there are no limits, or they find themselves able
to exceed the limits, they become more insecure.

Authoritarian parents and permissive parents both love their
children, but are going about it in the wrong way. Do you
need to change your approach from one of these styles to
a more democratic approach? Again, decisions about parenting
approaches should not be based on your own experiences as
a child, but should be based on what has been proven as
most effective. If you tend to be more of a dictator or
authoritarian, you may find the chapters on Codependency,

Unresolved Resentment, Dealing with a Loss, and Irrational Beliefs most helpful to you. If you tend to be more permissive, then consider first the chapters on : Low Self-Esteem, Frozen Needs, Vows and Dealing with a Loss. Obviously another place to look is back at your own childhood. Think about what approach your parents used in working with you and your siblings. Are you simply copying their approach and Recreating Your "At Home" Feeling, which is discussed in Chapter 2? You may be doing the complete opposite because you hated it so much, in which case Chapter 3 on Vows is important to read.

Another way to evaluate your method of parenting and illustrate the need to develop a de-parenting plan is through the use of the following chart:

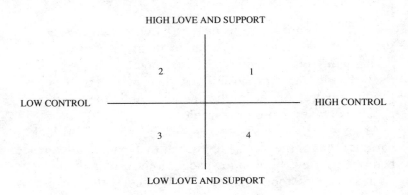

(Chart Concept from "What Kind of Parent Are You?" by Dennis Guetnsey, in Family Life Today, 1975, G/L Publications, Glendale, CA)

This basically shows that there are four parenting approaches, or four ways to be a parent: (1) High control and High love and support, (2) Low control and High love and support, (3) Low control and Low love and support, (4) High control and Low love and support.

It's very important, as was discussed in the first part of this chapter, for parents to communicate love to their children in ways that are received as love (High Love and Support). Parents always need to show high love and support to their children, therefore the only two healthy parenting styles would be number 1 and 2. When children are young, parents need to use high control. They must monitor behavior closely and require accountability on a daily basis. If you are too permissive and use low control with young children, they'll get into situations that they are not prepared to handle, and possibly suffer dire consequences for choices they are not prepared to make. As children get older, generally between the ages of 10 and 13, parents need to move toward the low control category. If you remain in the high control section with older children, then you take on the authoritarian approach to parenting.

As children grow into teenagers, parents need to gradually turn more and more areas over to them as they develop a de-parenting plan. Obviously, if a teenager is unable to effectively handle new responsibilities, then parents will need to resume control of the particular area until the teenager is capable of being more responsible.

An extremely important exercise for parents is to look at various areas of the teen's life, such as diet, church attendence, bedtime, curfew time, allowance, clothes, hair, homework, chores, care of room, dating, involvement with the family, etc. Periodically review the existing rules or expectations and revise the rules as the teenager demonstrates the maturity to have greater freedom. In this way, both the parents and the teenager will not only be aware of the rules, but both will realize that rules will be constantly reviewed and changed, to reflect the age and maturity of the teenager.

For Better Or For Worse by Lynn Johnston

For Better Or For Worse Copyright 1982, 1983, 1986, 1988 Lynn Johnston,
Reprinted with permission of Universal Press Syndicate.

The letting go process can be very difficult for parents.
Allowing your child to become more independent is necessary
and builds self-esteem.

Blondie

Reprinted with permission of King Features Syndicate, Inc.

Alexander is right to some degree. His parents need to develop a "De-Parenting" Plan, whereby they turn more things
over to him and allow him the opportunity to become more
responsible. He and his parents should enter some
negotiations to resolve the apparent problem.

DIGGING DEEPER

Are you holding on too tightly to your child or teenager? If so, consider re-reading Chapter 1 (Codependency) and Chapter 6 (Irrational Beliefs). Are you having difficulty showing High love and support? If so, consider Chapter 7 (Unresolved Resentments), and Chapter 8 (Dealing With A Loss). If you demonstrate too much low control at an early age, consider Chapter 5 (Frozen Needs), Chapter 3 (Vows), Chapter 4 (Low Self-Esteem), and Chapter 8 (Dealing With A Loss).

ENDNOTES

1. Dobson, Dr. James, *Hide or Seek*, Old Tappan, New Jersey: Fleming H. Revell Co., 1974, p. 7.
2. Campbell, Dr. Ross, *How To Really Love Your Child*, Wheaton: Victor Books, 1977.
3. Ibid., p. 15.
4. Campbell, Dr. Ross, *How To Really Love Your Teenager*, Wheaton: Victor Books, 1981.
5. Gordon, Thomas, *Parent Effectiveness Training*, New York: New American Library, 1970.
6. Campbell, *How To Really Love Your Teenager*
7. Campbell, Dr. Ross, *Your Child and Drugs*, Wheaton: Victor Books, 1988.
8. Wright, H. Norm, *Marital Counseling: A Biblically Based, Behavioral, Cognitive Approach*, Denver: Christian Marriage Enrichment, 1981, p. 248.
9. Gordon, Thomas, *Parent Effectiveness Training*.
10. Canter, Lee, *Parent Resource Guide*, Canter and Associates, Inc., Distributed by Harper & Row, 1985.
11. Eimers, Robert, and Robert Aitchison, Ph.D., *Effective Parents, Responsible Children*, New York: McGraw-Hill Book Company, 1977.
12. Ibid., pp. 35-42.
13. Gregory Bodenhamer, *Back In Control*, New York: Prentice Hall Press, 1983.
14. Dr. Joyce Brothers, Letter in the L.A. Times, December 5, 1989.

11

Self-Esteem And Stress

Improving Your Youngster's Self-Esteem

One of the most important tasks for a parent is to build high self-esteem in their children. If there were two or three things that I could just hand my children that would serve them well for the rest of their lives, high self-esteem would be among the top three.

I have several different stories or word pictures that may help explain self-esteem and its importance a little better. One is the *Poker Chip Theory*. If your child has lots of poker chips (high self-esteem) and the teacher says, "Who discovered America? If you miss, it will cost you two poker chips," the student with a lot of chips will take a chance and speak up. Learning involves risking yourself, speaking up and taking a chance. If a student has lots of chips, he won't worry so much about a wrong answer.

However, if a student is sitting there with only one or two chips (low self-esteem), he won't be so eager to speak up and take a chance. Our task as parents (and teachers) is to give our children lots of chips, or high self-esteem. It is also important in using this analogy, to not take away many chips when a child tries something and is not successful. That is something that we have control over.

If a student feels he'll lose 100 chips for a wrong answer, then he will rarely speak up. The same thing applies at home. If your son or daughter feels that he or she will drop in value when unsuccessful at something, then the child will not risk trying it. As parents, we need to make mistakes and failures less costly to our children's self-esteem. We need to reward and reinforce our youngsters as much, if not more, for attempting something as well as achieving something.

The other description of self-esteem comes from an experiment that I heard about where scientists put a fish in an aquarium with lots of guppies. The fish would very often eat the guppies when hungry. Then they put a glass partition in the aquarium, with the fish on one side, and the guppies on the other side. The fish kept trying to get the guppies, but finally gave up after running into the wall several times. Then they removed the glass partition and let the fish swim amongst the guppies once again. The fish starved to death. It had been thwarted so many times by the wall that, even though the wall was not there any longer, it was not going to take a chance. It gave up and died. So it may be with students. They may have been thwarted so many times that they simply do not try any longer. They just give up.

Low self-esteem is hard to see. When a child has a broken arm or leg, it's pretty easy to notice the cast, and therefore make some allowance for this handicap. It is hard to see low self-esteem. Maybe the youngster with low self-esteem fights with other children a lot, is a behavior problem in class, has few friends, or doesn't attempt to answer questions.

Ask yourself the following questions about your child:

1. Is my child willing to take on new tasks?
2. Does he show self-direction and independence in activities?
3. Does he ask questions when he does not understand?
4. Does he readily adapt to changes in procedures?
5. Does he talk appropriately about his school accomplishments?
6. Does he deal with mistakes or failures easily and comfortably?
7. Does he take criticism or corrections in stride —without over-reacting?
8. Is he popular with his his peers?
9. Does the child refer to himself in positive terms?
10. Does the child readily express his opinions, and is he receptive to the opinions of others?

It's important to consider these as possible indicators to measure the child's self-esteem, and take the necessary corrective action if needed. Remember, our challenge as parents is to identify problem areas our youngsters have and take action, develop a corrective strategy, and put a plan into action to remediate the problem.

Your child's self-esteem will affect many things in his life: how he does in school, what kind of friends he will choose, how many new things he will be willing to try, how he deals with peer pressure, how he withstands the pressures from peers to become involved with drugs or alcohol, and ultimately the kind of occupation he will strive for, and his selection of a spouse.

What Can Parents Do To Enhance Their Youngster's Self-Esteem?

Many techniques for building high self-esteem have already been discussed in the preceeding chapter entitled, "Creating a Positive Home Climate." Additionally, all of the discipline strategies which are discussed in the following chapter are presented in an order which, when used appropriately, is aimed toward protecting and building your child's self-esteem. The approach to parenting that is most effective in enhancing self-esteem is a democratic approach. Research studies have shown that youngsters raised in this type of environment will have a higher self esteem than those raised in an authoritarian or overly permissive environment.

In an authoritarian environment, the child's behavior is controlled by an outside force (the parent), and the child doesn't develop inward control. In this environment, the youngster makes few choices on his or her own, and is not allowed independence when he or she can handle it. In the overly permissive environment, the child sees the parent as weak. Since the child is allowed to do anything, the behavior soon becomes so obnoxious that the parent rejects them. In this environment, there are no constraints placed on what the child can do, and he or she may fail attempting something that he or she is ill-equipped to be successful at. High self-esteem develops in youngsters when they receive parental warmth, respectful treatment, and when there are clearly defined limits.

I will first list some of the areas that have already been discussed, so you can refer to those sections to remind yourself of some specific strategies to build self-esteem. Then I will list some other ideas that will also be helpful.

In the preceeding chapter the following were discussed:

- Showing unconditional love to your child.
- How to praise and reward your youngster for appropriate behavior.

- How to get your child to express feelings.
- How to be a good model for your youngster.
  Are you modeling high self-esteem?

In chapter 13 the strategies for dealing with inappropriate behavior are presented in a sequence that is aimed at helping a child's self-esteem to remain intact.

The following are important methods for developing and improving high self-esteem in your youngster.

Examine The Values in Your Home

When parents value sports and their child is good in music, the child's self-esteem can be affected in a negative way. Parents need to really study their child, evaluate his strengths and weaknesses, and steer him in the direction of his strengths, not towards what the parents value. One teenager I counseled was an excellent student in a "gifted program" at school. His brother was good in sports. The father's emphasis seemed to be in the area of sports, so the boy I was counseling felt that he was not OK. It seemed to him that sports were more valued in their home than academic achievements were. Examine what you value and be sure to support your youngsters in areas of their strengths and interests. Do not force them to go along with your values, or to be active in things you may be interested in if it is not their interest as well.

Admit Your Faults And Mistakes

It is very important for parents to admit it when they make a mistake. After all, our youngsters know when we make a mistake, so why not admit it to them? When parents always appear to be right, that leaves the youngster only one choice— he must be wrong. This will adversely affect his self-esteem. We also need to convey the message that it is OK to make a mistake. That's how we learn. When youngsters are afraid to make a mistake, their self-esteem will inevitably be lowered with each mistake they make. Rather than looking at it as a learning experience, they will consider it a failure.

Examine Your Expectations

This is a very important area, and one that I discussed previously in Chapter 6—the Dragon of Irrational Beliefs. Youngsters will rarely question their parents' expectations, they will only question their self-worth when they fail to achieve the parents' expectations. When my son, Matt, was about 11 or 12 I was trying to help him work on 5 Scout Merit badges at the same time, The poor guy was getting stressed out and frustrated. He wasn't able to say (few kids are), "Dad, your expectations are unrealistic!" I finally realized it and apologized to him, and said that I was wrong and unrealistic. Parents need to have reasonable expectations for their children. When your expectations are too low, you will not encourage your child to strive harder to reach a goal. When expectations are too high or not high enough, self-esteem will be eroded.

Encourage Independence

Parenting is a lot like flying a kite. If you hold on too tight, the string will break. If you let go too quickly, the kite will fall. As parents, we need to encourage our children to become independent, and to strive to do more and more on their own. If you attempt to hold on too long, teenagers will not only rebel more, but their self-esteem will also suffer. If you allow your teenagers to do things when they aren't mature enough to handle them, (let go too quickly), then their self-esteem will also suffer.

As you have already read in **Part I** of this book, there may be many Dragons or hidden factors from your own childhood that can interfere with your ability to let go. At a seminar that I attended given by Howard Hendricks, he made the statement, "If you do anything for your child that they could be doing for themselves, then you are making them a marital cripple." It's a good phrase to think about before you step in and do something for your child.

What task have you not trained your child to do that he or she ought to be learning by now? _____ .

What can your child do for himself that you are still doing for him? _____ .

Ask your child the above questions. You might be surprised at the response, and you might gain insights on some changes you may need to make.

Allow Your Child To Make Decisions

This concept is very similar to the previous one. When you go to a restaurant, do you order for your child? Are you still picking out their clothes to wear to school? You may feel that if they don't dress appropriately with the "right" colors, it may reflect on you as a parent. Are you still telling your teenager what to do with his room, or what time to go to bed? Parents need to let their children make decisions and experience the consequences of their decisions. That is the only way they will learn. If you constantly tell them, "It will be cold today, wear a jacket," then they will never learn to think for themselves. Don't carry this concept too far. You would not let your children decide whether or not they wanted to go to school, church, or the doctor. Parents should only turn over decisions to their children when they have some confidence that they will make the correct decision or a decision that if made poorly, will not jeopardize the health or welfare of the youngsters.

Praise their appropriate choices. Areas where they make poor choices you may have to take back under your control until they are more capable of making responsible decisions. For example, if you have decided to let your child decide when to take a nap or go to bed at night, and they make unhealthy decisions, then it's time to take that back under your control. If you give your teenager a clothing allowance but he blows it on candy, then go back to taking him with you to buy the clothes, and monitor more closely what he buys.

Help Your Child To Compensate

Parents need to study their children to really understand them, and in order to really determine their strengths and weaknesses. Too often, schools and parents keep trying to help a child to get better in an area where they may never improve. To me, it is far better to help the youngster compensate. The clearest example of this is in the area of handwriting. Some of us, including myself, do not have the best handwriting in the world. It is not one of our gifts. Should I continue to practice handwriting, or should I find a way to compensate for this weakness?

Fortunately, I am typing this book on a computer, not writing it longhand. In this day and age of computers, and "spell-check" programs, it makes little sense to me to practice handwriting, but more sense to find a way to compensate for that weakness. All adults and children have different learning styles. Some people are auditory learners, some visual learners, and some kinesthetic. We need to understand this and how each child learns best and help them to compensate for areas of weakness.

Discuss Round Spots And Flat Spots

Another way to help children with self-esteem is to discuss "round spots" and "flat spots." Draw a circle and accentuate some flat spots and some round spots on the circle. Explain that no one is perfectly "round." Each person has round spots or strengths, and each person has flat spots, or weaknesses. High self-esteem does not mean we are perfectly round. It means we learn to recognize and accept both our flat spots and round spots. We can get into positions that require our round spots and not get discouraged because of our flat spots. My son Matt once shared that he felt bad in his spelling class because each student had to say aloud to the class how many he or she had missed on a spelling test. (Not a very good classroom technique.) Nearly everyone had said they missed one or two, while Matt had to say he missed eight. Spelling is one of his flat spots, and it's hard when your flat spot is compared to other's round spots. But remember, good self-esteem does not mean we are perfectly round. Help your youngster to realize this. Continue to help them identify and compensate and work hard on their flat spots, but also recognize their round spots.

The No Knock Policy Or Positive Self-Talk

Help your child to develop positive self-talk. David Stoop's book on *Self Talk*[1] was one of the first books my children were aware of that I used in counseling. We talk aloud at the rate of approximately 200 words per minute, while our self-talk, things we are thinking, is going on at the rate of 1200 to 1300 words per minute. Teach your children to think positively. Ignore it when they knock themselves, and if it becomes a serious problem, make a more concentrated effort to help them to change their self-talk. I have coached soccer for over 10 years, and I encourage my children and other children to ignore the jerk on the sidelines who may be yelling at them, and to talk to themselves in a positive, encouraging way. People need to recognize they can have a positive coach with them all day long, no matter what they are doing. That coach can be themselves. They can talk to themselves in a positive, encouraging way, or they can choose to be critical, negative, and pessimistic. Helping your children develop positive self-talk is a tremendous tool to give them which will build their own self-esteem.

Help Your Child To Set And Reach Goals

Helping your children set and reach goals is a very effective way to help them develop high self-esteem. One Friday, when Chrissy was five and in kindergarten, she came home from school and imformed us that she was not good in jumping rope. She went out to the garage, got a rope, and said, "Would you give me 5 cents for every time I'm successful after five jumps in a row?" We said she had a deal. By the end of the weekend, she was jumping 25 to 30 times in a row without missing, while turning a complete circle. What a great example of goal setting! You can begin it at any age.

Chrissy also decided at age 9 or 10 to take the whole family out to an expensive restaurant. She saved her allowance and birthday money for five or six months. Boy, was she proud when she paid the bill for dinner! We were all proud of her too. We all had water to drink and no desserts, so we weren't too hard on her, but the bill still came to about one hundred dollars. Help your child to set goals. Make sure the goals are reasonable, reward them along the way, and encourage them to achieve the goals. One year we were in charge of taking a soccer team of 12-year-olds that our son Matt was on, to Hawaii for a tournament. Each boy had to earn $950.00 over a period of 6 months and all the boys achieved that goal. (I must slip this in as well, we beat 11 other teams in Hawaii and won the tournament.) The boys gained a great deal in self-esteem, not only from winning, but from working hard and achieving a long term goal.

Review And Take An Interest In Your Child's Schoolwork

It is very important for parents to review and take an interest in their children's schoolwork. It is also appropriate to help them set goals with school grades and reward them for achieving those goals. Rewards for grades and effort in school can be very effective for all students. One major difference for teenagers and rewards for school work is that the teenager must first decide that he or she wants to get good grades. In other words, they have to "buy into" the plan. Many parents try rewarding their teenagers for good grades, but the teenager hasn't bought into the plan, so it doesn't work. After a teenager has decided to get better grades, the reward system will be effective.

Post your child's school work on a bulletin board or on the refrigerator. Go to parent-teacher conferences. Volunteer to work in the classroom or on school fundraisers. All these things will help you convey to your youngster that what they are doing in school is important.

SUMMARY

Building high self-esteem in your children should be one of your major goals. Books are listed in the Suggested Reading section at the end of this book that you may want to add to your library. Low self-esteem parents have trouble building high self-esteem in their children. As you are aware, low self-esteem is a Dragon that many parents bring into their adult lives that can seriously interfere with applying proper parenting strategies (review Low Self-Esteem in Chapter 4). It is important for you to recognize and determine if low self-esteem is one of your Dragons and deal appropriately with it.

Helping Your Child And You Deal With Stress

An extremely important area for parents to become more involved in and accept more consciously is the need to help their children deal more effectively with stress . Unfortunately, many parents do not deal with stress effectively, so they are unable to pass on the correct information to their youngster.

Helping children deal with stress and anger (see Chapter 10) are two very important responsibilities of parents that often are neglected. Again, the lack of training that parents have in these areas makes it difficult for them to realize the importance of passing this information on to their youngsters, and they lack the knowledge of how to do it.

I have defined Dragons as things or issues that people bring into their roles as parents which will interfere with their effectiveness. The inability to deal effectively with stress is definitely an issue that will interfere with a parent's ability to respond appropriately to their children. The inability to deal with stress can also be considered a Dragon that parents bring into their adult lives from childhood, since many adults were not taught as children how to deal with stress. When parents are too frazzled by busy schedules and other stressors, they definitely are hindered in their application of the parenting strategies previously discussed. Therefore, I am including a discussion on stress management at this point for two reasons:

1. To give parents insights on how to deal with their own stressors, in order to be able to approach parenting more effectively.

2. To give parents a simple format for dealing with stress that they can use as well as pass on to their children.

It is my opinion that the inability of children and adults to deal with stress and anger effectively is the basis of much alcohol and drug abuse, teenage suicide, and the poor performance of students in school.

There are many excellent books on stress management—some references are presented at the end of this book. I strongly encourage the reader to follow up on this topic through additional reading. My intent is to get you started with some basic information that will help you begin to deal with stress more effectively, and will give you a model for helping your youngsters deal with stress. In all areas of parenting and especially this area, parents need to realize that it takes time to instill new and more effective life coping skills into your own behavior patterns.

It takes time and repetitions of the information in order to instill these new coping skills in your children. In other words, do not expect to sit down one night and tell your youngsters how to deal with stress and expect it to become part of their tool kit for life. Parents will need to go over and over the techniques, and point out how and when the different strategies can be utilized. I will discuss how to deal with stress, both from the standpoint of parents dealing with their own stress as well as how to impart the knowledge to your children.

Before looking at how to deal with stress, it is important for parents to realize and recognize when stress may be the reason for their behavior and for their child's. Stress symptoms can be divided into three categories: physical, emotional, and behavioral.

PHYSICAL

Physical symptoms include headaches, backaches, frequent colds or flus, diarrhea, vague stomach problems, chronic fatigue, loss of appetite, or excessive overeating and sleep difficulties. The list goes on. Parents need to be aware that stress affects everyone differently. Not all people will experience stress in the same way. Additionally, what causes stress to one person may have little effect on another.

EMOTIONAL

Emotional symptoms include feelings of failure, nervous laughter, excessive worrying, feelings of being unworthy, nightmares, dramatic mood changes.

BEHAVIORAL

Emotional symptoms include stuttering, fighting, stealing, attention-getting antics, alcohol or drug use, loss of interest in school or work, inability to concentrate, impulsive behavior, poor attitude toward others.

The lists does not include all the possible symptoms of stress, but hopefully these are enough to help you realize how many behaviors may be explained by stress, and to help you become alert to your need to help your youngsters deal with stress more effectively.

If you as a parent are experiencing any of the above symptoms, it will be very difficult to be effective. Thus, parents need to learn effective methods of dealing with stress to be effective parents, and to pass on the information to their youngsters.

The next step in dealing with stress is to identify the stressors. What is causing the stress? Learn to identify the stressors in your life as an adult. Are you worried about: a job interview, a work performance review, meeting the monthly bills, giving a lecture, having your in-laws visit, going on vacation, meeting with your child's teacher, going to a new church? Do you try to follow a frantic schedule, with little time to relax? You fill in the blank: _____ .

Help your children to identify the stressors in their lives. After you recognize that some of your physical, emotional, and behavioral symptoms may be due to stress, it is then important to identify the stressors in order to deal with them effectively. Here are some of the possible stressors in a child's life:

- Entering school for the first time.
- Having to take a test.
- Riding the bus to school for the first time.
- Being involved in too many activities.
- The arrival of a baby brother or sister.
- Playing in a soccer or baseball game or other team sport.
- Going to the school prom.
- Trying to decide on which college to attend.
- Wondering when or if a nuclear war will break out.

- Worrying about your parents getting a divorce when you hear them fighting.

- Worrying about whether or not the school bully will approach you today.

- Hearing awful things on television such as murders and kidnappings and wondering if it could happen to you.

- While eating breakfast you see a picture of some missing child on the milk carton and wonder if that could happen to you.

And the list goes on and on. The important point is for parents to get more tuned in to the stressors in their child's life, and become more effective in helping them to deal with the stress.

A major source of stress for both adults and children is change. All changes are stressful, even good changes. A major time of change for youngsters is when their parents are going through a divorce. The youngster may move, change schools, neighborhoods, or friends. I explain it as though one were on a hike with a backpack. Someone says, "here's 10 pounds of food, carry this in your backpack." That wouldn't be a problem for most people. But then someone else says, "here's another 20 pounds," "here's another 50 pounds." Each change adds weight to the backpack, and pretty soon the person is no longer able to walk. They become overloaded with change and stress.

Two excellent scales or tools to use to compute the amount of "weight" you are carrying in your backpack are: *The Life Change Units scale* or *Holmes Test*[2] from the University of Washington and one for children from David Elkind's book, *The Hurried Child.*[3] These scales can be very effective in not only determining how much "weight" you are carrying around, but in pinpointing specific causes of the stress that may often point to the corrective action to take. Just knowing that a youngster's school performance has dropped because of an overload of changes can help the parent relax and realize that part of the solution is time. Expectations of continued good school performance during times of many changes is not realistic. Unrealistic expectations will only serve to frustrate everyone. Not only must a parent and youngster deal with all the changes during a divorce, but they must grieve the loss, which is discussed in **Part I**, Chapter 8.

The next step is to decide how to deal with the stressors. The approach is very simple. There are four major ways in which a person can deal with stress. One morning when I took my daughter Robyn out to breakfast, I described the four ways. I wanted to write them down, but she really didn't want to get that formal. About a month later I said, "Robyn, I'll give you $10 if you can tell me the four ways of dealing with stress." She got 2 of the 4 and no $10. Chrissy and Matt soon realized I had this deal going with Robyn, so I went over the four ways with them. They felt it would be pretty easy money.

About a month after our discussion, Chrissy and I were in the check-out line at the store and Chrissy was going to buy some candy (yes, we let them spend their allowance on things they want, but we place some limits on the amount of candy, and other junk food). I said, "Chrissy, if you can tell me the four ways of dealing with stress, I'll buy that for you." She got three out of the four ways, and bought the candy with her own money. I give these examples for a reason. Again, you can not expect to help your children in a one-time lecture. Time and repetitions of the same ideas are important. I guarantee, however, if you accept your need to help them deal more effectively with stress, and consistently bring in examples you will definitely see an improvement in their ability to handle stress, and you will be giving them a "tool" that will serve them well for the rest of their lives. Following the cartoon I will discuss four ways to deal with stress.

Peanuts by Charles M. Schultz

Reprinted with permission of UFS, Inc.

Unless parents learn effective parenting tools and learn to deal with stressors effectively, they will definitely get worn down, because "Kids have better bench strength."

Take Care Of Yourself

This means many things. What kind of foods do you eat? What do you drink? Do your children consume lots of sugar and other junk foods? Do you get enough sleep? Do you take time to relax, to kick back and do nothing? Do you reward yourself with small gifts? Do you get enough exercise? When I ride the stationary bike at home or at the gym, I not only feel the sweat leaving my body, but stress along with it.

Taking care of ourselves and teaching our children to take care of themselves is one of the major things that we can do to deal with stress. One of the main reasons for this is because it is something we CAN do, regardless of the nature of the stressor. I have noticed lately that Chrissy makes more of an effort to get to sleep earlier, as she realized this has helped her to deal with the stress symptom of headaches.

Remember, nothing changes if nothing changes. What do you plan to do in the future in the area of taking care of yourself to deal with stress more effectively? _____
_____ .

Again, this way of dealing with stress is extremely important to implement, because regardless of the nature of the stressor, this method will help you to deal with it more effectively.

Take Constructive Action

In other words, do something about the stressor. Remember, first you have to identify the stressor before you can determine if there is some action you can take. When Robyn was stressed about her Advanced Placement Physics class, we got a tutor for her. When I begin to worry about an upcoming seminar, I try to prepare for it in advance. This is a good time to remind you that complaining about a stressor is not a very effective way to deal with stress.

It's OK to vent some frustrations and anger, but for the long-term solution, we need to attempt to take some constructive action. If your child is doing poorly in school and is stressed over school, take constructive action. For example: get them a complete physical or eye exam, have them tested for a possible learning disability, or set up the school to home communication system that is described in the next chapter.

It's impossible to list all the possible constructive action that a parent or child can take, because it's impossible to list all the possible stressors and situations that a person finds themselves in, but if you identify the stressor, you are well on your way toward figuring out some constructive action to take. Counseling with a professional or a good friend may help you expand your thinking in order to come up with a solution.

Determine if your life is in balance. There are at least eight life dimensions. I will list the eight life dimensions, then ask you to evaluate how you feel about each area with regards to your current life situation. Using the scale of one to 10, are you in the "pits" (1, 2, 3, 4), are you in the average range (5, 6, 7), or are you soaring (8, 9, 10)? As you consider these areas in your life, take time also to evaluate your children in these areas. The eight life dimensions are:

SPIRITUAL	1	2	3	4	5	6	7	8	9	10
PHYSICAL	1	2	3	4	5	6	7	8	9	10
PROFESSIONAL	1	2	3	4	5	6	7	8	9	10
MARRIAGE	1	2	3	4	5	6	7	8	9	10
SOCIAL	1	2	3	4	5	6	7	8	9	10
PERSONAL GROWTH	1	2	3	4	5	6	7	8	9	10
FINANCES	1	2	3	4	5	6	7	8	9	10
CHILDREN	1	2	3	4	5	6	7	8	9	10

A brief note about each might help you to rate them. Don't compare yourself to someone else or someone else's expectations.

Spiritual
- Do you attend a church?
- Are you working on a relationship with God?

Physical
- Do you exercise?
- Are you watching what you eat and drink?
- Are you staying away from junk food?
- Do you take time to relax?

Professional
- This may relate to your work inside the home or outside the home—how you feel about your professional component?

Marriage
- How do you feel about your marriage relationship? If not married, rate your relationships with others.

Social

- Do you go out with others?
- Who do you socialize with?
- Are they positive influences in your life or do they tend to drag you down or depress you?

Personal Growth

- Have you taken any classes lately in areas of interest?
- Have you read any books recently that are designed to help you with relationships or your own self-esteem?

Finances

- How do you rate your financial situation?
- Are you meeting your financial obligations?
- Are you spending more than you make?

Children

- How do you feel about your relationship with your children?

This inventory of seeing if your life is in balance is another way of taking constructive action in dealing with stress. Many times adults or children will focus on one area of their lives and become obsessed with it and ignore the other areas of their lives. One man I counseled was in the pits in all areas of his life. When I asked him what he could do about it, he said if he doubled his salary in the next two months, life would be great. I asked him if he could do this, and he said no. He didn't come back to see me after my next comment, but I'll share it with you anyway.

I said, "If you walk to church, you could take care of the spiritual, social, physical and personal areas of your life." And furthermore that is something you CAN do. Most people cannot double their salary in two months. Another man was in the "pits" in all areas of his life, but all he was looking at was the physical area of his life. He kept a record of everything he ate, and was starting to read a book about what the iris in his eye was telling him about his life.

Many times I see parents focused solely on what their children are doing or not doing. This is also related to Codependency (Chapter 1). Parents become obsessed with getting their children "squared away," and they ignore the other 7 areas of their lives. This is a big mistake. Sometimes in spite of what parents do for their children, in spite of applying all the correct principles of parenting, children will not respond the way we think they should. If your total focus is on that one area of your life, you become too dependent on your children for how you feel about your life, and you'll try to force them into changes faster than it is possible for them to change.

One of the best ways to deal with stress is to make sure your life is in balance. After evaluating your life with the scale, set specific goals in each area that needs improving. Don't dismiss certain areas as unimportant—they are all important. If you have become turned off to religion or the spiritual aspects because of painful childhood memories, reconsider that area. Make a decision about that area out of your **adult mode**, not the child in you. If you do not like to socialize with others because as a child you were a loner, or had no one to talk to, don't write off that area, develop the confidence to begin to socialize.

Another way to look at the "life in balance scale" is to consider that you may derive your self-esteem from each of the above areas. Is your source of self-esteem in balance, or are you counting on getting 90% of your self-esteem from what your children say or do? Boy, are you in trouble if this is the case! You have then put your well-being and self-esteem in the hands of a 7-year-old or a 13-year-old. That's pretty shaky, isn't it? Are you basing 80% of your self-esteem on the physical aspect, or how you look or feel? Do you base 80% of your self-esteem on how your finances are going, or who you have socialized with lately, or how your marriage is going?

Adults should go through the above exercise at least every six months. Then, make changes to get your life in balance. Are your childrens' lives in balance? Granted, they may not have all the areas to deal with that you do, but they definitely have some of the areas. Are you helping them to make sure their life is in balance? Recently, I counseled a 15-year-old who was jilted by his girlfriend and was very upset. He wondered if he should ever get involved with girls again.

Naturally, he will need to grieve the loss of this girlfriend, but he also needs to make sure his life is in balance, and not count on all his happiness to come from relationships with girls. He needs to think about his school work, his involvement with the band at school, his youth group at church and his exercise, as well as his friendships with other boys and girls. He will be much more capable of dealing with stress if his life is in balance.

Another constructive strategy for dealing with stress at any level comes from the "Serenity Prayer":

God grant me the serenity to accept the things I cannot change, the courage to change the things I can, and the wisdom to know the difference.

All of our lives would run a lot more smoothly if we could incorporate that belief into our everyday living. There are many things in life that we cannot change. Adults as well as children need to accept that. However, there are also areas of our lives where we can make changes. We need to identify those areas and have the courage and wisdom to make the needed changes.

Change Our Attitude About The Stressor

What is your self-talk? What are you saying about the stressor?

Do you get up every morning and say, "I don't want to go to school or work," or "I hate having to do so much work"? Is your attitude: "Oh no! I know something bad is going to happen," or "I hate it when I have problems." Scott Peck in *The Road Less Traveled*[4] says, "Life is difficult . . . . Life is a series of problems. Do we want to moan about them or solve them? Do we want to teach our children to solve them?" Recently I counseled a man who was worried about losing his job. We discovered that his parents did not deal with problems, and were overwhelmed by life. Thus, he did not learn that when you have problems, you deal with them. He saw his parents ignore problems, so that is what he did at work. He ignored the problems of missed deadlines, etc., to such a degree, that he may lose his job. This is another example of how we all need to dig deeper and look at our childhood to gain more understanding of our current behavior as adults. What attitudes did your parents have about problems? How did you see your parents deal with stress? Parents need to watch their own self-talk and attitudes about stressors, and be a good model for their children.

For several weeks, Chrissy listened to me talk about being frustrated with some situations at work. One morning at breakfast, I told her that complaining about school wasn't really a good way to deal with stress. She caught me. She said that I was complaining about things at work, and she was right. Worrying and complaining are not very effective ways to deal with stress. Unfortunately, these were the only "tools" that many of us observed our parents using.

Help children develop more healthy attitudes about taking a test in school, choosing a college to go to, trying out for a sport, being asked to the prom, having trouble with a friend, etc.

Another way of describing this aspect of dealing with stress comes from the Rational Emotive Therapy approach to life and counseling. I have discussed irrational beliefs and Rational Emotive Therapy in Chapter 6, but will mention them briefly at this point. According to the theory, it's not the A (event) in our life that causes C (emotional pain), its our B (beliefs), or how we look at the event. When our beliefs or self-talk is irrational or "junk thought," we will end up more angry and stressed. When our self-talk and beliefs are more rational, we will end up less stressed and less angry.

One of the sayings that my kids know is, "Life is 10% what happens to you, and 90% how you look at it." One weekend morning, we drove 3 hours to go skiing—only to find the slopes closed due to high winds. That was the first time I mentioned, "life is 10% what happens to you and 90% how you look at it." We can complain and gripe, or we can say we had a nice car ride, fellowship with friends, and ate lots of junk food, or we can say life is not fair.

Eliminate The Stressor

The fourth way to deal with stress is to eliminate the stressor. Obviously, one cannot always do this but we need to keep this way in mind a little more than we do. One parent came to me because his four-year-old was stuttering. After discussing the child's daily schedule, it became obvious that she was over scheduled. It was necessary to cut out some of her activities. Why was she in so many activities? For the answer to that, look to Part I of this book. The parents wanted to give their child things they did not have as children (see the chapter on Frozen Needs and Parenting).

With Robyn's struggles in the Advanced Placement Physics class, the first three ways of dealing with stress were not much relief of the stress symptoms so we suggested that she drop the class and take regular Physics. There are many times when adults and children can and should deal with a stressor by eliminating the stressor from their lives. Keep this option in mind. We definitely cannot use this option in all occasions, but we need to be more open to the possibility of eliminating a stressor, especially if you have already attempted to utilize the first three approaches discussed.

SUMMARY

In order to be effective as parents we need to deal with stress in our lives. Stress symptoms will take away from your ability to parent your children. It is also extremely important for parents to teach their children how to deal with stress. Teaching involves ongoing instruction as situations come up, to help our youngsters incorporate stress management techniques into their tool kit.

ENDNOTES

1. Stoop, Dr. David, *Self Talk*, Old Tappan, New Jersey: Fleming H. Revell Co., 1982.
2. Miller, Mary Susan, The Holmes Rahe Life Event Scale *Childstress*, Garden City, New York: Doubleday & Co., 1982.
3. Elkind, Dr. David, *The Hurried Child*, Menlo Park, California: Addison-Wesley Publishing Co., 1981, pp. 22-23.
4. Peck, Scott, *The Road Less Traveled*, New York: Simon & Schuster, 1978.

12

Techniques For Dealing With Inappropriate Behavior

Several common errors that parents make when dealing with their youngster's inappropriate behavior are illustrated in two of my favorite cartoons. In the first one, a boxer is getting beaten to a pulp, and his trainer says, "Try ignoring him." Parents often do the same thing. They may be very frustrated with their child's behavior problem, but they chose to ignore the problem, hoping that it will somehow go away. The second cartoon depicts another very similar approach that is also not recommended. In this scene, the boxer is again getting beaten to a pulp, but his trainer simply says, "Forget strategy, . . . think survival." Many parents are simply trying to survive. Their children may only be 4 or 5-years-old, but they are already counting the years until they will be 18 and out of the house.

It is our job as parents to become motivated to develop a strategy, or to seek help to develop one. The following point is very obvious, but I have found it helpful to verbalize it to parents to help them become more relaxed and confident in their role. Your job as a parent is not to raise a "perfect" child, or to hope that by applying all the proper parenting techniques your child will not experience any problems. Your role is to identify the problems your youngster may be experiencing, and to develop a strategy to resolve the problem.

I have discussed many different parenting concepts that have hopefully helped you to develop a more accurate perspective on your role as a parent and the challenges you face. I have also discussed what parents must do in order to create a positive home climate. I stated that in addition to creating a positive home climate, you could also help prevent discipline problems. One can not totally prevent children from misbehaving, but there are certain procedures that will minimize the discipline problems. In spite of all our efforts, children will misbehave. When this happens, parents need to be able to deal with the misbehaviors in an effective manner. Parents need three major ingredients in their approach to parenting:

- They need to show their children unconditional love.
- They need to praise them for appropriate behaviors.
- They need to deal with misbehaviors appropriately.

Many parents have said to me, "Well, I've been positive and that doesn't work, so now tell me how to use punishment." Remember, you always need to have all three ingredients in your approach to parenting.

This chapter will present various strategies for dealing with inappropriate behaviors. A word of caution—do not rush into this section looking for ways to deal with inappropriate behaviors until you have really studied and have begun in the previous chapter to create a positive climate in the home. Parents are often amazed that the problem behavior seems to disappear when they create a positive home climate. I frequently tell parents (no matter what their present problem is), to go home and show unconditional love, and praise the child. Then they come back in two weeks to talk about what misbehavior they may still need to deal with.

The techniques for dealing with inappropriate behavior are presented in the sequence in which they should be considered, in order to help you in thinking through correct strategies.

Punishment

Events that occur following a behavior which weaken the future rate of such behaviors are called punishers. One cannot determine if a child has been punished by what the parent did. You can only determine if you punished your child by what happened to the behavior. If the behavior was reduced or eliminated, then it was punished.

Undoubtedly there is no other area in behavioral psychology where more emotion, misunderstanding, and confusion exists than in the area of punishment. Utilizing the definition above, "events that occur following a behavior which weaken the future rate of such behaviors are called punishers," parents will learn during this next section that punishers can include many different techniques. Parents often think only of physical punishments when they think of punishment, and not the variety of techniques that would also meet the definition described above. The following techniques can be considered punishers:

- Ignoring
- Mild Social Punishment
- Time-out
- Punishment or "X" Charts
- Physical Punishment or Spanking
- Logical Consequences

It's essential for all parents to set a positive climate in the home. The methods to accomplish this were discussed in the previous section on preventative approaches to behavior problems. Additionally, all parenting approaches need to include techniques to use when children choose to misbehave.

Therefore, the question is not "should we ever punish our child," but a question of how severe of a punishment is needed to deal with the behavior and the particular child. A saying I once heard is, "Don't take an elephant gun to kill a fly." Problems occur when parents use punishments that are too severe for the offense and the child. Some children are much more sensitive than others. For some youngsters, a stern look from the parent will affect the behavior significantly, whereas another youngster may require a physical spanking in order to "get the message."

Parents need to study and understand their children in order to know what is required to get them to discontinue the inappropriate behavior. Stated in a different way, parents need to understand each child's unique personality and temperament when considering what punisher or negative consequences to utilize. Another mistake parents frequently make is to try to rely only on the use of punishers to change a child's behavior. If parents are not showing unconditional love, praising appropriate behaviors, modeling appropriate behaviors, and allowing their youngsters to express their feelings, then the punishers used will be very ineffective. This creates a very poor relationship between parent and child.

When the punishment is too severe there can be several negative aspects associated with it:

1. When youngsters anticipate a severe punishment, they may be more inclined to lie to their parents in an attempt to escape the punishment. The severe punishment could be anything from a physical spanking, to being grounded for two months, or longer (like Richie on the sit-com, *Happy Days*, who was once grounded for life).

2. When youngsters are grounded for an extended period of time, or are not allowed to watch TV or play Nintendo, etc. for several weeks or a month, then parents lose (for that period of time) activities that they can utilize to reinforce their children's appropriate behaviors. Extensive punishment periods often become more of a punishment for the parents who must try to enforce it, than for the youngsters. Frequently, the parent will just give in or the child gradually gets all the privileges back, as the enforcement of the penalties becomes too difficult for the parents.

3. When punishments are too severe, youngsters tend to want to avoid the person who dispensed the punishment. Parents need to have their children come to them when they have a problem, and the use of severe punishments will cause youngsters to stay away from the parent instead.

4. When the punishment is physical spanking, children often learn that it is OK to use physical force to solve a problem. I was really embarrassed after spanking two of my children when they were young for fighting with each other. They were trying to settle their problems with physical force, and I was trying to teach them not to fight, by using physical force. It really doesn't make much sense when you really think about it. A parent of a five-year-old boy was upset that his boy was fighting with other kids at school. The father stated that he spanked his son every day that he heard that his son had been in a fight at school, but he still kept fighting. Using physical punishment is modeling to children that it is OK to solve problems with physical force.

The pros and cons of the punishers listed above will be discussed in the forthcoming sections. The sequence to use in applying them will also be discussed. All of the techniques listed above are utilized following a particular behavior and serve to eliminate that behavior.

The first three techniques that I will review are thoroughly discussed by Robert Eimers and Robert Aitchison, Ph.D., in their book *Effective Parents, Responsible Children.*[1] The three techniques are: *Ignoring, Mild Social Punishment and Time-out*. I encourage you to consult their book for additional information on these three techniques.

Ignoring

One major reason that children misbehave is to get attention. For this reason, ignoring is often a very effective technique. When parents pay a lot of attention to their child's misbehavior, they are teaching their children that inappropriate behavior pays off. Ignoring works best on behaviors that are obvious efforts to gain parental attention.

Some examples would include temper tantrums, sulking, whining, crying from their beds at bedtime, and fighting over a toy. Ignoring can also be used for behaviors that have just occurred for the first time. An example would be the time when your child says his first profane word. Just don't be like one parent who was upset with Dear Abby because she had told the parent to ignore her son's profanity—18 years later, the son was still swearing. I am sure that Abby did not mean to ignore the swearing for 18 years.

Eimers and Aitchison spell out the following basic components of proper **ignoring**:[2]

1. *Look away from your child.*

    Direct eye contact can be a reward, and is therefore not desirable.

2. *Move away from your child.*

Physical proximity can be rewarding to a child. Research data suggests that parents must move at least three feet away from a misbehaving child for ignoring to be maximally effective. Parents could even leave the room.

3. *Neutral facial expressions.*

Remember a smile can be a reward, so your facial expression should be matter-of-fact.

4. *Ignore your child's verbalizations.*

Do not respond to any of your child's verbalizations. It is alright for you to say something like "I'm going to ignore you when you whine," but only say it once.

5. *Ignore immediately.*

The sooner you can ignore the misbehavior the better.

6. *Begin to praise and reinforce appropriate behaviors as soon as you see them after having ignored some misbehavior.*

SALLY FORTH by Greg Howard

Reprinted with permission of North American Syndicate, Inc.

This mother has decided to use the technique of "ignoring" inappropriate behavior (whining and complaining). She will be successful if she can hang in there and realize that the whining and complaining will get worse before it gets better. The mother also needs to reward appropriate behaviors, not simply ignore inappropriate ones.

There are several other points to consider about ignoring that are extremely important. To be effective in eliminating an undesirable behavior, the behavior must be ignored completely. If you and your spouse ignore a particular behavior but another child gives it attention, then the behavior is not being ignored. When Matt was about three-years-old, he began to stutter. Well, the appropriate technique is ignoring, which my wife and I were doing quite well. Robyn who was about 7 at the time, was calling Matt "Porky Pig" because of the way he was talking.

We had to elicit her help in ignoring Matt's stuttering, and before long he was over it. In the classroom, a teacher could ignore a spit ball flying across the room, but I doubt that 30 students would ignore it. Ignoring would probably not be the best technique to use in that situation. There is another reason why ignoring would not be effective in that situation. An important principle to remember is that when you ignore a behavior, it will get worse before it gets better. If you can't allow the behavior to get worse, ignoring is not the technique to use.

Parents often do a very good job of ignoring a particular behavior one, two or maybe three times, then they slip and give it attention. This will set you back more than you might realize. It's also, as previously stated, vitally important that both parents, other children, and grandparents if they are involved, learn to ignore the target behavior. If everyone involved with the youngster will not or cannot ignore the behavior, then you'll be better off selecting another approach.

Mild Social Punishment

A second technique used in dealing with inappropriate behavior is mild social punishment. This sounds pretty complicated, but it is a very simple, yet effective technique. It does require the parents to get up out of the easy chairs and stop what they are doing to move closer to their child, and deliver a brief statement in a calm voice. The technique is designed to terminate a low intensity inappropriate behavior, and keep an explosive situation from exploding into something bigger.

Mild social punishment is a useful technique that causes relatively little pain. It is one of the least severe of all punishment techniques. It is a little more severe than ignoring, but much less severe than other techniques which will be mentioned later. The following are the seven components of mild social punishment as discussed in the book by Eimers and Aitchison[3]. It is important to utilize all seven components to make its application most effective.

1. Look at your child.
2. Move close to your child (within three feet).
3. Demonstrate a disapproving facial expression.
4. State in one or two sentences what you expect of your child, or want them to stop. For example, "stop fighting right now."
5. Do not yell and scream, but speak in a normal voice level.
6. Use a non-verbal gesture consistent with disapproval.
7. Deliver Mild Social Punishment as soon as you observe the target behavior.

Mild Social Punishment must be delivered calmly, smoothly and quickly in order to be maximally effective. Similar to the technique of ignoring, and the next technique, time-out, it is important to follow the technique with praising your child for appropriate behavior, possibly through the use of the Marbles In the Jar idea.

Time-out

Time-out is an abbreviated way of saying "time-out" from any positive rewards or attention. Time-out involves placing a child in a situation where he receives no attention, nor does he have the opportunity to engage in any rewarding activites. The place for time-out is up to you as long as it meets this criteria. Parents could use a bathroom, bedroom or a corner in the kitchen. Use time-out for only one behavior at a time, otherwise, your child will become confused, and will not remember what you want him to stop doing. According to Eimers and Aitchison, the following points should be followed when using **time-out**:[4]

1. Remain matter of fact. Don't lose your temper.

2. When you see the target behavior, simply state the rule and the consequence, and have the child go to the time-out location. Some children may have to be carried there, or put in their room, after which you hold the door closed.

3. Ignore all the child's verbalizations or pleas for a reprieve.

4. Deliver time-out as soon as you see the target behavior.

5. A rule of thumb is that the length of time-out should be one minute per year of the child's age. Thus a four-year-old would be in time-out 4 minutes.

As with ignoring and mild social punishment, remember to praise your youngsters after they leave time-out and demonstrate an appropriate behavior. It is very good practice to reward a behavior that is opposite to the inappropriate target behavior. For example, use the Marbles In the Jar idea, and praise your youngsters when you see them playing together nicely if you are using time-out for fighting. Punishment tells your children what you do not like, but it does not tell them what you want. A child learns appropriate behavior mainly through rewards.

The techniques of ignoring, mild social punishment, and time-out are probably most effective with children between the ages of one and nine. The techniques can often be used in sequence, going from ignoring, to mild social punishment, to the use of time-out. Initially, parents should zero in on one particular behavior, study the techniques, then apply them consistently while monitoring the effect it has on the behavior.

In this way, you will become more comfortable with the techniques, and applying them will become much more natural. The next section will discuss several charts that can be used to deal with inappropriate behaviors. These charts utilize procedures that are stronger than these three techniques. They may also be more appropriate when it is difficult to apply time-out procedures. The charts can be used for children from about five-years-old up to the teenage years, thus they cover a somewhat different range of ages than the three techniques just discussed.

Punishment Or "X" Charts

Ignoring, mild social punishment, and time-out are very effective techniques for a variety of behaviors and ages. However, there will be some situations where these techniques will be inappropriate or ineffective. Ignoring, mild social punishment and time-out are generally most effective with younger children. The following punishment charts are stronger techniques and may be much easier for parents to utilize, based on your youngster's temperament and what you may have already tried with them. The "X" charts will also be easier to use and more effective with teenagers than the technique of time-out.

The punishment, or "X" charts are especially effective for behaviors such as fighting or talking back, but can also be used for behaviors such as getting ready for school on time. The steps are simple but must be followed carefully if the results are to be successful.

When our oldest daughter Robyn entered kindergarten (15 years ago), we began to have hassles every morning about getting her to school. We had hassles over getting her hair combed, getting her dressed, and getting her shoes and socks on. I am always amazed to remember how long we hassled with her before we thought of a strategy and implemented it. About the first of November (school started in September), my wife and I decided that we should "think strategy, not survival." We set up the following chart (Figure 1) to deal with her behavior:

FIGURE 1

Punishment Chart Or "X" Chart

	MON.	TUES.	WED.	THUR.	FRI.	
Put shoes on	★					Watch T.V.
Put clothes on	NO					Dessert
Get hair combed						Play with a friend

★: Indicates the child put his/her shoes on.

No: Indicates the child did not perform the task.

Steps To Take To Implement The Chart

FIRST STEP

Define very specifically the behaviors you expect of your child. Do not say "be good" or "be nice." Use statements such as:

1. Get dressed in the morning before school without complaining.
2. Put your shoes on in the morning before school without complaining.
3. Feed the dog every night before dinner.
4. Put your toys in the toy box before going to school.

Involve your child in defining those behaviors whenever possible as this will make it very clear what you expect of him or her.

As shown in Figure 1, we zeroed in specifically on factors related to Robyn getting ready for school on time without all the hassles.

SECOND STEP

Determine what your child likes to do or would be willing to work for if given free time. Examples may be: eat some dessert, watch TV after school, or play with a friend. You must select things your child really likes. To determine this, just watch him for a few days to see what he does with free time. You also need to select things that you have some control over. In other words, if you work at night and cannot monitor his TV watching, then don't select that as the activity that you will restrict.

THIRD STEP

Set up a chart to post in his room or in the kitchen. See Figure Number 1. If your child cannot read, draw pictures of each item as a reminder of what your expectations are. If your child performs the desired task, draw a star, or write "yes," or draw a happy face on the square under the day of the week. If he does not perform the task, place a "no" or a sad face in the square. After several days of using the chart, our daughter began to draw her own stars in the spaces.

FOURTH STEP

Explain the chart to your child. You may want to say that you are tired of the hassles you and he have been having over certain things, and that from now on, it will be his responsibility to decide if he wants to perform the desired behavior. On the sample chart shown, explain that if he feeds the dog, he will get to watch TV after school. If he doesn't, don't hassle him, just deprive him of watching TV for the day. The next day he will get another chance—it will be a whole new ball game and you can both start fresh. You must impress upon the child that he is responsible for deciding what he will do. Whether or not the desired behavior will be accomplished will be his choice.

FIFTH STEP

Verbally praise your child when he completes the desired behavior. Catch him being good throughout the day, and praise some desirable behavior at least three times a day. It may also be helpful to reinforce your child's efforts over the period of the entire week, such as telling him, "you can earn 1 cent (or five cents) for each star or 'yes'. When you earn 10 to 15 stars, we'll go to a movie or take a trip to the beach."

SIXTH STEP

After several weeks to a month, you will probably be ready to phase out the chart. This may happen naturally, such as at Christmas break, or when a long term goal has been reached, such as a trip to the beach. You may just stop doing it if the child's behavior appears to have improved so that few reminders are necessary for him to complete the desired tasks. But you must keep on praising his good behavior if you expect it to continue. Do not be in a big hurry to eliminate the chart. Remember, it takes time to change a behavior, and the chart helps make very clear what you expect and what the consequences (both positive and negative) are. This can reduce arguing over rules and consequences.

Cautions

1. Do not argue with your child as to whether he performed the desired behavior. Spell out the behavior, so there is no question as to whether or not the task was performed. In other words, if you told me the behavior, and I came to your house, there should be no doubt in my mind as to whether or not the behavior occurred. It is very important never to argue with your youngster. If you argue, you will not be effective, nor will you be in control—your child will be.

2. Verbally praise your child for successful behavior when marks are placed on the chart for each day. Do not lecture if the desired behavior was not performed, just say, "I know you will choose to do better tomorrow, so good luck."

3. Remind the child that it is he who is deciding whether or not to earn the reinforcer.

4. Be consistent. Do not give in to crying or pleading from your child if he did not perform the desired task.

This procedure is very similar to the previously mentioned chore charts. However, this system is more focused on specific behavior, and ties the child's performance to preferred activities. Thus, the system is stronger than Mild Social Punishment or Time-out, and can be more effective in changing behavior, at least initially, than a chore chart.

For Inappropriate Behavior
That May Occur Throughout The Day

A different type of chart (Figure 2) is necessary for behavior that may occur more than once during the day. Inappropriate behavior that could occur many times during the day include:

- Talking back
- Fighting with a sibling
- Interrupting you while you are on the phone
- Using profanity

FIGURE 2

Punishment Chart Or "X" Chart

	Warning	Dessert	Play with a Friend	T.V.	Go to Bed Early
MONDAY					
TUESDAY					
WEDNESDAY					
THURSDAY					
FRIDAY					
SATURDAY					
SUNDAY					

STATE THE "TARGET" BEHAVIOR THAT YOU ARE WORKING ON:

List the days of the week down the left hand edge of the paper and across the top list "warning", and then any items your child would not like to have happen. Examples are:

- no dessert
- no TV
- no playing with friends
- going to bed early

These are only examples. You need to pick activities that your son or daughter would not like to miss out on, and also items over which you have control. Each time your child demonstrates the inappropriate behavior, calmly state the rule, "Remember, there will be no talking back" and with his/her knowledge place an "X" under the box headed "warning." Remember to work on only one behavior at a time. It's too confusing to both parents and children to use the chart for more than one, or at the most two behaviors at one time. Then, each time your child demonstrates the inappropriate behavior, calmly place an "X" under the next activity on the list. Be sure to calmly let your youngster know that you are marking the chart, by stating the rule and the consequence.

This system will change his behavior much more quickly and with less hassle than yelling and spanking. Additionally, you can take the chart with you to a friend's house or to a restaurant. In fact, after using it for a while, you will not need to take it with you, but you can simply state the rule and say, "you have received one 'X'." The youngster will remember what that means.

This system for dealing with inappropriate behaviors incorporates many of the important principles of changing behaviors:

1. The rule or behavior needs to be spelled out very specifically.
2. Follow through needs to be consistent.
3. Parents should not use anger and emotion.

Physical Punishment Or Spanking

Punishment is something that follows a particular behavior and causes that behavior to weaken or cease happening. One can not determine if they are punishing the child by the parent's behavior, but only by observing what happens to the child's behavior. As I stated earlier, if your child draws a picture on the wall with a crayon and you spank his hand, this may be a punishment or it may be a reward. If the behavior stops or weakens, then you have punished the child. If the child draws a bigger picture the next day, then you rewarded the child. In other words, spanking or the use of physical punishment is not necessarily "punishment."

I encourage parents to show unconditional love, increase the amount of praise and rewards for appropriate behavior, and determine what punishers are necessary to deal with the still existing misbehavior. Often parents report that much misbehavior has been eliminated as a result of showing more unconditional love and rewarding appropriate behavior.

Parents particularly need to reward behavior that is in contradiction to the misbehavior. In other words, if fighting is a problem with your children, then praise them or use the Marbles In the Jar idea to reinforce them for getting along together and for sharing toys with each other. If your child interrupts you while you are on the phone, then be sure to reward him through praise, etc. for waiting patiently while you were talking on the phone.

The question is not whether or not to use punishment when dealing with children. The question or concern for parents needs to be about the correct use of punishers. I have already discussed several different punishers in this section:

- Ignoring
- Mild Social Punishment
- Time-out
- Punishment Charts

All of these are negative consequences or punishers that can be utilized when a youngster misbehaves. The important point is that parents must be aware of all the possible negative consequences that they can use, and must apply the right one at the right time with the right child. Frequently, parents only have one tool in their parenting tool kit—spanking or physical punishment. They are unaware of all other possibilities. There is definitely a place for spanking, but there are also some things to look out for when using this technique or any other punishment that may be too severe for the "crime."

Physical punishment or spanking should be used:

1. When your child is young, up until about age four or five.

2. When there is no other technique that will have an impact on the youngster.

3. When the child is in danger of hurting themselves. For example, if he is going to touch a hot plate, spank him on the hand and say "No! Do not touch that!" If your toddler has run into the street, spank him on the bottom, and say "No! Stay out of the street!" If possible, spank him while you both are still in the middle of the street. That way, he will associate pain with the middle of the street. Obviously, if cars are coming down the street, you both need to get out of the way.

> One of my favorite cartoons depicts a young boy hurting from a spanking and saying to his parents, "If you're trying to get something into my head, you're working on the wrong end!" Although physical punishment is an appropriate technique, when used at the right time, teens and children learn best through rewards for appropriate behavior, rather than punishing inappropriate behavior.

When any form of punishment is too severe, the parents may cause other behaviors in their child that they also do not like. Children tend to avoid a person who is too strict or who mostly dishes out punishment. We want our children to come to us when they have a problem. However, if you apply punishments that are unreasonable, your youngsters may not come to you when they have a problem.

Parents should start with negative consequences that are less harmful, then move to more severe consequences if the behavior does not change. If you've **ignored** sibling fights and they still continue, move to **mild social punishment**, or **time-out**. If those are not successful, move to the use of "X" charts. You don't always have to go through this sequence, but it should at least be considered.

When parents use too much physical punishment, there can be other harmful side effects in addition to the one stated above. Physical punishment teaches children that it is OK to use force to solve a problem. Consequently, they may use fighting at school if they have a problem with another student.

When any punishment is too severe, children may develop negative avoidance behavior such as: cheating, truancy, running away, lying, or hiding.

Parents need to be aware that spanking is reinforcing to the user. When a parent spanks a child, they may see the behavior change for the moment, so they may be reinforced to use it again. When parents spank, they relieve some of their frustrations, and may also feel that spanking is effective. Parents need to consider the long-term effects, not just the short-term effects of spanking. A study was done with two groups of students and mathematical achievement. With one group the teacher was more punishing and demanding. This group did more work than the group which the teacher encouraged and praised.

However, 10 years down the road, the group that was punished did not even want to balance a checkbook, because they had been turned off to math. The group that had been encouraged still enjoyed math, even though their initial output was much lower than the "punished" group.

Many parents have heard and read that physical punishment or spanking is the correct procedure in the case where a child has been willfully disobedient. If you tell a child not to do something, and 2 seconds later he does it anyway, then possibly it's a case of willful disobedience, and spanking is in order. However, it has been my experience that many parents have trouble differentiating willful disobedience from childhood irresponsibility. Many parents end up interpreting all misbehavior as willful disobedience to justify to themselves that physical punishment is in order. **Part I**, Chapter 6 on Irrational Beliefs will help you investigate how your interpretation of your child's behavior affects your subsequent reaction to them.

DIGGING DEEPER

How did your parents discipline you? Did they use a lot of physical punishment? If your parents used a lot of physical punishment, you may have made a vow that you would never spank your children. In this case, reread Chapter 3 (Vows). Or possibly, you may feel very justified in spanking regularly, in which case Chapter 2 (Recreating Your "At Home" Feeling) would be important to reread. In either case, you need to deal with your past, then investigate other forms of punishment and make sure the punishment fits the crime.

Sometimes adults who had very punitive parents are willing to use a technique such as logical consequences, but then want to add on some physical punishment. They may say to their child, "If you don't eat dinner then you'll have to go to bed hungry," but then they'll also feel it is appropriate to spank the child as well. If your parents used physical punishment a great deal, then you may feel you are just disciplining your child when you yourself use physical punishment.

Other Dragon chapters that may be of assistance if you find yourself using excessive physical punishment are:

Codependency—Chapter 1, Unresolved Resentment—Chapter 7, and Dealing With a Loss—Chapter 8.

Husbands and wives frequently disagree on the use of physical punishment. It's important for parents to discuss their own childhood experiences with each other, to be able to resolve differences in this area. Frequently, one parent is very strict and the other parent becomes too lenient in order to offset the strict parent. This type of approach is detrimental to the children as well as the husband and wife relationship.

Logical Consequences

Another very powerful technique for dealing with inappropriate behaviors is called logical consequences. Logical consequences can be used for children of all ages, and it is successful in dealing with many types of problems. Although I am discussing it following the techniques of ignoring, mild social punishment, and time-out, the use of logical consequences does not have to follow the use of these three techniques. Several books have been devoted entirely to the principles of logical consequences, and I encourage the reader to consult them for a more detailed discussion. One book, by Rudolf Dreikurs and Loren Gray, is entitled: *A New Approach to Discipline: Logical Consequence*.[5] Another book is *Help! I'm a Parent*, by Bruce Narramore.[6]

I will present a brief description of the concepts, and give you some practical situations where a logical consequence would be a very effective intervention to eliminate undesirable behavior.

The term natural consequence has been defined as denoting the natural results of ill-advised acts. If a child runs into the street, he or she may get struck by a car. That's a natural consequence of running into the street. If a youngster were to touch a hot plate, they would be burned. That's a natural consequence of touching the hot plate. If a child plays with matches, he may burn himself or the house. That would be a natural consequence of playing with matches. Parents need to help protect their children from natural consequences, not allow them to happen as a teaching tool. Parents must also educate their children to help them from engaging in behaviors that could result in harm to themselves or others.

The term logical consequence has been used to define situations where the consequences are arranged by the parent or another adult, and are not solely the result of the child's own acts. Additionally, with logical consequence there will not be severe physical or psychological harm to the youngster.

As discussed earlier in the book, youngsters today do not have the respect for authority figures that children had 20 or 30 years ago. Children no longer simply agree with authority figures but have begun to question authority to a much greater extent. I am not condoning this, or saying it's OK, but I am just stating a fact that we need to consider in our approach to parenting.

Dreikurs and Gray have utilized the following criteria to contrast logical consequences from punishment:

1. Logical consequences express the reality of the social order, not of the person. Punishment is the power of a personal authority.

2. The logical consequence is logically related to the misbehavior whereas punishment rarely is.

3. Logical consequences involve no element of moral judgement. Punishment inevitably does.

4. Logical consequences are concerned only with what will happen now. Punishment is concerned with the past.

5. The voice of the parent is friendly when logical consequences are invoked. There is anger in punishment, either open or concealed.

The technique of logical consequences is very useful. With this technique, the parent needs to remain calm, avoiding the use of anger and emotion to change the child's behavior. Allowing a youngster to experience a logical consequence is often much more effective than 10 lectures on the subject. It's much more effective than constantly nagging or reminding your child of something he needs to do or not do. It's often however, very hard for many parents to keep quiet and allow the logical consequence to teach the lesson.

Before listing some example behaviors and a logical consequence, I must let you know that logical consequences will not be appropriate for some behaviors. Do not continue to rack your brain thinking of a logical consequence for behaviors such as swearing, or low grades in school. Other techniques are needed in these situations, such as the "X" Chart or fine system for swearing, and the school-to-home communication system for low grades in school.

Here are are some examples of using logical consequences. The voice of the adult needs to be friendly when discussing the logical consequence, the consequence must be logically related to the misbehavior and it should be presented to the child as a choice.

BEHAVIOR

A young child does not get ready for school on time.

Logical Consequence

Explain to the child that if he is not ready for school when a timer goes off, then you will take him to school the way he is dressed. This seemed to be a very common problem among teachers who I worked with as a school psychologist. They would struggle to get their young children dressed and to the babysitter or preschool before they had to be at work. After explaining the techniques, one mother simply said to her three-year-old, "If you are not ready for school when the timer goes off, I will take you to school the way you are. Do you understand?"

The next day, the child tested the limit. I told the mother

she could let him take his clothes with him in the car. Have you ever seen a three-year-old get dressed in the back seat of a car with three other kids? It happened, and there were fewer hassles the next day. Remember also to set up a reward system, concurrently, such as the Marbles In the Jar idea, for getting dressed on time.

BEHAVIOR

Your children come home late for dinner.

Logical Consequence

When this happens, simply tell them that from now on when they are late for dinner, they will have to eat a cold dinner or go without dinner. Remember, you need to remain calm. Do not state these things in an angry, hostile manner.

BEHAVIOR

Your child breaks something around the house, or loses some particle of clothing or a baseball glove, etc.

Logical Consequence

Since it is our responsibility to teach our children, if they break or lose something, we should pay at least half the cost. Besides, if you charged them the whole amount they would probably be in debt for 3 years.

BEHAVIOR

Your children waste their money on candy or toys then do not have money for the fair when it comes to town.

Logical Consequence

The logical consequence is that they don't have any money for the fair, and hopefully they will plan better the next year. Does this sound cold and heartless to you? Remember, your job as a parent is not to be a pal to your children, but to teach them how to be responsible adults. It's OK to remind your children that the fair is coming and they need to save their money ahead of time. Doing that may also help you to feel less guilty when they choose to spend their money and not save it for the fair.

BEHAVIOR

Your children do not put their dirty clothes in the hamper.

Logical Consequence

A logical consequence would be that the clothes do not get washed. Do not nag them about it. If you can't stand the clothes smelling up the house, then it would probably be OK to wash the clothes, just do not give them to the children for a week.

BEHAVIOR

Your children do not eat their dinner.

Logical Consequence

To me, it's logical that if children do not eat their dinner, they do not get dessert and they go to bed hungry. Remember you present this to the child as a choice. "If and when you eat your dinner, you can have dessert (if we are having dessert)." Ignore all the subsequent whining and complaining.

BEHAVIOR

Your children leave toys out.

Logical Consequence

It would be logical to simply put the toys in a box or on top of the refrigerator and tell them they will not get the toys for three days. If they don't miss the toy, that may tell you that you are spoiling them and they have too many toys. Also, the particular toy may not be that important. Don't give up. Using this technique will help you to avoid getting angry, and eventually you will seize a "meaningful" toy and the lesson will be taught.

BEHAVIOR

Your children spill something at a meal.

Logical Consequence

Simply have them clean it up. Remember to stay calm. (Refer to Chapter 11 where I wrote about how to stay calm.) You could also not give the child anything else to drink at that meal.

BEHAVIOR

Your children fight over a game, such as Nintendo.

Logical Consequence

It would be logical to forbid them to play with it until they can play cooperatively, or put it away for the day and let them try to get along with it the next day. Parents should also help the youngsters to figure out a way to resolve their disagreement. Parents can suggest possible solutions and allow the youngsters to choose one.

For Better Or For Worse by Lynn Johnston

For Better Or For Worse Copyright 1982, 1983, 1986, 1988 Lynn Johnston,
Reprinted with permission of Universal Press Syndicate.

This mother is trying the technique of nagging and is becoming very frustrated. She could possibly use logical consequences or set up a chore chart to reward appropriate behaviors. Nagging and reminding will definitely not work.

Logical consequences is a very powerful technique. The lesson might not be learned the first time, since children will continue to test the limits, but eventually they will get the message, and you will feel less stressful and angry as you use **logical consequences**. When using this technique, remember to not nag or remind your children constantly, but warn them, and then follow through depending on the choices they make. Remember, there is not a **logical consequence** for every behavior. Also, **logical consequences** will not be effective unless you are doing the things discussed in Chapter 10—Creating A Positive Home Climate.

DIGGING DEEPER

If you have found it difficult to implement the tool of logical consequences, there may be several Dragon chapters that you need to reread.

Codependents (Chapter 1) often need to be in control, and often try to force children to do the right thing. They may have difficulty in giving their youngster choices and allowing them to experience the consequences of their choices. If you were raised in a very punitive or overly coercive environment, then you may be Recreating Your "At Home" Feeling (Chapter 2) and thus are unable to allow your youngster to experience the consequences of their choices. Irrational Beliefs (Chapter 6) may be present, if you think that a child should make the right choices, and not make mistakes.

School-To-Home Communication System To Resolve School Problems

The school-to-home communication system is a very effective program to help deal with a variety of school problems. I have used this system for over 12 years in a variety of settings for youngsters from four-years-old to high school students. If your child is experiencing academic or behavioral problems in school, then the school-to-home communication system is an excellent program to use to improve and maintain appropriate school behaviors. This system can be used at the beginning of the school year to help your student get off to a good start. Parents and teachers are often reluctant to do this. They want to give the student a fair chance to have a good year, even if his previous year was poor.

Why take a chance? Why wait till the youngster digs himself a hole and then try and help him? All students tend to be on their best behavior the first week or two of school, so we ought to take advantage of this, and utilize this system to help get the students off to a good start. This system can also be implemented any time during the school year.

Parents and teachers often meet during the school year to discuss the problems a student may be experiencing. Very often, all the problems are discussed and the meeting is concluded without any plan of action suggested to improve the student's behavior. This can be very frustrating to all parties. The school-to-home communication system is an excellent approach to utilize in many cases.

This program is generally designed for students who have the potential to succeed academically but who are demonstrating significant behavioral difficulties. These students may demonstrate one or more of the following behaviors:

- Disruptiveness in class
- Chronic truancy or tardiness
- Constant arguing
- Refusal to follow directions
- Failure to complete work they are capable of completing
- Being highly unorganized
- Having an inconsistent work pattern and grades or Attention Deficit Disorder With or Without Hyperactivity.

Treatment approaches and philosophies vary on Attention Deficit Disorder With or Without Hyperactivity (ADD), from diet to vitamins to medications. I strongly recommend that parents and teachers utilize the school-to-home communication system before pursuing medications or other interventions from a doctor. The use of medication should be the last resort. This system, when applied correctly, is very effective, and has frequently resolved situations in which it appeared medication was needed. I am not saying you should use this for years before considering medication. A trial period of 2 to 4 weeks should be sufficient to determine what effect a well structured system with good motivators will have on the child's behavior. Prior to considering medication, parents also need to look at their approach to discipline, and make sure they are effectively and consistantly using all the parenting tools discussed in this book. If medication is ultimately utilized (this should only be considered after an in-depth study of all the factors), the daily system should still be used to reinforce positive behaviors, and to help the school and parents work together effectively.

Setting Up The Program

FIRST STEP

The first step toward setting up the school-to-home communication system is to define and list the desired behaviors. The teacher and parent can work together to establish the list of desired behaviors. It is also possible, depending on the student's age and willingness to cooperate, to involve him in selecting the target behaviors. Sometimes parents have a good knowledge of the problems, because they have already talked to the current teachers or know from previous years, and can present a list to the teachers of possible behaviors to work on.

Parents do not have to sit around and wait for the teacher to come up with the idea. Parents do need to try to solicit the teacher's cooperation in using the program. It will require some additional time on the part of the teacher, but in the long run, it will reduce the amount of attention she has to devote to your child. Letting the teacher know how you plan to follow up at home, as well as starting out with a trial period of three weeks will aid you in getting cooperation from the teacher.

SECOND STEP

Once you decide on the target behaviors, the next step is to put the behaviors on a form that can be easily completed by the classroom teacher. Examples include:

1. A form with 20 behaviors (page 300), which could be used from grades 1 or 2 to 5 or 6. This form can be shortened to fit the circumstances as well as the age of the child.

2. A form with 5 behaviors (page 301) and space to fill in for 7 teachers. This format is more suitable for middle school or high school where the youngster has more than one teacher. This form could also be used by one teacher, on a weekly basis, simply by changing the numbered periods to the days of the week.

In this situation, the form could be sent home at the end of the week and the teacher could establish her own agreement with the student, and not necessarily involve the parents. I only suggest this in cases where the parent might not be able to or willing to cooperate with the necessary follow through at home.

NAME _____ DAY/DATE _____

HOME/SCHOOL COMMUNICATION SYSTEM

BEHAVIOR DESIRED	YES	NO	COMMENT
1. Came to school and class on time			
2. Completed Math Assignment			
3. Completed Spelling Assignment			
4. Completed Reading Assignment			
5. Completed Assignment			
6. In the morning: Raised hand before talking			
7. Followed teacher's direction			
8. Used proper language			
9. Got permission to leave seat			
10. Allowed others to work			
11. In the afternoon: Raised hand before talking			
12. Followed teacher's direction			
13. Used proper language			
14. Got permission to leave seat			
15. Allowed others to work			
16. A.M. Recess: Followed playground rules			
17. Noon Recess: Followed playground rules			
18. P.M. Recess or P.E.: Followed playground rules			
19. Caught doing something good			
20. Caught doing something good			
TOTAL YES			

TEACHER'S SIGNATURE _____

PARENT'S SIGNATURE _____

This form will be taken home each day and returned the next day.

Home/School Communication System

Student's Name _____   Day/Date _____

Period Teacher's Init.	1	2	3	4/5	6	7	8
1. Comes to class on time.	yes - no	yes - no	yes - no	yes - no	yes - no	yes - no	yes - no
2. Brings the necessary materials to class	yes - no	yes - no	yes - no	yes - no	yes - no	yes - no	yes - no
3. Completes classroom assignments.	yes - no	yes - no	yes - no	yes - no	yes - no	yes - no	yes - no
4. Follows classroom rules.	yes - no	yes - no	yes - no	yes - no	yes - no	yes - no	yes - no
5. Treats teacher and students with respect.	yes - no	yes - no	yes - no	yes - no	yes - no	yes - no	yes - no
						TOTAL "Yes"	

- -

(a)   This form will be taken home each day, signed by the parent and returned to the office.

(b)   Student receives all "no's" for a period when sent to the office.

(c)   Teachers and parents can write comments on this side.

COMMENTS: _____

_____

_____

_____

_____

Parent's Signature

THIRD STEP

Establish the criteria level or goal. All parties should be involved in this decision. The goal would be a certain number of "Yes" responses on the chart which appears to be a reasonable amount for the student to shoot for. If there are:

- 20 behaviors—13 to 18 "Yes" responses
- 8 behaviors—the goal might be 5 to 7
- 5 behaviors and 7 teachers (or a possible 35 "Yes" responses)—the goal might be anywhere from 20 to 30

The above numbers should serve as a rough guideline. Obviously the age of the child, his ability level, and his current level of performance are all factors to be considered.

FOURTH STEP

Develop the contract by first selecting the short-term and long-term reinforcers. Possible short-term or daily reinforcers include:

1. Playing with friends after school.
2. Riding a bike after school or to school.
3. Going to the Boy's Club or Girls Club.
4. Watching TV.
5. Listening to the radio or record player.
6. Staying up somewhat longer than the normal bedtime.
7. Earning 25 cents a day.
8. Getting dessert that night.
9. Practicing baseball, soccer, etc.
10. Riding a skateboard.
11. Going shopping with the family.
12. Using the telephone.

Parents should choose two or three of these that they feel would be very important to their child, or think of similar types of activities that the child would hate to miss out on.

If the child achieves his goal for that day, then he would receive the selected reinforcers. Parents can use the same 2 or 3 reinforcers for each day. If the student falls short of the goal for the day, he loses out on those 2 or 3 privileges for that day, but can start over the very next day.

Many parents and teachers set up systems where a student is on restriction for weeks or months. I do not suggest this, at least not initially. In my opinion, the shorter the restriction the better, provided some improvements are seen in the student's behavior and performance in school. Parents and teachers should also give the student plenty of verbal praise for his efforts in school and his achievement of the goals. Possible long-term reinforcers include:

1. Buying a ball, bat, record, skateboard, doll, etc.
2. Spending the night with a friend.
3. Earning money to take the family out to dinner.
4. Going to the show with mom or dad.
5. Going fishing with dad or mom.
6. Going out to lunch with mom or dad.

Each contract should include at least one long-term reinforcer. The long-term reinforcer would be earned when the student earns a certain number of "yes" responses. For example, if the student can earn up to 20 "yes" responses a day, then the long-term reinforcers could be earned when the student reaches 100 or 150 total "yes" responses. Each day, the parent should help the student add that day's total to the previous day's. In this way, even if the student doesn't reach his criteria level for that day, the student would be allowed to add up the day's total toward a long-term goal.

Once the short-term and long-term reinforcers have been selected, a contract could be drawn up and signed by all interested parties.

I Have An Offer You Can't Refuse

If Johnny earns 16 YES responses out of a possible 20 by the end of the day; Then he can:

   (1)   Watch TV

   (2)   Earn 25 cents

   (3)   Stay up until 9:00 p.m.
            (normal bedtime is 8:30 p.m.)

When Johnny earns 150 YES responses Dad and he will go fishing.

Teacher _____

Student _____

Parents/
Principal _____

If necessary, the contract could be revised after each week. The target behaviors could be changed, as could the criteria level, dependent on how the student performs.

Since it takes time for a student's behavior to change, it may be appropriate to continue using the contract for several months. If this is the case, new long-term reinforcers would have to be selected. As a student improves on certain target behaviors, it may be helpful to change them to other behaviors that the student needs to work on. Parents and teachers are often in a hurry to stop the system. Don't be. It becomes very easy to complete the form, it provides tremendous positive strokes to the student, and it keeps the parents informed and involved with the educational process.

It will be necessary at some point to discontinue the system. This may occur at a natural break in the school year, such as Christmas vacation or spring break. You may also decide to discontinue the daily system after several long-term goals have been achieved. Achieving goals greatly enhances a student's self-esteem. When you discontinue the daily system be sure to request at least a weekly report for several weeks before discontinuing the regular school-to-home communication.

Benefit To The Parents

The school-to-home communication provides parents with detailed, objective information each day about how their child has done in school. This objective information serves as a basis for awarding home privileges to the youngster. Frequently, parents receive notes from their child's teacher with good comments and negative comments, and then are unsure whether to reward or punish the youngster.

With this system it is very clear to the parents what the youngster has done that day in school. It is also very clear to the parents what positive or negative consequences should be given to their child. Often parents have control over more powerful positive and negative consequences than the school does, and thus can become a strong ally of the school in helping the student achieve his potential. Can you imagine how the grades of some high school students would skyrocket if they had to achieve a certain level each day in order to use the car?

Benefit To The Student

The school-to-home communication system also provides the students with a very specific list of behaviors or actions that are expected of them at school. Frequently parents and teachers expect the students to "be good," but do not spell out what that means. With this system the youngsters know exactly what is expected, and equally important, what the consequences will be at home based on their school performance that day. This brings to mind another benefit of this system. It works on a daily basis.

Therefore, if a youngster does poorly on Monday and fails to achieve at the expected level, or forgets the form at school, he will experience the negative consequences on that day. However, he is then able to start over the very next day. Responsibility is also placed upon the youngster to have the form filled out, taken home, and returned to the teacher. The student must learn to work and maintain progress without making excuses for his behavior due to external factors.

Benefit To The Teacher

The school-to-home communication system will help the teacher to spell out very specific behaviors, with the cooperation of the parent and student, that he expects the student to perform. The form is very easy for the teacher to complete, and if all parties cooperate, it will greatly reduce the amount of time they need to spend with the student on behavioral problems. Understandably, since the home is actively involved in the process and will offer strong positive and negative consequences, the likelihood of the behavior changing quickly is much greater than a system used just within the school. Another positive feature is the fact that the teacher will know in a very short time whether or not the system is working. It will only take a few days to decide if it is working, although the program should probably be maintained for several weeks to a month or two, depending on circumstances.

Typical Problems And Suggestions

1. The student "forgets" the paper at school.

    Solution: Calmly explain that if the paper doesn't come home, you'll assume zero points and follow through with the contract.

2. The student forgets the teacher's signature and marks the paper himself.

    Solution: Plan to check with the teacher by phone at least for the first few days, and at least once a week after that.

3. The student says he doesn't care about not getting enough points, and that he doesn't care about TV or 25 cents, etc.

    Solution: Hopefully you picked short-term reinforcers that are important to your child. Calmly state, "I'm glad you didn't want those things, because you did not earn them today, but you may decide to earn them tomorrow." You might need to change the short-term reinforcers, but don't do that too quickly. Wait a week before changing reinforcers.

ENDNOTES

1. Eimers, Robert, and Robert Aitchison, Ph.D., *Effective Parents, Responsible Children*, New York: McGraw-Hill Book Company, 1977.
2. Ibid., pp. 87-96.
3. Ibid., pp. 49-70.
4. Ibid., pp. 71-86.
5. Dreikurs, Rudolf, and Loren Gray, *A New Approach to Discipline: Logical Consequences*, New York: Hawthorn Books, 1968.
6. Narramore, Dr. Bruce, *Help! I'm a Parent*, Grand Rapids: Zondervan Publishing House, 1982.

Parenting Quiz—Answers

---

1. Your four-year-old comes running into the house after playing with several older neighborhood kids and yells a profane word. It's the first time you've heard him use the word. The best thing to do is:

   B. *Ignore it.*

      For first time behaviors such as this, the best approach is to ignore it. If the behavior continues, you would need a stronger technique such as **mild social punishment**, then **time-out**. If these fail to change the behavior, a light tap on his mouth with your hand might work. Also consider restricting his play so he no longer plays with these children.

2. You've caught your two-year-old in the middle of the street in front of your home. The best thing to do is:

   C. *Spank your child while still in the middle of the street.*

      In this way he will associate pain with the middle of the street. Obviously, if a car is coming down the street, you need to get him onto the sidewalk before spanking him.

3. Johnny, age 6, and Bobby, age 8, who are brothers, are fighting in the living room. The best thing to do is:

    A. *Ignore it.*

       Give them some time and see if they are able to work it out by themselves. Be sure to praise appropriate behaviors. If fighting has been going on for some time then use:

    C. *Send each of them to a different place in the house to sit for five minutes.*

       This is **time-out**. Do not try to determine who started it, but simply state the rule and the consequence, and put them both in **time-out**.

4. The worst time of the day for children and their parents is:

    B. *The hour before dinner.*

       This usually gets the most votes. Everyone is hungry, tired, and it's near the end of the day. If you find this to be true, then be sure and make some changes in your routine, to cut down on behavior problems. For example, have the kids work on their homework at this time, or give them special toys to play with that they can only play with at this time.

5. Your first-grader says she hates school. You should:

    D. *Say to her, "You really don't like school, do you?"*

       In this way, you will hopefully be encouraging her to talk more about her day in school, and she may become more specific as to why she does not like school.

6. Your two children are coloring quietly in the living room. You should probably:

    D. *Go in and tell them that you like the way they are coloring quietly.*

    It is very important for parents to catch their children being good and praise them for appropriate behaviors and not just give attention to misbehaviors.

7. Your kindergartner does not get ready for school on time. The thing to do is:

    (There are two possible answers.)

    A. *Let him go to school partially dressed.*

    This is the technique of **logical consequences**; or

    D. *Set up a chart so that the child can earn rewards for the appropriate behavior.*

8. Giving your children rewards for doing well in school and for doing their chores:

    C. *Is OK to do.*

9. Which of the following can never be a reward:

    E. *None of the above.*

    This is a trick question. All of the answers—praise, candy, money, and spanking—can be rewards. The only way to tell if you have punished your child is to observe their behavior following the "punishment." If the behavior ceases, then you have used a punisher. If the behavior increases, then you have used a reward.

10. Your seven-year-old boy complains every night about going to bed, and it takes you 30 to 45 minutes each night to get him to bed. The thing that would probably not help resolve this would be:

   C. *Wrestling with him before bedtime to tire him out.*

11. Johnny has always done well in math, but has started bringing home incomplete math papers and low grades. You should:

   B. *Wait another month and see what happens, then*

   D. *Call his teacher and set up an appointment to discuss it, possibly along with the school counselor.*

   Also consider setting up the school-to-home communication system which was discussed in **Part II**.

12. Suzie, age 8, refuses to eat her entire dinner each night. The thing that would probably not help this situation is:

   B. *Making her stay at the table until she is finished.*

A Study Guide

Putting It (The Tools) Into Action

This questionnaire and study guide can help you put what you have learned about tools in **Part II** into action. It can be very difficult to make changes in what you are already doing as a parent. It can be impossible if you do not have a plan of action. As you read the following questions, evaluate what you have been doing, and make a specific plan or commitment to change.

You will not feel better as a parent unless you do something different. Each question stems from information presented in **Part II**. If you are unsure of a course of action to take, go back and read the appropriate sections. It may be easier for you to also think of one of your children as you go through the study guide the first time, then go back over it again as you think about your other children.

CHILD'S NAME _____

1. Think of a recent time when your child misbehaved. Why do you think that he misbehaved?

2. Most parents concentrate on their youngster's misbehavior (B), then wonder what consequence (C) to apply. What antecedent (A) could possibly be changed in the example above (or other situations) that would reduce or eliminate the misbehavior (B)?

   (The ABC's of Parenting)

3. What behavior is your youngster demonstrating which you may be trying to simply ignore without developing a strategy?

   (Ignore The Problem? Think Survival? or Develop A Strategy?)

4. What area of discipline do you and your spouse need to agree about dealing with?

   (Parental Agreement And Teamwork)

5. What behavior are you modeling for your child that is a positive behavior?

   What behavior are you modeling for your youngster that is a negative behavior?

   What positive behavior are you modeling that needs to be discussed with your youngster?

   (Model Appropriate Behavior)

6. Which of the three ways to show unconditional love that Campbell discusses (eye contact, physical contact, and focused attention) do you need to demonstrate more?

   How, when, and where do you plan to do it?

   Think of a recent time when your youngster's misbehavior was probably due to the fact that his emotional tank was empty.

What specific temperament traits does your child have?

How is your temperament different from that of your child?

How does your temperament match or fit with that of your child?

What is your youngster's language of love? State one or two specific things or activities that are really important to your youngster. Be sure to show love to him using his language of love, not yours.

(Demonstrating Unconditional Love To Your Child)

7. When do you need to work harder at simply accepting your youngster's feelings?

   What did you do as a child when you were angry?

   Take time to discuss the anger ladder with your child.

   What area of conflict are you having with your teenager in which you need to reach a compromise or resolve?

   (Accepting Feelings, Encouraging Communication and Teaching Your Children To Express Anger Appropriately, Resolving Conflicts)

8. I plan to implement the Marbles In the Jar idea and catch my kids being good. I will praise them and put marbles in the jar for the following behaviors . . .

   When the jar is full, our entire family plans to . . .

   A specific behavior that I would like to see my child develop is . . .

   I plan to reward that behavior with one of the following techniques: "Fill in the spaces on a picture," "Hershey Kiss Faces," "Three Quarters at Bedtime," or another method that I think of which incorporates the essential ingredients of effective reinforcement principles.

   When I praise my youngsters I need to be sure that I . . .

   (Rewards or Approval For Appropriate Behavior)

9. The following is a list of chores that I would like my child to accomplish . . .

   I will ask him what he thinks of these chores and possibly negotiate some of them with him.

   The rewards that would probably be most effective with my youngster would be . . .

   (Chores, Children, and Character—They Go Together, How Do You Make It Work?)

10. Now I am ready to consider what inappropriate behavior my youngster is demonstrating, provided I have worked consistently in the past two weeks to accomplish the above goals. (Do not jump down to this section, until you have first worked at providing a positive home climate.)

    State in very specific terms a behavior that you would like to see your youngster stop performing.

    Remember to reward your child for behavior that is opposite of this. For example, if you want your child to stop fighting, be sure you are rewarding him in some way for playing nicely. If you want him to not interrupt you when you are on the phone, then be sure and reward him when he waits until you get off the phone.

    Determine if one of the following techniques would be appropriate: *ignoring, mild social punishment, time-out.*

    Can you use **logical consequences** in any of the above situations?

    If you decide to use the Punishment or "X" Chart, then determine what the activities will be that your child will miss out on.

    Make a chart, then discuss the consequences with your youngster.

    (Techniques For Dealing With Inappropriate Behavior)

11. In reviewing the section on Self-Esteem, list specific ideas that you plan to discuss with your youngster and implement in your approach to building his self-esteem over the next few months.

(Improving Your Child's Self-Esteem)

12. Is your life in balance? If not, what goals do you need to set for yourself to get it in balance?

Sit down with your child and list five to ten possible stressors in his life at this time.

Next to each stressor list which of the four ways to deal with stress you could use in the future to deal effectively with that stressor. You can use more than one method in many cases.

(Helping Your Child and You Deal With Stress)

Afterword

A Final Note Of Encouragement

Imagine a city some distance from your house that you and your family have visited, which may take 8 to 10 hours to get to. For our family, it's a trip from Ventura to San Francisco, where my wife's family lives. The trip takes about 8 or 9 hours, which was an especially long time when our three children were 3, 5, and 8 (or younger). Sometimes it seemed like we would never get there. We'd drive and stop, drive and stop, and wonder if we would ever make it. The kids would constantly be saying, "How much further?" I am sure that you have probably felt the same way in your travels.

In my mind, the trip to effective parenting is very clear cut. It is as clear as the road map you have to a favorite city. You know how to get there; you just have to be persistent enough to stay on the road to get to your destination. The very same thing is true of effective parenting. Hopefully, this book has given you an accurate road map of how to get to "effective parenting." Each parent may have to spend more time at certain spots. It may take you time to deal effectively with certain Dragons, and it may take you time to learn some "new tools." But rest assured, you will get to your destination if you stay on the road long enough, and get back on it when you drift away.

Beetle Bailey by Mort Walker

Reprinted with permission of King Features Syndicate, Inc.

You may not know what to do to make things better in your family, but once you decide that you want things to be better and quit arguing with yourself, then you have begun the journey to more positive parenting.

Obviously, the arguing is over for you. The fact that you are at this point in this book indicates you have begun the trip. Hopefully this book has offered encouragement to continue the trip, and given you the insight necessary to reach your destination.

Suggested Reading

DIVORCE

Despert, J. Louise, M.D., *Children of Divorce*, A Dolphin Handbook, Garden City, New York: Doubleday & Company, Inc., 1962.

Grollman, Earl, *Explaining Divorce to Children*, Boston: Beacon Press, 1969.

Jewett, Claudia L., *Helping Children Cope With Separation & Loss*, Harvard, Massachusetts: The Harvard Common Press, 1982.

> A compassionate, practical book for any adult who wants to help a child recover from the stages of denial and mourning that can follow the loss of a loved one. Whether the loss is great or small, whether it arises from death or divorce, moving or hospitalization, or simply the politics of friendship, this book offers warm advice and specific techniques for dealing with the situation.

McKay, Matthew, Peter Rogers, and others, *The Divorce Book*, Oakland, California: New Harbinger Publications, 1984.

> A practical guide to: understanding the emotional stages of divorce, avoiding the psychological traps, mourning and mending, attorneys and the law, divorce mediation, telling the children, effects on children, single and second parents, coparenting, surviving as a single, sex, and re-marriage.

Phillips, Carolyn, *Our Family Got A Divorce*, Regal Books, 1979.

> This book is designed for children of ages 7 through 11 to read (or it can be read to them) to help them understand and work through the various feelings associated with a divorce. The author wrote the book following her divorce after 9 years of marriage and based it on experiences with her two children.

Teyber, Edward, Ph.D., *Helping Your Children With Divorce*, New York: Pocket Books, 1985.

> Most libraries also have many books for children and teenagers to read that deal with divorce. Other books in this area are:

Laurene Brown, *Dinosaur's Divorce*
Patricia Perry, *Mommy And Daddy Are Divorced*
Eric E. Rofes, *The Kid's Book Of Divorce*
Jill Krementz, *How It Feels When Parents Divorce*

SELF-ESTEEM

Anderson, Jill, *Thinking, Changing, Rearranging: Improving Self-Esteem In Young People*, Eugene, Oregon: Timberline Press, 1981.

Based on concepts found in Rational Emotive Therapy, this book guides children in examining their own thinking, inner language, and belief system to learn for themselves how they go about creating those "rotten" days. A workbook is also available.

Briggs, Dorothy Corkville, *Your Child's Self-Esteem*, Dolphin Books, Garden City, New York: Doubleday & Company, Inc., 1975.

How to help create strong feelings of self-worth is the central challenge for every parent and teacher. The author offers excellent insight and practical suggestions for building your child's self-esteem.

Briggs, Dorothy Corkville, *Celebrate Your Self*, Garden City, New York: Doubleday & Company, Inc., 1977.

This book offers step by step specifics on how to free yourself from those things that keep you from fully enjoying life. The book utilizes the concepts of Transactional Analysis, Parent-Adult-Child, as a model in helping adults feel better about themselves.

Dobson, Dr. James, *Hide or Seek*, Power Books, Old Tappan, New Jersey: Fleming H. Revell Company, 1974.

The author exposes the false value system of our society and presents ten comprehensive strategies through which parents and teachers can cultivate self-esteem in every child.

Smalley, Gary & John Trent, *The Blessing*, Nashville, Tennessee: Thomas Nelson Publishers, 1986.

An excellent book on specific strategies for parents to build the self-esteem of their children. The book also discusses adult self-esteem, and offers suggestions for adults who did not get the blessing (high self-esteem) from their parents. Giving the blessing back to our parents is also discussed and encouraged.

PARENTING TEENAGERS

Campbell, Dr. Ross, *Your Child And Drugs*, Wheaton, Illinois: Victor Books, 1988.

The author discusses our drug culture and the confusing world that our teenagers are growing up in. The relationship between anger, depression, the child with learning problems, and drugs is explored. Treating your child's drug habit and keeping your child drug free are also discussed.

Campbell, Dr. Ross, *How To Really Love Your Teenager,*
Victor Books, 1981.

> This book elaborates on the techniques of showing unconditional love
> to your teenager that were first presented in his book *How To Really Love
> Your Child.* Additionally, the author discusses teenage depression, letting
> go, and how to help teenagers to express anger utilizing the anger ladder
> concept.

Elkind, David, *All Grown Up & No Place To Go*, Menlo Park,
California: Addison-Wesley Publishing Company, 1984.

> Raising teenagers today is tougher than ever. The author helps parents
> cope with the pressures facing today's adolescents and offers insightful advice
> that will help parents guide their teenagers through these turbulent years.

Sanderson, J.D., *How To Stop Worrying About Your Kids*, New York:
W. W. Norton & Company, 1978.

> "Give up the power before they take it" is the title of one chapter in
> this book, and in many ways describes the book. The author and his wife
> developed a five-year plan (called Adult at Eighteen), and introduced it
> to each of his children on his or her thirteenth birthday. Typical problems
> and practical solutions are presented to help parents develop an effective
> de-parenting plan.

PARENTING CHILDREN

Bodenhamer, Gregory, *Back In Control*, New York:
Prentice Hall Press, 1983.

> This book does an excellent job discussing two major reasons that parents
> get out of control: unclear rules and inconsistent follow through. The author
> emphasizes the concept of never arguing with your child, the reasons why,
> and how to get out of that pattern. The book is not very strong in the
> areas of praise or showing unconditional love, but is a must for all parents
> because of the attention it gives to rules and follow through.

Campbell, Dr. Ross, *How To Really Love Your Child*, Wheaton, Illinois:
Victor Books, 1979.

> This book is a must for all parents. Campbell states that the foundation
> for good parent-child relationships is showing the children unconditional
> love, and he gives practical ideas for doing this. He discusses the affect
> of congenital temperament on a child's behavior and the need for parents
> to solidify their marital relationship.

Canter, Lee, *Assertive Discipline*, Parent Resource Guide, Santa
Monica, California: Canter and Associates, Inc., 1985

This is a very practical book for parents to use in pinpointing problem
behaviors, and developing the assertive discipline plan, which includes stating
the rule, using rewards, and using negative consequences. Practical charts,
stickers, and contracts are also included.

Dreikurs, Rudolf, and Loren Grey, *A New Approach To Discipline:
Logical Consequences*, New York: Hawthorn Books, 1968.

This is an excellent resource for more information about the theoretical
aspects of **logical consequences,** as well as presenting practical examples
of problems and the appropriate logical consequences. The author describes
the difference between logical or natural consequences and punishment.

Eimers, Robert and Robert Aitchison, Ph.D., *Effective Parents,
Responsible Children*, McGraw-Hill Book Company, 1977.

This is a very practical book for parents when attempting to apply the
techniques of **ignoring, mild social punishment,** and **time-out.** The authors
also look at the "slow learner," the withdrawn and fearful child, and the
hyperactive child. Special incentive programs are also discussed.

Elkind, David, *The Hurried Child*, Menlo Park, California:
Addison-Wesley Publishing Company, 1981.

The author explores the unique burdens we have brought upon our children
and offers insights, advice, and hope for solving those problems. He looks
at the pressures and stresses that children are a force to cope with.

Gordon, Dr. Thomas, *Parent Effectiveness Training*, New American
Library, 1970.

Gordon's book discusses effective listening and communication skills. Many
parents have difficulty simply accepting their child's feelings. This book will
help you in that area. The "no-lose" method for resolving conflicts is also
covered.

Ilg, Frances, Louise Bates Ames, Sidney Baker, *Child Behavior,
Specific Advice on Problems of Child Behavior*, New York:
Harper & Row Publishers, 1981.

This book will help parents get a better handle on what is normal for
different age levels. The authors discuss topics such as: eating behavior,
sleeping and dreams, elimination, tensional outlets, and fears. Brother-sister
and parent-child relationships at different age levels are also discussed.

ADULTS

Bloomfield, Harold, *Making Peace With Your Parents*, New York: Ballantine Books, 1983.

"No matter how old you are and whether or not your parents are alive, you have to come to terms with them. This wise and practical book will show you how to deal with the most fundamental relationship in your life and, in the process, become the happy, creative, and fulfilled person you are meant to be." Making peace with your parents is a key to all areas of your life. The book discusses how to express love and anger toward your parents, and gives practical suggestions on how you can become a better parent to yourself.

Buhler, Rich, *Pain and Pretending*, Nashville, Tennessee: Thomas Nelson Publishers, 1988.

A must book for all adults who have experienced pain in their childhoods. When children are not helped to deal with pain, pretending takes place, which not only carries over into adult life, but also results in vow making and reassigning anger to someone in the present. The why's and how's of forgiveness are also presented.

Halpern, Dr. Howard, *Cutting Loose, An Adult Guide To Coming To Terms With Your Parents*, A Bantam Book, 1977.

In this book, psychotherapist Howard M. Halpern describes how people get stuck in frustrating parent/child patterns and how to get out of them. He talks about the tactics of the Martyred Mom, the Despotic Dad, moralistic parents, seductive parents, aging parents, and more. He shows how you can break the old routines and begin to have better, happier relations with your parents—as adults, as equals, even as friends.

Wright, H. Norman, *Making Peace With Your Past*, New Jersey: Fleming H. Revell Co., 1985

H. Norman Wright explains that although we can never erase our memories and past experiences, we can choose to be free from their effects. He helps you take inventory of the excess baggage that hinders your journey through life. By showing you how to practice the presence of Jesus Christ in your life, Wright reveals how you can live your life unburdened by the past.

MISCELLANEOUS

Beattie, Melody, *Codependent, No More*, Hazeldon Publications, 1987.

An excellent overview of codependent issues and behaviors, along with practical suggestions for dealing with codependency. Topics discussed include: detaching, enabling or rescuing, and anger.

Beattie, Melody, *Beyond Codependency*, Hazeldon Publications, 1989.

> A sequel to her first book, Melody Beattie reinforces points made in greater depth and deals with issues such as relapse and relationships, and codependency in the work setting.

Bloomfield, Harold, *Making Peace With Yourself*, New York: Ballantine Books, 1985.

> Through a series of exercises, case studies, and personal growth techniques, you'll learn to analyze your weakness, and most important, strip it of the power it has over you. Chapters include: "I'm afraid of getting hurt again," "When I look in the mirror, I'm never quite satisfied," "I can't stand criticism," and "I wish I could be happier."

Buhler, Rich, *Love, No Strings Attached*, Nashville, Tennessee: Thomas Nelson Publishers, 1987.

> This book discusses three essential ingredients in every marriage: Love, Approval, and Disapproval. It is an excellent book for couples to use to enhance their marriage. These three ingredients are also essential in every effective approach to parenting.

Davis, Martha, Elizabeth Eshelman, and Matthew McKay, *The Relaxation & Stress Reduction Workbook*, Oakland, California: New Harbinger Publications, 1982.

> This book is an excellent resource of techniques for dealing effectively with stress. Chapters include: Thought Stopping, Refuting Irrational Beliefs, Assertiveness Training, and Time Management.

Ellis, Albert and Robert Harper, *A New Guide To Rational Living*, North Hollywood, California: Wilshire Book Company, 1961.

> This book takes an in-depth look at various irrational beliefs and how they affect one's reaction to the events in their life. It also tells the reader how to refuse these irrational beliefs and what to replace them with.

Gravitz, Herbert, and Julie Bowden, *Guide To Recovery, A Book For Adult Children Of Alcoholics*, Florida: Learning Publications, Inc., 1985.

> This is an excellent book for adult children of alcoholics. It discusses the roots of Adult Children Of Alcoholics (ACA) behaviors, survival strategies, core issues facing ACA's and what to do to break out of the destructive patterns that develop in childhood.

Harris, Thomas, *I'M OK, YOU'RE OK*, New York and Evanston, Illinois: Harper & Row Publishers, 1967.

> This book distinguishes three active elements in each person's make-up: the Parent, the Adult, and the Child. Each aspect is defined, and the model is used individually and in relationships.

Martin, Sara Hines, *Healing For Adult Children Of Alcoholics*, New York: Bantam Books, 1988.

> This is another excellent book for adult children of alcoholics. The author reveals how growing up in an alcoholic home affects one's work, marriage, health, children, judgement, self-image, and relationship with God. How to deal with, and even forgive, your drinking parents is also discussed.

Missildine, W. Hugh, *Your Inner Child Of The Past*, Pocket Books, 1963.

> Much distress, fatigue, loneliness, and inner emptiness could be eliminated if people had a deeper understanding of how to live fruitfully with their 'inner child of the past'. Such understanding could help married couples meet one another's needs more fully. It should help parents create a childhood for their own children that will be free of the attitudes that pile up future trouble. This book is an effort to provide, in understandable language, a working knowledge of the root causes of emotional disturbance, and a method of dealing with them.

Stoop, Dr. David, *Living With A Perfectionist*, Nashville, Tennessee: Nelson Publishers, 1987.

> Dr. Stoop looks at the causes of perfectionism along with the results of this behavior, and suggests a variety of practical approaches to correct this behavior and create more of a balance in your life.

Wright, H. Norman, *Marital Counseling: A Biblically Based, Behavioral, Cognitive Approach*, Denver, Colorado: Christian Marriage Enrichment, 1981.

> The author concisely analyzes the causes of marital conflict, presents an overview of marital counseling theory, gives practical "how to do it" counseling direction, and illustrates his points with helpful examples and case histories.

Books & Tapes by Starburst Publishers

(Partial listing—full list available on request)

Dragon Slaying For Parents
—Tom Prinz, M.S.

Subtitled: Removing The Excess Baggage So You Can Be The Parent You Want To Be. Shows how Dragons such as Codependency, Low Self-Esteem and other hidden factors interfere with effective parenting. This book by a marriage, family, and child conselor, is for all parents—to assist them with the difficult task of raising responsible and confident children in the 1990's. It is written especially for parents who believe they have "tried everything!"

(trade paper) ISBN 0914984357 **$9.95**

Courting The King Of Terrors
—Frank Carl
with Joan Hake Robie

Why are so many people turning to Mental, Spiritual and Physical suicide? This book probes the relentless ills that are destroying the American family, and offers counsel to families in crisis. "I know about suicide," says Frank Carl. "I lost a Brother and a Sister to that monster!"

(trade paper) ISBN 0914984187 **$7.95**

Reverse The Curse In Your Life
—Joan Hake Robie

A handy "guidebook" for those who wish to avoid Satan's snares. Includes Biblical Curses, Forbidden Practices, Warfare Prayers, and much more. This book is the result of author Joan Hake Robie's over ten years of research on the subject of the occult, demons, and Satanism.

(trade paper) ISBN 0914984241 **$7.95**

Man And Wife For Life
—Joseph Kanzlemar, Ed.D.

A penetrating and often humorous look into real life situations of married people. Helps the reader get a new understanding of the problems and relationships within marriage.

(trade paper) ISBN 0914984233 **$7.95**

Alzheimer's—Does "The System" Care?
—Ted Valenti, M.S.W. & Paula Valenti, R.N.

Experts consider Alzheimer's disease to be the "the disease of the century." More than half the one million elderly people residing in American nursing homes have "senile dementia." This book reveals a unique observation as to the cause of Alzheimers's and the care of its victims.

(hard cover) ISBN 0914984179 **$14.95**

Inch by Inch . . . Is It a Cinch?
—Phyllis Miller

Is it a cinch to lose weight? If your answer is "NO," you must read this book. Read about the intimate details of one woman's struggle for love and acceptance.

(trade paper) ISBN 0914984152 **$8.95**

Books & Tapes by Starburst Publishers—cont'd.

Allergy Cooking With Ease
—Nicolette N. Dumke

A book designed to provide a wide variety of recipes to meet many different types of dietary and social needs, and, whenever possible, save you time in food preparation. Includes: Recipes for those special foods that most food allergy patients think they will never eat again; Timesaving tricks; and Allergen Avoidance Index.

(trade paper-opens flat) ISBN 091498442X **$12.95**

Off The Floor . . . and Into Your Soup?
—Charles Christmas, Jr.

A shocking account of what goes on behind the scenes at many resturants—high class or not. Author looks at the restaurant itself, its employees, and the food that is served to the customer. He also reveals the practical jokes, and more, that kitchen employees do to each other, and the not-so-kind things they do to patrons.

(trade paper) ISBN 0914984381 **$7.95**

Like A Bulging Wall
—Robert Borrud

Will you survive the 1990's economic crash? This book shows how debt, greed, and covetousness, along with a lifestyle beyond our means, has brought about an explosive situation in this country. Gives "call" from God to prepare for judgement in America, Also lists TOP-RATED U.S. BANKS and SAVINGS & LOANS.

(trade paper) ISBN 0914984284 **$8.95**

You Can Eliminate Stress From The I.R.S.
—Fulton N. Dobson

Almost everyone can expect to undergo a tax audit at least once or twice in their lifetime. This book gives common sense actions to take that will make the audit easier to face. Answers questions like: What are my rights as a taxpayer? What can I expect from my tax accountant? How can I prove to the IRS my ability (or inability) to pay back taxes?. . . and much more.

(trade paper) ISBN 0914984403 **$7.95**

Get Rich Slowly . . . But Surely!
—Randy L. Thurman

The only get-rich-quick guide you'll ever need. Achieving financial independence is important to young and old. Anyone who wants to be financially free will discover the way to financial independence easier by applying these long-term, time-tested principles. This book can be read in one sitting!

(trade paper) ISBN 0914984365 **$7.95**

What To Do When The Bill Collector Calls!
Know Your Rights
—David L. Kelcher, Jr.

Reveals the unfair debt collection practices that some agencies use and how this has led to the invasion of privacy, bankruptcy, marital instability, and the loss of jobs. The reader is told what he can do about the problem.

(trade paper) ISBN 0914984322 **$9.95**

The Quick Job Hunt Guide
—Robert D. Siedle

Gives techniques to use when looking for a job. Networking, Following the Ten-Day Plan, and Avoiding the Personnel Department, are some of the ways to "land that job!"

(trade paper) ISBN 0914984330 **$7.95**

Horror And Violence—The Deadly Duo In The Media
—Phil Phillips
and Joan Hake Robie

Americans are hooked on violence! Muggings, kindappings, rape and murders are commonplace via your TV set. This book not only brings you up-to-date on what is happening in the media in general, but also will help you and your children survive with integrity in a complex media environment.

(trade paper) ISBN 0914984160 **$8.95**

Turmoil In The Toy Box II
—Joan Hake Robie

This book takes a hard look at the popular "Nintendo" games, the "Batman" craze, "Ghostbusters," "Freddy" from *A Nightmare on Elm Street,* Dungeons and Dragons and much more. Seeks to make every parent aware of the potential for mental, emotional and spiritual harm from allowing their children access to toys and TV that will give them more of a foundation in the occult than in God's teaching.

(trade paper) ISBN 0914984209 **$8.95**

Turmoil In The Toy Box II—audio
—Joan Hake Robie

60 minute audio cassette narrated by Joan Hake Robie, author of the book *Turmoil In The Toy Box II.*

(audio cassette tape) ISBN 0914984268 **$7.95**

Turmoil In The Toy Box
—Phil Phillips

A shocking expose of the toy and cartoon industry—unmasks the New Age, Occult, Violent, and Satanic influences that have invaded the once innocent toy box. Over 150,000 in print.

(trade paper) ISBN 0914984047 **$8.95**

Turmoil In The Toy Box—video
—Phil Phillips

This eye-opening video, featuring Phil Phillips and host Gary Greenwald, takes an indepth look at the rise of the occult and pagan religions within the toy and cartoon industries. Contains actual examples of toys and film clips from popular TV cartoons.

(90 min. tape—VHS only) 0006563589 **$34.95**

The Truth About Dungeons And Dragons
—Joan Hake Robie

Explains the game of Dungeons and Dragons and lists the bizarre cast of characters which includes demons, dragons, witches, zombies, harpies, gnomes and creatures who cast spells and exercise supernatural powers. It tells how Dungeons and Dragons dabbles in the occult, encourages sex and violence and is a form of Devil worship.

(trade paper) ISBN 0914984373 **$5.95**

Books & Tapes by Starburst Publishers—cont'd.

The Truth About Dungeons And Dragons—audio
—Joan Hake Robie

60 minute audio cassette narrated by Joan Hake Robie, author of the book *The Truth About Dungeons And Dragons.*

(audio cassette tape) ISBN 091498425X **$7.95**

The Rock Report
—Fletcher A. Brothers

An "uncensored" look into today's Rock Music scene—provides the reader with the necessary information and illustrations to make intelligent decisions about rock music and its influence on the mind.

(trade paper) ISBN 0914984136 **$6.95**

The Quest For Truth
—Ken Johnson

A book designed to lead the reader to a realization that there is no solution to the world's problems, nor is there a purpose to life, apart from Jesus Christ. It is the story of a young man on a symbolic journey in search of happiness and the meaning of life.

(trade paper) ISBN 0914984217 **$7.95**

A Candle In Darkness (novel)
—June Livesay

A heartwarming novel (based on fact), set in the mountains of Ecuador. This book is filled with love, suspense, and intrigue. The first in a series of books by June Livesay.

(trade paper) ISBN 0914984225 **$8.95**

Purchasing Information

<u>Listed books are available from your favorite Bookstore,</u> either from current stock or special order. You may also order direct from STARBURST PUBLISHERS. When ordering enclose full payment plus $2.00* for shipping and handling ($2.50* if Canada or Overseas). Payment in US Funds only. Please allow two to three weeks minimum (longer overseas) for delivery. Make checks payable to and mail to STARBURST PUBLISHERS, P.O. Box 4123, LANCASTER, PA 17604. **Prices subject to change without notice**. Catalog available upon request.

★ We reserve the right to ship your order the least expensive way. If you desire first class (domestic) or air shipment (overseas) please enclose shipping funds as follows: First Class within the USA enclose $4.00, Airmail Canada enclose $5.00, and Overseas enclose 30% (minimum $5.00) of total order. All remittance must be in US Funds.

03-92